Applied Mathematics **9**

**Addison-Wesley
Secondary
Mathematics
Authors**

Elizabeth Ainslie
Paul Atkinson
Maurice Barry
Cam Bennet
Barbara J. Canton
Ron Coleborn
Fred Crouse
Garry Davis
Mary Doucette
Bonnie Edwards
Jane Forbes
George Gadanidis
Liliane Gauthier
Florence Glanfield
Katie Pallos-Haden
Carol Besteck Hope
Terry Kaminski
Brendan Kelly
Stephen Khan
Ron Lancaster
Duncan LeBlanc
Kevin Maguire
Jim Nakamoto
Paul Pogue
Linda Rajotte
Brent Richards
Kevin Spry
David Sufrin
Peter Taylor
Paul Williams
Elizabeth Wood
Rick Wunderlich
Paul Zolis
Leanne Zorn

Robert Alexander

Lynda Cowan   **Antonietta Lenjosek**
Peter J. Harrison   **Nick Nielsen**
Rob McLeish   **Margaret Sinclair**

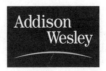

Addison
Wesley

Toronto

Developmental Editor
Ingrid D'Silva

Senior Consulting Mathematics Editor
Lesley Haynes

Coordinating Editor
Mei Lin Cheung

Production Coordinator
Stephanie Cox

Editorial Contributors
Kelly Davis
Gay McKeller
Alison Rieger
Judy Wilson
Christina Yu

Product Manager
Susan Cox

Managing Editor
Enid Haley

Publisher
Claire Burnett

Design/Production
Pronk&Associates

Art Direction
Pronk&Associates

Electronic Assembly/Technical Art
Pronk&Associates

Reviewers

Joe DiGiorgio
Cardinal Carter Catholic High School
York Catholic District School Board
Aurora

Rod Forcier
Head of Mathematics and Computers
Christ the King Secondary School
Georgetown

Duncan LeBlanc
Head of Mathematics
Sir Robert L Borden Business and
Technical Institute
Toronto

Gizele Price
Holy Name of Mary Secondary School
Dufferin-Peel Catholic District School Board
Mississauga

Bill Sherman
Lasalle Secondary School
Sudbury

Wendy Solheim
Head of Mathematics
Thornhill Secondary School
Thornhill

ISBN: 0-321-15451-7   Preprint Edition
ISBN:0-201-77119-5   Final Edition

Preprint Contents

Preprint Contents

Chapters 7, 8, and 9 are not a part of this preprint.

1 Relationships

By the end of this chapter, you will:

- Describe possible situations for graphs.
- Represent data with tables of values and graphs. Describe and analyse relationships.
- Collect, organize, and analyse data, with and without technology. Decide whether results are reasonable for the situation.
- Communicate findings of an experiment and solutions to problems. Justify your conclusions.
- Pose and solve problems about investigations and experiments.
- Decide whether relations are linear or non-linear.
- Decide whether situations are proportional.

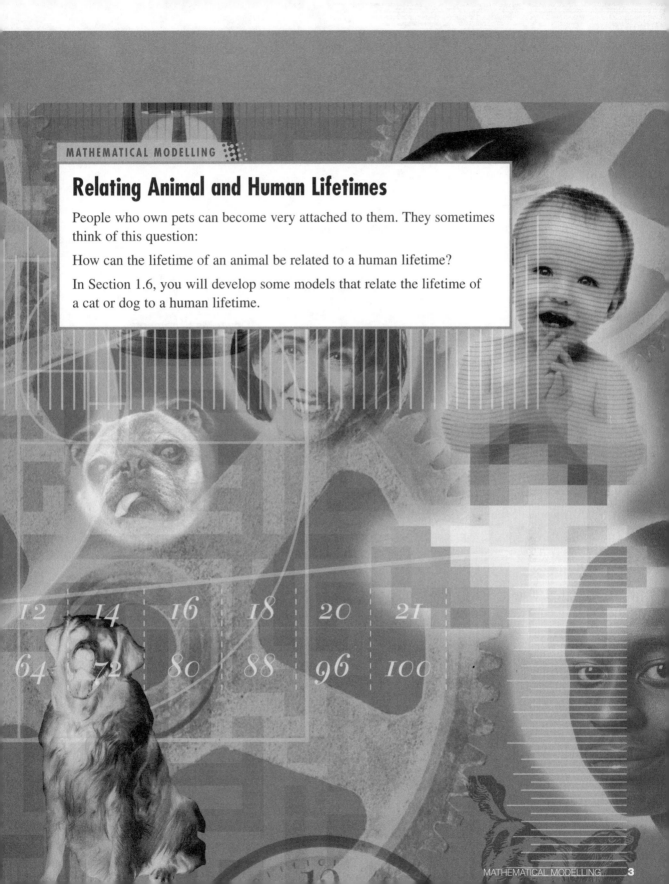

Relating Animal and Human Lifetimes

People who own pets can become very attached to them. They sometimes think of this question:

How can the lifetime of an animal be related to a human lifetime?

In Section 1.6, you will develop some models that relate the lifetime of a cat or dog to a human lifetime.

12   14   16   18   20   21

64   72   80   88   96   100

Necessary Skills

Graphing Data

Example

Describe the relationship in the table. Graph the data.

Centimetres	0	20	40	60	80	100	120	140	160	180	200
Metres	0	0.2	0.4	0.6	0.8	1.0	1.2	1.4	1.6	1.8	2.0

Solution

In the table, the number of centimetres is 100 times the number of metres since 1 m = 100 cm.
Plot *Centimetres* along the horizontal axis and *Metres* along the vertical axis.
Choose a horizontal scale of 1 square represents 20 cm, and a vertical scale of 1 square represents 0.2 m. Mark the points to represent the data. Join the points.

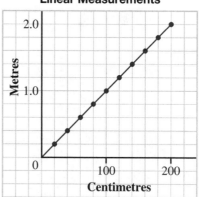

Exercises

1. Calculate each length in centimetres. Use or extend the above table or graph to check whether your answers are reasonable.

   a) 0.4 m b) 1.5 m c) 1.93 m d) 0.7 m e) 2.14 m

2. Use the graph above to estimate each length in metres. Use the table above to check.

   a) 120 cm b) 86 cm c) 54 cm d) 2 cm e) 197 cm

3. a) Copy and complete this table.

Distances Travelled at 40 km/h

Time (h)	0	2	4	6	8	10	12	14	16	18	20	22	24
Distance (km)	0	80	160	240									960

b) Graph the data. Plot *Time* along the horizontal axis and *Distance* along
   the vertical axis.

4. Calculate the distance travelled at 40 km/h for each time. Use or extend the
   table or graph in exercise 3 to check.

a) 6 h   b) 11 h   c) 20.5 h

d) 17 h   e) 26 h   f) 27.5 h

Distance = speed × time

Reading a Graph

Example

This graph shows the fuel needed by a car owner.

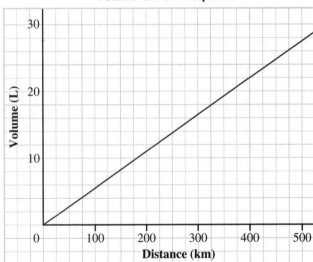

Volume of Fuel Required

How much gas is required to drive 400 km?

Necessary Skills

Solution

Place a ruler vertically from 400 km to the graph. Then place a ruler horizontally from the graph to the vertical axis. The ruler meets the axis at 22 L.

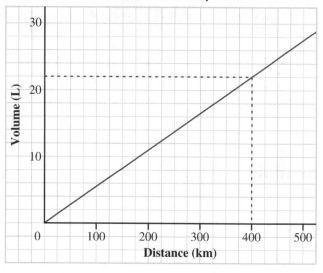

Volume of Fuel Required

Exercises

1. Use the graph in the *Example*. Estimate the amount of gas for each distance.

    a) 50 km   **b)** 200 km   **c)** 475 km   **d)** 500 km

2. How far do you think the car owner can drive on 10 L of gas?

3. Use the graph *Population of Canada*.

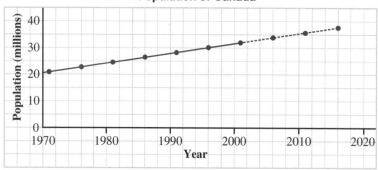

Population of Canada

a) Estimate the year that Canada's population was about 30 000 000.

b) Estimate Canada's population in 1980 and in 2040.

c) What assumptions are you making about the population in 2040? Explain.

A graph is a picture of a relationship between two quantities.
A graph shows how one quantity is related to another.

Relating Height and Time at Canada's Wonderland

Vikings Rage™, a ride at Canada's Wonderland, is a large ship that swings higher and higher.

1. Imagine you are on *Vikings Rage*. Visualize how your height above the ground changes from the beginning to the end of the ride.

   Which graph best represents the relationship between your height above ground and the length of time you are on the ride? Explain your choice.

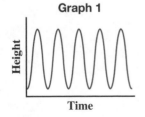

Graph 1

Height / Time

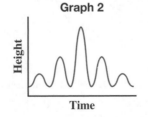

Graph 2

Height / Time

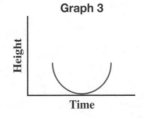

Graph 3

Height / Time

Drop Zone Stunt Tower™ is a 23-storey free-fall ride. People in open seats are lifted to the top of the ride, where there is brief stop. Then they are dropped straight down, reaching speeds of 100 km/h before coming to a complete stop.

2. Imagine you are on *Drop Zone Stunt Tower*. Visualize how your height above the ground changes from the beginning to the end of the ride.

   Which graph best represents the relationship between your height above ground and the length of time you are on the ride? Explain your choice.

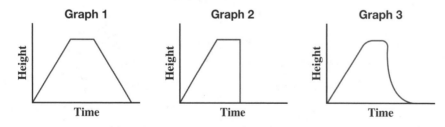

In the *Investigation*, each graph is a *distance-time graph* because distance (or height) is plotted against time. A distance-time graph is *not* a picture of the motion taking place; it shows how the distance changes with time.

In part 1 of the *Investigation*, Graph 2 best represents the ride. Over time, the height for each swing increases to a maximum, then decreases.

In part 2 of the *Investigation*, Graph 3 best represents the ride. The time to go up is greater than the time to come down. On the way down, your height above the ground changes quickly as you come to an abrupt stop.

Example 1

a) Describe the relationship represented by each graph.

i) 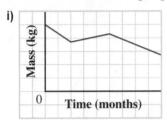 ii)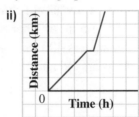

b) Describe a possible situation for each graph.

Solution

a) **i)** As time passes, the mass in kilograms decreases, then increases a little, then decreases.

   ii) As time passes, the distance in kilometres increases, then stays the same, then increases at a faster rate than before.

b) **i)** A possible situation is a person on a diet. During the first months, the person loses mass quickly. Then the person gains some mass over a longer period of time, and then loses even more mass.

   ii) A possible situation is a person driving a car. The graph shows she drives at a constant speed, stops for a short time, then continues at a faster speed.

Example 2

Draw a graph for each situation. Describe how each graph fits the situation.

a) the motion of a person on a trampoline

b) the heights and ages of a family

c) the money in the wallet of a person on a shopping trip

Solution

a) The person gets on a trampoline, bounces to a height of 0.75 m, falls, bounces higher to 1.0 m, falls, bounces higher to 1.25 m, falls, bounces higher to 1.5 m, then falls and stops.

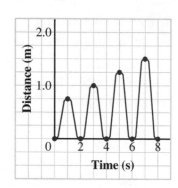

b) There are 5 people in the family. A 6-year-old child is 1.0 m tall. A 12-year-old child is 1.5 m. Another person is 20 years old and 1.85 m. A parent is 40 years old and 1.75 m. The other parent is 45 years old and 1.65 m.

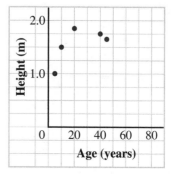

c) The person starts with $70. After 2 h, he spends $20. After another hour, he spends $5. About an hour and a half later, he goes to a bank machine and withdraws $35. He then has $80 in total.

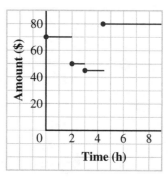

Discuss

How are these graphs similar? How are they different?

---

 1. Which graphs show both quantities increasing?

| **Graph A** | **Graph B** | **Graph C** | **Graph D** |

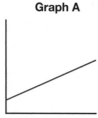      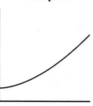   

2. Which graphs show one quantity decreasing then increasing?

Graph A  **Graph B**   **Graph C**   **Graph D**

3. Which graph best represents each situation?

a) the height of a tree over time

b) the height of a Ferris wheel seat as the wheel rotates

c) the number of hours you sleep each day over your lifetime

Graph 1 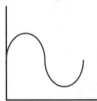 **Graph 2**  **Graph 3**

4. This graph shows the height of water in a bathtub over a period of time. Think about the label on each axis and the changes in the graph. Describe what happened to the water in the bathtub.

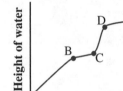

5. Describe the relationship indicated by each graph.

a)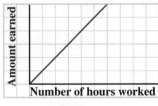

b)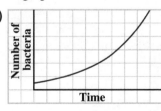

c)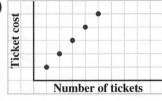

d)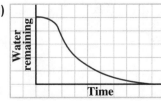

6. Knowledge/Understanding This graph shows Shakira's distance from home during a walk. Describe the walk.

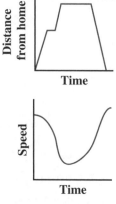

7. This graph shows the speed of Raoul's bike as he rides to school. Describe Raoul's ride.

8. Application In a science experiment, students suspended an object on a spring. They pulled the object down and released it to measure its motion. The graph shows the height of the object above the floor during the first few seconds of the experiment.

Motion of Object on a Spring

a) Find the height of the object at 1 s, 2 s, and 3 s.

b) Find when the object was:
   i) 6 cm above the floor
   ii) 10 cm above the floor

c) How long does it take the object to move up and down once?

9. Communication Suggest a possible situation for each graph. Describe the significance of any key points or changes in the graph.

a)   b)   c)   d)

10. For each activity, draw a graph with the axes shown. Label the units.

a) Graph the height above sea level for a person walking along a level road, climbing a hill, stopping to rest at the top, then walking down the hill.

b) Graph the height, above the water surface, for a person diving off a board.

c) Graph the height, above the bottom of a hill, for a ski-jumper.

d) Graph the height, above the bottom of a hill, for a skier in a slalom race.

11. Thinking/Inquiry/Problem Solving Draw a graph to represent each statement. Suggest two quantities that could be described by the graph. Record them on the axes.

a) When one quantity increases, the other increases.

b) When one quantity decreases, the other decreases.

c) When one quantity decreases, the other increases.

d) When one quantity increases, the other decreases.

12. Select one graph you drew in exercise 11. Describe how your graph fits the situation.

By conducting experiments and measuring, we can discover relationships between data.

A Pendulum Experiment

Work with a partner.

You need:

- about 1 m of string
- a small object such as a key or washer
- tape
- a metre stick or measuring tape
- a watch that measures tenths of a second

1. Copy this table.

A Pendulum Experiment

Length of pendulum (cm)	Time for 5 swings (s)

2. Make a pendulum by tying an object to a string. Tape the string to the edge of a desk so the object hangs freely close to the floor.

3. **a)** Measure the length of the pendulum. Record it in the table.

   b) Pull the object to an angle of about 30° from the rest position. Release it. One partner counts 5 swings back and forth, while the other measures the time and records it in the table.

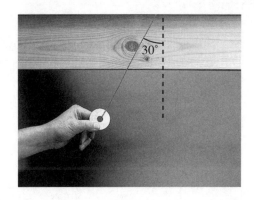

4. Repeat exercise 3 for shorter and shorter pendulum lengths. To shorten the length, lift the tape and pull up the string. Use 6 different lengths, including very short lengths.

5. Graph the data, using appropriate scales. Decide whether to join the points.

6. **a)** How does the amount of time change as the length of the string decreases? Explain whether this makes sense.

   b) Describe the relationship between the amount of time for the pendulum to swing 5 times and the length of the string.

A Pendulum Experiment

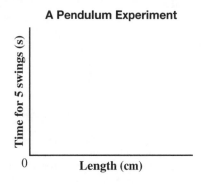

7. Use the graph to estimate how long it takes a 45-cm pendulum to swing back and forth 5 times.

8. Write a report to describe your experiment and what you found out. Include the graph in your report and justify your findings.

Graphs and tables of data show relationships between quantities.
A relationship between two quantities is a *relation*.

Example 1

Students measured the space occupied by identical books on a shelf.
Describe patterns in their table of values and graph.

Number of books, x	Shelf space (cm), y
1	3
2	6
3	9
4	12
5	15

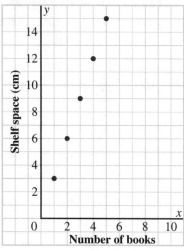

Space Used by Books on a Shelf

Solution

The table shows that as the number of books
increases by 1, the shelf space increases by 3 cm.

Start at any point on the graph. Move horizontally
and vertically to the next point. Each move is
1 unit right and 3 units up. The points lie on a
straight line. This is a result of constant changes
in the table of values.

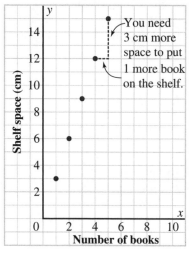

Space Used by Books on a Shelf

You need
3 cm more
space to put
1 more book
on the shelf.

Discuss

Why are the points not joined?

Example 2

This table of values and graph show the heights and bases of triangles whose area is 30 square units. Describe patterns in the table of values. Relate the patterns to the graph.

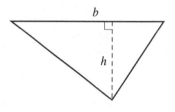

For a triangle, $A = \dfrac{bh}{2}$
A represents the area, b represents the base, and h represents the height.

Height, x	Base, y
1	60
2	30
3	20
4	15
5	12

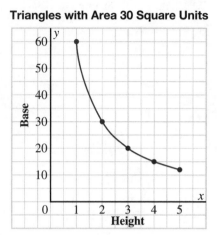

Solution

In the table, the height increases by a *constant* amount; the base decreases by a different amount.
As the height increases, the base decreases.
This pattern results in a curved graph that goes down to the right.

A small increase in the height results in a large decrease in the base.
A large increase in the height results in a small decrease in the base.

Each product of the height and base is 60.

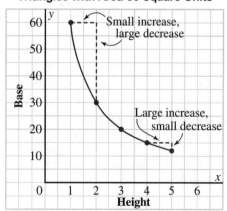

Discuss

Why are the points joined?

Example 1 illustrates a linear relation.
Example 2 illustrates a non-linear relation.

Differences in *y*-coordinates

We can also identify a linear relation by *differences*. We include a third column in each table of values in *Examples 1* and *2*. To complete the *Difference* column, take each *y*-coordinate and subtract the previous *y*-coordinate.

Number of books, *x*	Shelf space (cm), *y*	Difference
1	3	
		$6 - 3 = 3$
2	6	
		$9 - 6 = 3$
3	9	
		$12 - 9 = 3$
4	12	
		$15 - 12 = 3$
5	15	

Height, *x*	Base, *y*	Difference
1	60	
		$30 - 20 = -30$
2	30	
		$20 - 30 = -10$
3	20	
		$15 - 20 = -5$
4	15	
		$12 - 15 = -3$
5	12	

In *Example 1*, the *x*-coordinates increase by the same amount, and the differences in *y*-coordinates are equal.

In *Example 2*, the *x*-coordinates increase by the same amount, but the differences in *y*-coordinates are not equal.

TAKE NOTE

Linear and Non-Linear Relations

- The points on the graph of a *linear relation* in *x* and *y* lie on a straight line. If the numbers in the *x*-column of the table of values change by a constant amount, the differences in the *y*-coordinates are equal.

- The points on the graph of a *non-linear relation* in *x* and *y* do not lie on a straight line. If the numbers in the *x*-column of the table of values change by a constant amount, the differences in the *y*-coordinates are not equal.

A **1.** Does each graph represent a linear relation or a non-linear relation? How do you know?

a) 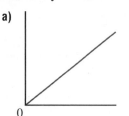   b) 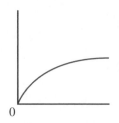   c) 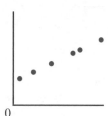   d)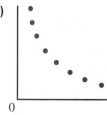

2. Does each table of values represent a linear relation or a non-linear relation? How do you know?

a)

x	y	Difference
2	3	
		3
4	6	
		3
6	9	
		3
8	12	
		3
10	15	

b)

x	y	Difference
1	12	
		−6
2	6	
		−2
3	4	
		−1
4	3	
		−1
6	2	
		−1
12	1	

c)

x	y	Difference
6	12	
		−3
5	9	
		−3
4	6	
		−1
3	5	
		−2
2	3	
		−2
1	1	

d)

x	y	Difference
2	12	
		−3
4	9	
		−3
6	6	
		−3
8	3	
		−3
10	0	

B **3. Knowledge/Understanding** For each table of values, calculate the differences. Describe the relationship between each pair of quantities.

a)

Mass suspended from a spring, x (g)	Extension of the spring, y (mm)	Difference
1	24	24
2	48	24
3	72	24
4	96	24
5	120	

b)

Distance from the basket, x (m)	Percent of baskets sunk, y	Difference
2	82	
3	68	
4	50	
5	30	
6	25	

c)

Time of day, x	Temperature, y (°C)	Difference
10:00	22	
11:00	25	
12:00	28	
13:00	27	
14:00	25	

✓ **4. a)** Graph the data. Plot *Number of coins* horizontally.

Number of coins	4	8	12	16	20
Mass (g)	100	200	300	400	500

b) Describe patterns in the data. Relate the patterns to the graph.

c) What is the mass of one coin? 18 coins?

5. a) Graph the data. Plot *Length of side* horizontally.

Length of side (cm)	1	2	3	4	5
Area of square (cm²)	1	4	9	16	25

b) Describe patterns in the data. Relate the patterns to the graph.

c) What is the area of a square with side length 3.5 cm?

d) What is the side length of a square with area 20 cm²?

e) Look at the table. When the length of one side is doubled does the area double? Why or why not?

> For a square, $A = s^2$
> A represents the area and s represents the side length.

6. a) Graph the data. Plot *Number of stairs climbed* horizontally.

Number of stairs climbed	5	10	15	20	25
Heart rate (beats/min)	70	80	98	119	147

b) Describe patterns in the data. Relate the patterns to the graph.

c) What is the heart rate after climbing 18 stairs? 13 stairs?

d) About how many stairs were climbed when the heart rate was 85 beats/min? 130 beats/min?

e) Suppose you climbed a very long flight of stairs. Would your heart rate change more rapidly near the beginning or the end of your climb? Explain.

7. a) Graph each relation in exercise 3.

b) For each graph, describe how one quantity changes as the other changes.

8. Investigation: Mass of Textbooks You need a scale that measures up to 20 kg.

a) Copy the table. Measure and record the masses of increasing numbers of your mathematics book.

Number of books	1	2	3	4	5	6	7	8	9	10
Mass (kg)										

b) Graph the data in the table. Plot *Number of books* horizontally.

c) Describe any patterns in the table. Relate the patterns to the graph.

d) Is the relation between the number of books and the mass linear or non-linear? How do the table and the graph show this?

e) Summarize your experiment and what you found out. Include the graph and table of values.

f) Pose a problem regarding the mass of books in the Investigation. Exchange problems with a classmate. Solve the problem posed by your classmate.

9. Communication Suppose the mass in exercise 8 was measured in grams. Would this affect whether the relation is linear or non-linear? Use the table and graph to support your answer.

10. Investigation: Comparing Ounces with Millilitres
Find cans with capacities labelled in both millilitres (mL) and fluid ounces (fl. oz.).

mL is a metric unit. fl.oz. is an imperial unit.

a) Record the capacities in a table.

Description	Capacity (mL)	Capacity (fl. oz.)

b) Predict the shape of the graph that represents the relation between these capacities.

c) Graph the capacities. Plot *Capacity (mL)* horizontally.

d) Is the relation between millilitres and fluid ounces linear or non-linear? How do the table and graph support your answer?

e) How does the graph compare with your prediction? Explain any differences between your prediction and the results.

f) Use the graph to convert each capacity to millilitres.

i) 15 fl. oz.　**ii)** 22 fl. oz.　**iii)** 20 fl. oz.　**iv)** 30 fl. oz.　**v)** 32 fl. oz.

✓ 11. Application The chart shows stopping distances on a dry, clean, level
pavement. This information is used in drivers' education courses. Stopping
distance is the sum of the driver reaction distance and the braking distance.

a) What is meant by "driver reaction distance"?

b) What is meant by "braking distance"?

c) Graph the data. How did you join the
points? Explain.

d) What is the average stopping distance
for a speed of 65 km/h? 95 km/h?

e) How does a wet road affect stopping
distance?

f) How would the graph change in each
situation?

  i) The road is wet.

  ii) The road is not level.

  iii) The road is gravel.

g) What other factors affect stopping distance?

Speed (km/h)	Average stopping distance (nearest metre)
20	8
30	12
40	17
50	23
60	31
70	41
80	52
90	66
100	81
110	99
120	120
130	143

✓ 12. Thinking/Inquiry/Problem Solving Psychologists have conducted
experiments to measure how much people remembered what they learned.
The results of the experiment are shown in the table and in the graph.
Sketch what the graph *Percent Forgotten vs. Time in Days* would look like.
Explain how you came up with your graph.

Time (days)	Percent remembered
1	84
5	71
15	61
30	56
60	54

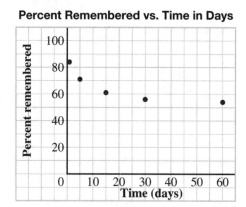

Percent Remembered vs. Time in Days

1. This graph represents the distance from shore during a boat ride. Describe the boat ride.

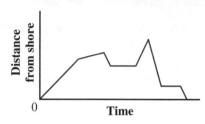

2. Describe the relation between the two quantities. Explain how one quantity changes as the other increases or decreases.

Temperature (°C)	0	20	40	60	80	100
Temperature (°F)	32	68	104	140	176	212

3. a) Copy and complete this table for the perimeters of equilateral triangles.

For an equilateral triangle, $P = 3s$
P represents the perimeter and s represents the side length.

Side length (cm)	1	2	3	4	5	6
Perimeter (cm)						

b) Graph the data. Plot *Side length (cm)* horizontally.

c) As the side length increases, what happens to the perimeter?

d) Is the relation linear or non-linear? Explain how the table of values and graph show this.

e) Use the graph to estimate the perimeter of a triangle with each side length.

   i) 3.5 cm   ii) 4.25 cm   iii) 0.5 cm   iv) 0.75 cm

f) Write a problem regarding side length. Solve your problem.

4. Frieda walks to the corner store to buy milk, then returns home. Which graph best represents her walk?

a)

b)

c)

d)

Using a Graphing Calculator to Investigate Relationships

A small company cuts lawns in the summer and clears driveways in the winter. It considers printing and distributing flyers to advertise.

Flyer Advertising

Work with a partner. You need a graphing calculator.

This price list shows the prices for printing and distributing flyers.

FULL PAGE FLYERS

Quantity	Printing ($)	Distribution ($)
1000	56.95	45.00
2000	78.90	90.00
3000	100.85	135.00
4000	122.80	180.00
5000	144.75	225.00
10,000	254.50	450.00
15,000	364.25	675.00
20,000	474.00	900.00
25,000	583.75	1125.00

One ink colour and one paper colour.
Artwork is $50.00 extra.
GST is extra.

Step 1. Enter the data.

- Press [STAT] **1** to go to the list editor.
  If there are any numbers in the columns, move the
  cursor into the column heading, then press [CLEAR] [ENTER].

- Move the cursor to the space
  below L1.
  Enter the first number from the
  Quantity column.
  Press [ENTER].

- Enter the other numbers from
  the *Quantity* column into list L1.

- Move the cursor to the space
  below L2.
  Enter the numbers from the
  Printing ($) column into list L2.

Step 2. Set up the graph.

Your calculator can draw the graph
you want, as well as plot the lists
along each axis.

- Press [2nd] [Y=] to get the STAT PLOT menu.
  This menu shows:
  - whether the plot is turned on or off
  - the type of graph
  - the lists plotted in the graph
  - the plotting symbol

- Press **1** to select Plot1. Press [ENTER] to turn on Plot1.

- Press [▼] [ENTER] to select the first plot type.

- Press [▼] [2nd] **1** to graph L1 horizontally.

- Press [▼] [2nd] **2** to graph L2 vertically.

- Press [▼] [ENTER] to select the first plotting symbol.

Step 3. Set up the window.

- Press [WINDOW].
- Enter Xmin = 0, Xmax = 25 000, and Xscl = 5000 to show quantities up to 25 000 on the horizontal axis.
- Enter Ymin = 0, Ymax = 600, and Yscl = 100 to show costs up to $600 on the vertical axis.

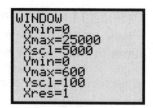

Step 4. Graph the data.

- Press [GRAPH] to graph L2, the cost of printing, against L1, the quantity.

  1. a) Does the relation appear linear or non-linear? Explain how you know.

   b) Explain whether the relation is reasonable for the data.

  2. Sketch the graph. Label the axes including units.

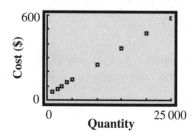

Operating with lists

The price list on page 24 states that artwork is $50.00 extra. You can use the calculator to add the cost of artwork to the printing cost.

- Press [STAT] **1** to go to the list editor. Move the cursor to the heading L3.
- Press [2nd] **2** [+] 50 [ENTER] to add 50 to each number in L2, and show the results in L3.

L1	L2	▮▮	3
1000	56.95	------	
2000	78.9		
3000	100.85		
4000	122.8		
5000	144.75		
10000	254.5		
15000	364.25		

L3 =L2+50

L1	L2	L3	3
1000	56.95	106.95	
2000	78.9	128.9	
3000	100.85	150.85	
4000	122.8	172.8	
5000	144.75	194.75	
10000	254.5	304.5	
15000	364.25	414.25	

L3(1)=106.95

  3. Predict how the graph of L3, the cost of printing with art, against L1, the quantity, will compare with the first graph for the cost of printing without art.

To check your prediction:

- Press [2nd] [Y=] to get the STAT PLOT menu.
- Press **2** to select Plot2. Press [ENTER] to turn on Plot2.
- Press [▼] [ENTER] to select the first plot type.
- Press [▼] [2nd] **1** to graph L1 horizontally.
- Press [▼] [2nd] **3** to graph L3 vertically.
- Press [▼] [▶] [ENTER] to select the second plotting symbol.

- Press GRAPH to graph the cost of printing without art on the same screen as the cost of printing with art.

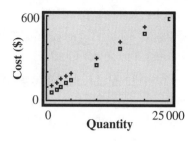

4. a) Sketch the graph. Label the axes, including units.

   b) How are the lists L2 and L3 related? Explain whether this is reasonable for adding the cost of $50 to the cost of printing each quantity.

   c) How does the graph show this relation?

Viewing coordinates of points

- Press TRACE. The flashing cursor is on a plotted point, with its coordinates at the bottom of the screen.

- Use the arrow keys to move the cursor.

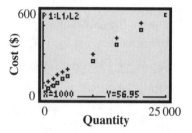

5. a) What happens when you press ◄ and ►?

   b) What happens when you press ▲ and ▼?

6. a) Trace to find the cost of printing 15 000 flyers without art.

   b) Trace to find the cost of printing 15 000 flyers with art.

Managing lists

The price list on page 24 shows the cost of distributing the flyers.
You can use the calculator to add the printing and distribution costs.

- Press STAT 1 to go to the list editor.
  Move the cursor to the heading L3.
  Press CLEAR ENTER to clear L3.

- Enter the distribution cost in L3.

- Move the cursor to the heading L4.
  Press 2nd 2 + 2nd 3 ENTER to add the printing cost in L2 and the distribution cost in L3, and show the results in L4.

L1	L2	L3	3
4000	122.8	180	
5000	144.75	225	
10000	254.5	450	
15000	364.25	675	
20000	474	900	
25000	583.75	1125	
------	------		

L3(10) =

L2	L3	L4	4
56.95	45	------	
78.9	90		
100.85	135		
122.8	180		
144.75	225		
254.5	450		
364.25	675		

L4 =L2+L3

7. Predict how the graph of the cost of printing plus distribution will compare with the graph of the cost of printing.

To check your prediction:

- Press 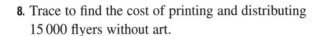 to get the STAT PLOT menu. Press **2** to select Plot2.
- Press ▼ ▼ ▼ [2nd] **4** to graph L4 against L1.
- Press [WINDOW]. Change window settings so that the whole graph will show. Enter Ymax = 2000 and Yscl = 200.
- Press [GRAPH].

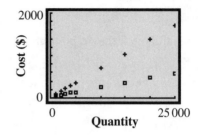

8. Trace to find the cost of printing and distributing 15 000 flyers without art.

The price list shows that GST is extra. You can use the calculator to multiply the cost by 1.07 to find the cost with GST.

- Press [STAT] **1** to go to the list editor.
- Move the cursor to the heading L5. Press [2nd] **4** [×] 1.07 [ENTER] to calculate the cost including GST, and show the results in L5.
- Press [2nd] [Y=] to get the STAT PLOT menu. Press **2** to select Plot2.
- Press ▼ ▼ ▼ [2nd] **5** to graph L5 against L1.
- Press [GRAPH] to display L5, the total cost, including GST, of printing and distributing flyers without art, against L1, the quantity.

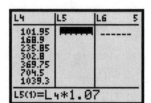

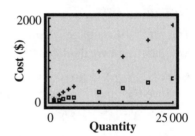

9. Trace to find the total cost, including GST, of printing and distributing 15 000 flyers.

10. Sketch the graph, and label the axes.

11. Communication Explain whether you would advise the company to advertise with flyers. Support your advice with data from the *Investigation*.

1.4 Using a Motion Detector to Investigate Relationships

You can use technology to gather data and display graphs. In this *Investigation*, you will use a TI-83 graphing calculator connected to a Calculator-Based Ranger™ (CBR™) unit. A CBR is a sonic motion detector that collects data and displays them on the calculator screen.

The instructions for the *Investigation* assume the RANGER program has been transferred to your calculator.

Checking for the Ranger program

To check whether the RANGER program has been transferred to your calculator:

- Connect the CBR to the calculator with the connecting cable.

- Turn on the calculator, then press [PRGM]. A list of programs stored in memory appears. If RANGER appears in the list, the program has been transferred. If RANGER does not appear, continue with the following steps.

Transferring the RANGER program to the calculator

- On the calculator, press [2nd] [X,T,θ,n] [▶] [ENTER].

  The calculator will show it is waiting to receive the program.

- On the CBR, open the pivoting head and press [82/83]. The CBR will send this program to the calculator.

Pendulum Experiment

You will use the CBR to measure its distance from a swinging pendulum. The calculator displays a graph to show how this distance changes as the pendulum swings back and forth.

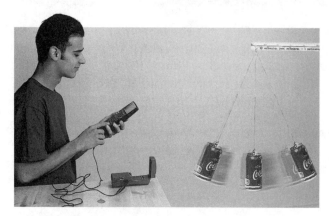

Work with a partner. You need:

- about 1 m of string
- an empty pop can
- a TI-83 graphing calculator
- a CBR and connecting cable
- a metre stick

Step 1. Set up the experiment.

- Set up the pendulum and CBR as shown. Use an object as large as a pop can for the weight. This is needed so that the CBR measures the distance to the object, not an object beyond it. Make the string as long as possible.
- Place the CBR at least 50 cm from the closest position of the object.
- Connect the CBR to the calculator with the connecting cable.
- Turn on the calculator. Press [PRGM].
- Choose RANGER. Press [ENTER].
- Press [ENTER] [ENTER] to display the main menu.
- Press **2** to choose SET DEFAULTS.
- Make sure the cursor is beside START NOW. If not, use the arrow keys to move it.
- Start the pendulum swinging.

```
MAIN MENU
1:SETUP/SAMPLE
2:SET DEFAULTS
3:APPLICATIONS
4:PLOT MENU
5:TOOLS
6:QUIT
```

Step 2. Collect and graph the data.

- Press [ENTER] when you are ready to begin. The calculator displays a distance-time graph that follows the motion of the pendulum.
- To make the calculator redraw the graph in a better position on the screen, press [ENTER] **1**.
- To repeat, press [ENTER] **3**. Repeat until you are satisfied with the result.
- Leave the graph on the screen while you complete the following exercises. Since the data for this graph are in your calculator, you can disconnect the cable so that someone else can use the CBR.

1. Look at the graph. What quantity is represented along

   a) the horizontal axis?   **b)** the vertical axis?

2. Sketch the distance-time graph, or use a computer linkup to print it. Label the axes with the units.

3. Is the graph linear or non-linear? How do you know?

4. Describe what happens to the plotted points in each case.

   a) The object is moving toward the CBR.

   b) The object is moving away from the CBR.

   c) The pendulum slows down.

Viewing coordinates of points

You can view the coordinates of some points on the graph. These correspond to the data the CBR gathered.

5. Press ⌞TRACE⌟ and the arrow keys to move the flashing cursor along the graph. Its coordinates appear on the screen.

   a) What was the maximum distance from the object to the CBR?

   b) What was the minimum distance from the object to the CBR?

   c) How many complete swings are represented on the graph?

6. The period of the pendulum is the time for one complete swing. Find the period of the pendulum as accurately as you can.

7. **a)** Suppose you pulled the object farther from the rest position before starting the pendulum. Predict how the distance-time graph would change.

   b) Use the CBR and calculator to check your prediction.

8. **a)** Suppose you repeated the experiment with a longer pendulum. Predict how the distance-time graph would change.

   b) Use the CBR and calculator to check your prediction.

9. **a)** Suppose you repeated the experiment with a shorter pendulum. Predict how the distance-time graph would change.

   b) Use the CBR and calculator to check your prediction.

10. **Communication** The graphs in the *Investigation* show the relation between two quantities. Describe these two quantities, and explain how they are related. Include sketches of graphs to illustrate your description.

The graph from page 16 is repeated here. It shows a relationship between two quantities.

- These quantities are related by multiplication and division.
- The points on the graph lie on a straight line through the origin.
- The line goes up to the right.

Any situation that has these properties is a *proportional situation*. To solve problems in proportional situations, use multiplication or division.

Space Used by Books on a Shelf

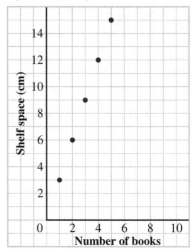

Example 1

Marcia works in a card store after school. In 4 h, Marcia earns $20.

a) What is Marcia's hourly rate of pay?

b) How much does Marcia earn in 8 h?

c) How long does Marcia work to earn $100?

d) Use the data from parts a to c. Make a table of values. Draw a graph to show how Marcia's earnings are related to the number of hours she works.

e) Do Marcia's earnings show a proportional situation? Explain how you know.

Solution

a) Marcia earns $20 in 4 h.
   So, in 1 h, Marcia earns $\frac{20}{4} = 5$.
   Marcia's rate of pay is $5/h.

b) Marcia earns $5 per hour.
   So, in 8 h, Marcia earns $8 \times 5 = 40$.
   Marcia earns $40 in 8 h.

c) Marcia earns $5 per hour.
   So, to earn $100, Marcia works $\frac{100}{5} = 20$.
   Marcia works 20 h to earn $100.

d)

Time (h)	Earnings ($)
4	20
1	5
8	40
20	100

Marcia's Earnings

(graph: Earnings ($) vs Time (h), points plotted at (4, 20), (8, 40), (20, 100) lying on a straight line through the origin going up to the right)

e) Marcia's earnings show a proportional situation. The quantities are the time Marcia works and the amount she earns. These quantities are related by multiplication and division. The points on the graph lie on a straight line through the origin. These points go up to the right.

Discuss

Suppose Marcia's hourly rate increased. How would the graph change?

Example 2

At the bulk-food store, Jerry bought 200 g of mixed nuts that cost $2.50.

a) What is the cost of 1 g of nuts?

b) What is the price for 450 g of nuts?

c) What mass of nuts would cost $6.25?

d) Show the results of parts a to c in a table. Draw a graph.

Solution

a) 200 g of nuts cost $2.50.

For 1 g: $\frac{2.50}{200} = 0.0125$

One gram of nuts costs $0.01.

The cost of 1 g of nuts is the unit price.

b) 1 g of nuts costs $0.0125.

For 450 g: $450 \times 0.0125 \doteq 5.63$

The price for 450 g of nuts is $5.63.

c) $0.0125 buys 1 g.

For $6.25: $\frac{6.25}{0.0125} = 500$

500 g of nuts would cost $6.25.

d)

Mass (g)	Price ($)
200	2.50
450	5.63
500	6.25

Cost of Mixed Nuts

Discuss

Suppose the price per gram decreased. How would the graph change?

Is this a proportional situation? How do you know?

In part b, why is the cost for 1 g of nuts written with more than 2 decimal places?

1.5   Exercises

Use mental math where possible.

A ✓

1. One cheeseburger costs $1.29. What is the cost for each number of cheeseburgers?

   a) 3   **b)** 5   **c)** 20   **d)** 12

2. One tennis ball costs $0.72. What is the cost for each number of tennis balls?

   a) 2   **b)** 4   **c)** 6   **d)** 13

✓ **3.** Find each unit price. Round to the nearest cent.

   a) A box of 15 sports drinks costs $23.99.

   b) A box of 12 markers costs $34.59.

   c) A package of 500 sheets of paper costs $5.99.

4. Find each unit price to the nearest cent.

   a) Message pads cost $4.40 for 10.

   b) Business envelopes cost $8.99 for 100.

   c) Blank CDs cost $11.99 for 10.

5. A customer buys 400 g of candy for $2.40. Find the cost of each mass. Check with a calculator.

  a) 800 g   **b)** 100 g   **c)** 200 g   **d)** 1600 g

6. A case of 24 cans of pop costs $6.96.

  a) What is the unit price per can?

  b) What is the cost of a dozen cans of pop?

7. Six bottles of motor oil cost $11.34.

  a) What is the unit price?

  b) What is the price for 10 bottles? 40 bottles? 100 bottles?

  c) Show the results in a table.

  d) Draw a graph. Plot *Number of bottles* horizontally and *Cost* vertically. Include the units.

  e) Does the graph represent a proportional situation? How do you know?

8. The gas tank in May's car holds 45 L of gas. The cost for a fill-up is $27.86.

  a) What is the price per litre? Round to the nearest cent.

  b) For this unit price, what is the cost of 35 L of gas?

  c) How many litres could May buy with $10.00?

9. The Red Shield Telethon raised $42 500 in the first 20 min.

  a) At this rate, how much would be raised in 1 h? 3 h? 8 h?

  b) Show the results in a table.

  c) Draw a graph to show the relationship between the time and the amount raised.

  d) At this rate, about how long would it take to raise $1 000 000?

  e) Suppose the amount raised per hour increased. How would the graph change? Explain.

  f) Is this a proportional situation? Explain how the table and graph show this.

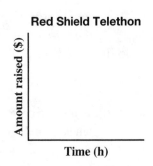

10. Knowledge/Understanding Tina works part-time for a landscaping company. She is paid hourly and earns $28.70 in 3.5 h.

  a) How much does she earn in 1 h? 9 h? 12 h? 20 h?

  b) How many hours would she work to earn $287?

  c) Show the results of parts a and b in a table.

  d) Draw a graph to show how the amount earned is related to the time worked. Plot *Time worked* horizontally.

e) Suppose Tina's hourly rate increased. How would the graph change? Explain.

f) Is this a proportional situation? Explain how you know.

11. a) Taborah had 12 hits in 30 attempts at bat. About how many attempts at bat would she need for 100 hits?

b) What assumption is made in part a? Do you think this assumption is realistic? Explain your reason.

✓ **12. Application** Which cola special is the better value?

1.5-L bottle	$1.29
Case of 24 x 355-mL cans	$5.99

13. A 5-kg bag of grass seed covers an area of 300 m^2.

a) What mass of grass seed is needed to cover a football field 150 m by 60 m?

b) Explain how you could estimate to check your answer.

✓ **14. Communication** Explain what is meant by a *proportional situation*. Use an example to illustrate your explanation.

15. Thinking/Inquiry/Problem Solving
The giant sequoia trees on the west coast of North America are among the world's tallest and oldest living things. Some of them are 3200 years old. An average sequoia pumps about 1000 L of water from its roots to its leaves every 24 h.

How long would it take to pump the amount of water that would fill a pop can? Explain how you got your answer.

1.6 Relating Animal and Human Lifetimes

On page 3, you considered the problem of comparing the lifetime of an animal with a human lifetime.

There is no exact formula. Several models have been proposed by veterinarians and scientists. Your task is to make a graph to show how the models relate the lifetime of a cat or dog to a human lifetime. You will compare the models, then determine which model you think is best.

You will need grid paper, some coloured pencils or markers, and a ruler.

1. Prepare a grid with axes as shown. Make the grid as large as possible. You may need to experiment to find the best way to set up the axes and the scales.

   a) Plot the animal's age along the horizontal axis. Since the expected lifetime for a cat or dog is no more than 20 years, label the horizontal scale from 0 to 20.

   b) Plot a person's age along the vertical axis. Label the vertical scale from 0 to 100.

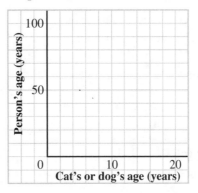

Model 1

One year of a cat's life is equivalent to 7 years of a person's life.

2. **a)** Copy and complete this table.

Cat's age (years)	1	2	3	4	5	6	7	8	9	10
Person's age (years)	7	14								

   b) Graph the data from your table. Decide whether it makes sense to join the points on the graph. Label your graph.

   c) Do you think this model is reasonable? Why?

Model 2

This model for cats appeared in an article in *Reader's Digest*.

The first year of a cat's life equals about 21 human years. For each additional year, count 4 human years for each year of the cat's life.

3. a) Copy and complete this table.

Cat's age (years)	1	2	3	4	5	6	7	8	9	10
Person's age (years)	21	25								

b) Graph the data on the same grid as Model 1. Label the graph.

4. Compare the graph of this model with the graph of Model 1.

a) State two ways in which Model 2 differs from Model 1.

b) Explain what these differences mean in terms of relating the lifetime of a cat to a human lifetime.

Model 3

This model for dogs appeared in an article in *The Toronto Star*.

The first year of a dog's life equals about 15 human years. The second year adds another 10 years. For each additional year, count 5 human years for each year of the dog's life.

5. a) Copy and complete this table.

Dog's age (years)	1	2	3	4	5	6	7	8	9	10
Person's age (years)	15	25	30							

b) Graph the data on a grid similar to the one in exercise 1.

c) How is Model 3 similar to Model 2?

d) Do you think it would be reasonable to use either Model 2 or Model 3 for both cats and dogs? Why?

6. Which graph shows a proportional situation? How do you know?

7. Choose the model that you think is the best one for relating the lifetime of an animal to a human lifetime. Explain your choice.

Relation

- A relationship between two quantities can be shown on a graph.

Linear Relation	Non-Linear Relation
• If the numbers in the x-column of the table of values change by a constant amount, the differences in the y-coordinates are equal.	• If the numbers in the x-column of the table of values change by a constant amount, the differences in the y-coordinates are not equal.
• The points on the graph lie on a straight line.	• The points on the graph do not lie on a straight line.
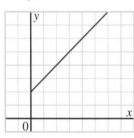	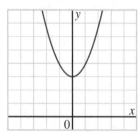

Proportional Situation

- Quantities are related by multiplication and division.
- Points on the graph lie on a straight line through 0.
- The graph goes up to the right.

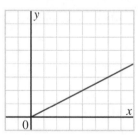

1. For each graph, explain how the quantities change.

a)

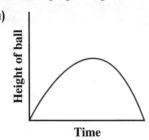

b)

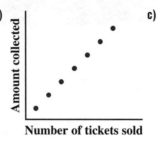

c)

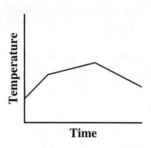

2. a) Sketch a graph to show the water level in a sink.
- Start with an empty sink with the plug in.
- Turn on the tap.
- Turn off the tap.
- Turn on the tap again.
- Turn off the tap.
- Take out the plug.

b) Describe how your graph shows the water level.

3. Describe the relationship between the two quantities.

Time a tap is on (min)	2	4	6	8	10	12	14	16	18
Depth of water in fish pond (cm)	1	2	3	4	5	6	7	8	9

4. a) Investigation: Metric and Imperial Units Measure the lengths of 6 objects in centimetres and in inches. Record the lengths in a table.

> Centimetre is a metric unit. Inch is an imperial unit.

Object	Length (cm)	Length (in.)

b) Does the table of values show a linear or non-linear relation? How do you know?

c) Graph the lengths.

d) Does the graph show a linear or non-linear relation? How do you know?

e) Use the data to write a problem about an object and its length.

f) Solve the problem you wrote in part e.

Metric and Imperial Units

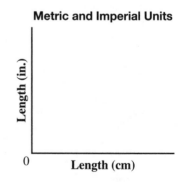

5. a) Suppose distances are measured in both metres and feet. Predict if there is a relationship between the two measures. Explain.

b) Choose 6 distances to measure in feet and in metres. Record the data in a table.

c) Graph the data.

d) Compare the table and the graph with your prediction. Explain any differences between your prediction and results.

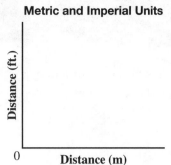

Metric and Imperial Units

Distance (ft.) vs *Distance (m)*

Metre is a metric unit. Foot is an imperial unit.

1.4 **6.** Suppose you use a graphing calculator and CBR to graph the distance between the CBR and a swinging pendulum.

a) Sketch a graph that could appear on the calculator screen.

b) How does your graph represents this situation?

1.5 **7.** What is the price per package for each kind of paper?

a) 10 packages of computer paper cost $119.90.

b) 10 packages of copy paper cost $109.70.

c) 10 packages of 3-hole punched paper cost $229.80.

d) 10 packages of green paper cost $149.90.

8. Raj earned $40.50 for working 6 h in a grocery store.

a) What is Raj's hourly rate of pay?

b) How much does Raj earn in 12 h? 24 h?

c) How long does Raj work to earn $216?

d) Show the results of parts a to c in a table.

e) Graph the data. Plot *Time worked* horizontally.

f) Do Raj's earnings show a proportional situation? How do the table and graph show this?

g) Suppose Raj took another job with a lower hourly rate. How would the graph change?

9. Marta's hockey team can buy a dozen black pucks for $16.95 or 3 dozen orange pucks for $45.95.

a) What is the unit price for each puck?

b) Which is the better price per puck?

1. This graph represents the speed of a ride at an amusement park. Describe how the speed changes.

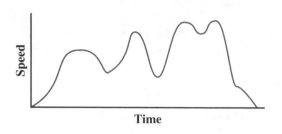

2. **Knowledge/Understanding**

   a) Copy and complete the table. It shows the dimensions of rectangles with area 24 cm².

Width (cm)	1	2	3	4	6	8	12	24
Length (cm)	24	12						

   b) Graph the data. Plot *Width* horizontally.

   c) Use the graph to estimate the length of a rectangle with width 5 cm.

   d) What happens to the length as the width increases? Why?

   e) Is the relation linear or non-linear? How do the table of values and graph show this?

   f) Do the graph and table show a proportional situation? How do you know?

3. **Thinking/Inquiry/Problem Solving** In exercise 2b, how would the graph change if the area of the rectangle was 36 cm²? Explain your ideas.

4. **Communication** This graph represents the cost for printing flyers. Pose a problem about this relation. Solve your problem.

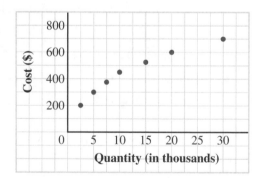

5. A package of 12 pens costs $15.48.

   a) At this rate, what is the cost of 1 pen? 36 pens? 50 pens? 100 pens?

   b) Show the data in a table.

   c) Graph the data. Plot *Number of pens* horizontally.

   d) Does the graph represent a proportional situation? Explain how you know.

   e) **Application** Describe how the graph in part c would change for each situation.
      i) The pens were on sale at a cheaper price.
      ii) The pens were purchased individually for $1.39 each.

1. Three sisters, Sam, Dina, and Nat, decided to race 60 m.

   • The youngest, Sam, was allowed to start ahead of the others.

   • The oldest, Nat, had to wait for 1 s after their father said "Go."

   Match each sister with the line A, B, or C, which represents her race.
   Explain your choices.

The Race

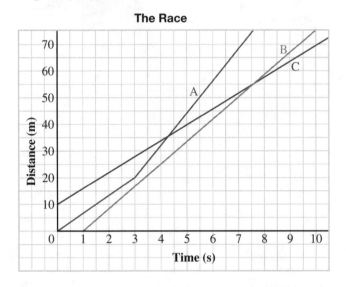

2. Avinash tried his new snowboard at "Snowboarders Only Resort."
   The following graph shows his first run.

Snowboarder

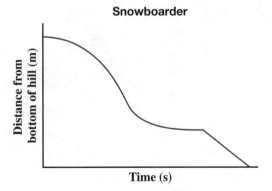

   • The vertical axis shows his distance from the bottom of the hill.

   • The horizontal axis shows time in seconds.

   Write a description Avinash's first run.

CHAPTER 2

Powers and Roots

By the end of this chapter, you will:

- Evaluate powers. Calculate with powers. Calculate square roots.

- Understand zero and negative exponents.

- Use patterns to find the rules for multiplying and dividing monomials.

- Evaluate powers with natural number exponents and rational number bases.

- Represent very large and very small numbers in scientific notation.

- Use the Pythagorean Theorem to calculate side lengths of right triangles.

- Use a scientific calculator for calculations with exponents.

- Decide whether answers are reasonable by considering likely results for the situations and by estimating.

- Communicate solutions to problems, and justify your reasoning in solving problems.

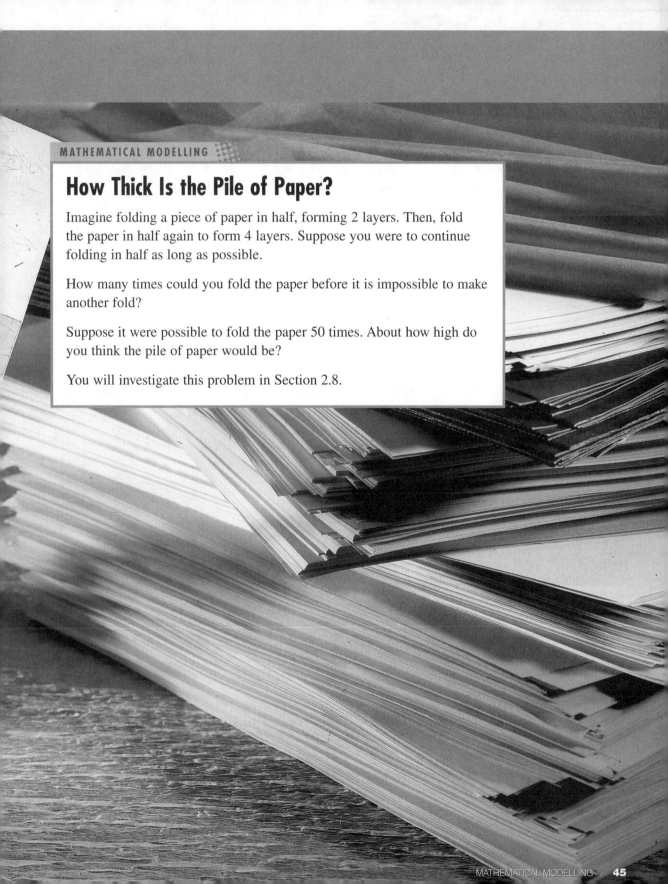

How Thick Is the Pile of Paper?

Imagine folding a piece of paper in half, forming 2 layers. Then, fold the paper in half again to form 4 layers. Suppose you were to continue folding in half as long as possible.

How many times could you fold the paper before it is impossible to make another fold?

Suppose it were possible to fold the paper 50 times. About how high do you think the pile of paper would be?

You will investigate this problem in Section 2.8.

Necessary Skills

Powers

For the *power* 2^5:

- the *base* is 2. The base is the number that is repeatedly multiplied.
- the *exponent* is 5. The exponent is the number of times that the base is multiplied.

$$\text{power } 2^5 \overset{\longleftarrow \text{ exponent}}{\longleftarrow \text{ base}}$$

We say "2 to the fifth" or "2 to the power 5."

We write: $2^5 = 2 \times 2 \times 2 \times 2 \times 2$
$\qquad\qquad = 32$

Example

Evaluate each power.

a) 4^2 **b)** 3^3 **c)** 1^4

Solution

a) $4^2 = 4 \times 4$ **b)** $3^3 = 3 \times 3 \times 3$ **c)** $1^4 = 1 \times 1 \times 1 \times 1$
$\qquad = 16$ $= 27$ $= 1$

Exercises

1. Evaluate each power.

   a) 10^2 **b)** 10^3 **c)** 10^4 **d)** 10^5

2. Look at exercise 1. How can you mentally evaluate a power with base 10?

3. Explain what each power means. Evaluate each power.

   a) 5^4 **b)** 7^3 **c)** 3^2 **d)** 10^5

4. Evaluate each power. Calculate mentally if possible.

   a) 6^2 **b)** 5^3 **c)** 4^2 **d)** 1^8

5. Write a rule about evaluating a power with base 1. Use a calculator to check your rule.

6. Use a calculator to evaluate each power.

   a) 21^3 **b)** 9^7 **c)** 130^4 **d)** 19^5

Recall the rules for multiplying integers.

When two integers have the same sign, their product is positive.

$$(+) \times (+) = + \qquad (-) \times (-) = +$$

When two integers have different signs, their product is negative.

$$(+) \times (-) = - \qquad (-) \times (+) = -$$

Recall that a power is a repeated multiplication. For example, $2^3 = 2 \times 2 \times 2$

Example 1

Write each power as a product. Then evaluate.

a) 4^5 **b)** $(-6)^8$ **c)** $(-5)^4$

Solution

Since these require several multiplications, use a calculator.

a) $4^5 = (4)(4)(4)(4)(4)$

Press: 4 $\boxed{\wedge}$ 5 $\boxed{\text{ENTER}\atop=}$

$4^5 = 1024$

```
4^5
           1024
```

b) $(-6)^8 = (-6)(-6)(-6)(-6)(-6)(-6)(-6)(-6)$

Press: $\boxed{(}$ $\boxed{(-)}$ 6 $\boxed{)}$ $\boxed{\wedge}$ 8 $\boxed{\text{ENTER}\atop=}$

$(-6)^8 = 1\ 679\ 616$

```
(-6)^8
          1679616
```

c) $(-5)^4 = (-5)(-5)(-5)(-5)$

Press: $\boxed{(}$ $\boxed{(-)}$ 5 $\boxed{)}$ $\boxed{\wedge}$ 4 $\boxed{\text{ENTER}\atop=}$

$(-5)^4 = 625$

```
(-5)^4
             625
```

In part c, the brackets are significant.

$$(-5)^4 = (-5)(-5)(-5)(-5) \qquad\qquad -5^4 = -(5)^4$$
$$= 625 \qquad\qquad\qquad\qquad\qquad = -(5)(5)(5)(5)$$
$$\qquad\qquad\qquad\qquad\qquad\qquad = -625$$

A rational number is a number that can be written as a fraction, a terminating decimal, or a repeating decimal. A rational number can be positive or negative.

Products of Integers and Rational Numbers

- The product of positive rational numbers is positive. $(+) \times (+) \times (+) = +$
- The product of an even number of negative rational numbers is positive.
  $(-) \times (-) \times (-) \times (-) = +$
- The product of an odd number of negative rational numbers is negative.
  $(-) \times (-) \times (-) = -$

A power with a rational-number base is evaluated in the same way as a power with an integer base.

We can use the rules for multiplying integers and rational numbers to predict whether a product is positive or negative.

Example 2

Write each power as a product. Then evaluate.

a) $\left(\dfrac{2}{3}\right)^3$　　　　b) $\left(-\dfrac{5}{4}\right)^2$　　　　c) $\left(-\dfrac{3}{10}\right)^5$

Solution

a) $\left(\dfrac{2}{3}\right)^3 = \dfrac{2}{3} \times \dfrac{2}{3} \times \dfrac{2}{3}$

$= \dfrac{2 \times 2 \times 2}{3 \times 3 \times 3}$

$= \dfrac{8}{27}$

b) $\left(-\dfrac{5}{4}\right)^2 = \left(-\dfrac{5}{4}\right)\left(-\dfrac{5}{4}\right)$

$= \dfrac{(-5) \times (-5)}{4 \times 4}$

$= \dfrac{25}{16}$

There is an even number of negative rational numbers. So, the product is positive.

c) $\left(-\dfrac{3}{10}\right)^5 = \left(-\dfrac{3}{10}\right)\left(-\dfrac{3}{10}\right)\left(-\dfrac{3}{10}\right)\left(-\dfrac{3}{10}\right)\left(-\dfrac{3}{10}\right)$

There is an odd number of negative rational numbers. So, the product is negative. Use a calculator.

Press: ( ) (-) 3 A% 10) ^ 5 ENTER =

$\left(-\dfrac{3}{10}\right)^5 = -0.002\ 43$

```
(-3⌐10)^5
        -0.00243
```

Example 3

Evaluate each power to 2 decimal places.
Estimate to check whether the answers are reasonable.

a) $(-1.25)^4$ **b)** 10.2^5 **c)** $(-2.9)^3$

Solution

a) $(-1.25)^4$

Use a calculator.
Press: (( ) ((-)) 1.25 ( )) (^) 4 [ENTER]

$(-1.25)^4 \doteq 2.44$

```
(-1.25)^4
            2.44140625
```

Check.
1.25 is greater than 1 and $1^4 = 1$; 2.44 is slightly greater than 1.
$(-1.25)^4$ has an even number of negative rational numbers, so the answer
is positive.
So, $(-1.25)^4 \doteq 2.44$ is reasonable.

b) 10.2^5

Press: 10.2 (^) 5 [ENTER]

$10.2^5 \doteq 110\ 408.08$

```
10.2^5
            110408.0803
```

Check.
$10.2 \doteq 10$ and $10^5 = 100\ 000$; $100\ 000$ is close to $110\ 408.08$.
So, $10.2^5 \doteq 110\ 408.08$ is reasonable.

c) $(-2.9)^3$

Press: (( ) ((-)) 2.9 ( )) (^) 3 [ENTER]

$(-2.9)^3 \doteq -24.39$

```
(-2.9)^3
            -24.389
```

Check.
2.9 is almost 3 and $3^3 = 27$; 24.39 is close to 27.
$(-2.9)^3$ has an odd number of negative rational numbers, so the answer
is negative.
So, $(-2.9)^3 \doteq -24.39$ is reasonable.

1. Evaluate. Round to 3 decimal places where necessary.

   a) $(-5)(-5)(-5)(-5)(-5)$

   b) $(6)(6)(6)(6)(6)(6)$

   c) $(-9.1)(-9.1)(-9.1)(-9.1)$

   d) $(2.85)(2.85)(2.85)(2.85)(2.85)$

   e) $\left(\frac{1}{4}\right)\left(\frac{1}{4}\right)\left(\frac{1}{4}\right)$

   f) $\left(-\frac{7}{3}\right)\left(-\frac{7}{3}\right)\left(-\frac{7}{3}\right)\left(-\frac{7}{3}\right)\left(-\frac{7}{3}\right)\left(-\frac{7}{3}\right)$

✓ **2.** Write each power as a product. Then evaluate.

   a) $(-2)^1$ **b)** $(-2)^2$ **c)** $(-2)^3$

   d) $(-2)^4$ **e)** $(-2)^5$ **f)** $(-2)^6$

✓ **3.** Write each power as a product. Then evaluate.

   a) $\left(-\frac{1}{2}\right)^1$ **b)** $\left(-\frac{1}{2}\right)^2$ **c)** $\left(-\frac{1}{2}\right)^3$

   d) $\left(-\frac{1}{2}\right)^4$ **e)** $\left(-\frac{1}{2}\right)^5$ **f)** $\left(-\frac{1}{2}\right)^6$

✓ **4.** Evaluate each power mentally.

   a) 4^1 **b)** 7^1 **c)** 1^1 **d)** 10^1

   e) $(-4)^1$ **f)** $(-7)^1$ **g)** $(-1)^1$ **h)** $(-10)^1$

 5. a) Evaluate.

   i) 10^2 **ii)** $(-10)^3$ **iii)** $(-10)^4$ **iv)** 10^5 **v)** $(-10)^6$

   b) How would you evaluate a power of 10 mentally?

✓ **6. a)** Evaluate.

   i) $(-3)^1$ **ii)** $(-3)^2$ **iii)** $(-3)^3$ **iv)** $(-3)^4$ **v)** $(-3)^5$

   b) Communication Explain how you know whether a power with a
   negative base is positive or negative.

7. Evaluate. Record only answers less than 1. Round to 3 decimal places
   where necessary.

   a) $\left(\frac{2}{3}\right)^4$ **b)** $(1.02)^3$ **c)** $(-0.6)^8$ **d)** $\left(\frac{6}{5}\right)^2$ **e)** $(-3.2)^5$

8. Write each power as a product. Then evaluate.

   a) $\left(\frac{1}{3}\right)^4$ **b)** $\left(-\frac{3}{5}\right)^3$ **c)** $\left(-\frac{10}{3}\right)^4$ **d)** $\left(\frac{5}{8}\right)^2$

9. Evaluate each power. Round to 2 decimal places where necessary. Estimate to check whether the answers are reasonable.

a) 3.8^4 **b)** $(-1.9)^5$ **c)** 2.25^6 **d)** $(-0.1)^2$

10. Knowledge/Understanding Evaluate each power. Round to 3 decimal places where necessary.

a) 3^6 **b)** $(-5)^9$ **c)** 2.1^5

d) $\left(\dfrac{2}{5}\right)^4$ **e)** $(-1.7)^4$ **f)** $\left(-\dfrac{3}{11}\right)^3$

11. a) Evaluate.

     i) $(-4)^2$ **ii)** -4^2 **iii)** $-(-4)^2$ **iv)** 4^2

b) Describe the differences among the four powers in part a.

12. a) Evaluate each power without rounding.

     i) $(0.25)^3$ **ii)** $\left(\dfrac{1}{4}\right)^3$ **iii)** $(-0.8)^4$

     iv) $\left(-\dfrac{4}{5}\right)^4$ **v)** $(-0.5)^2$ **vi)** $\left(-\dfrac{1}{2}\right)^2$

b) Which results from part a are equal? Why are they equal? How might you use this when entering powers on a calculator?

13. a) Application Evaluate each power. Make decisions about rounding you think are appropriate.

     i) Dinosaurs became extinct about 90^4 years ago.

     ii) In 2001, the population of Canada was about 6.8^9.

     iii) The area of Ontario is about 102.5^3 km^2.

b) Explain your decisions about rounding in part a.

14. Thinking/Inquiry/Problem Solving

     a) List the powers of $(-2)^n$ from $n = 1$ to $n = 8$. Evaluate each power.

     b) When is $(-2)^n$ positive? Explain.

     c) When is $(-2)^n$ negative? Explain.

     d) When is $-(-2)^n$ positive? Explain.

     e) When is $-(-2)^n$ negative? Explain.

Recall that a power represents repeated multiplication. In each *Investigation*, you will examine patterns you can use to multiply and divide powers efficiently.

Multiplying Powers

1. Copy and complete this table.

Product of powers	Product form	Power form
$10^2 \times 10^3$	$(10 \times 10) \times (10 \times 10 \times 10)$	10^5
$10^3 \times 10^4$		
$10^3 \times 10^6$		
$5^4 \times 5^5$		
$5^3 \times 5^1$		
$2^2 \times 2^9$		

2. Extend the table. Make up 5 more examples. Add them to the table.

3. Look at the table.

a) State a rule for multiplying powers of 10. Explain why your rule works.

b) State a rule for multiplying powers of 5.

c) State a rule for multiplying powers with the same base.

Investigation 1 shows this pattern:

Multiplying Powers

Since a^3 means $a \times a \times a$ and a^4 means $a \times a \times a \times a$,

$$a^3 \times a^4 = (a \times a \times a) \times (a \times a \times a \times a)$$
$$= a^7$$

The powers a^3 and a^4 have the same base. The base is a.

We find the product $a^3 \times a^4$ by writing the base a and adding the exponents: $a^3 \times a^4 = a^{3+4}$
$$= a^7$$

Dividing Powers

1. Copy and complete this table.

Quotient of powers	Quotient form	Power form
$10^5 \div 10^3$	$\dfrac{10 \times 10 \times 10 \times 10 \times 10}{10 \times 10 \times 10}$	10^2
$10^8 \div 10^5$		
$10^7 \div 10^3$		
$5^{10} \div 5^4$		
$5^5 \div 5^4$		
$9^8 \div 9^3$		

2. Extend the table. Make up 5 more examples. Add them to the table.

3. Look at the table.

a) State a rule for dividing powers of 10. Explain why your rule works.

b) State a rule for dividing powers of 5.

c) State a rule for dividing powers with the same base.

Investigation 2 shows this pattern:

Dividing Powers

Since a^5 means $a \times a \times a \times a \times a$ and a^3 means $a \times a \times a$,

$a^5 \div a^3 = \dfrac{a \times a \times a \times a \times a}{a \times a \times a}$

$\qquad = a^2$

The powers a^5 and a^3 have the same base. The base is a.

We find the quotient $a^5 \div a^3$ by writing the base a and subtracting the exponents: $a^5 \div a^3 = a^{5-3}$

$\qquad\qquad\qquad\qquad = a^2$

Exponent Law for Multiplying Powers

To multiply powers with the same base, write the base and add the exponents.
$a^n \times a^m = a^{n+m}$, where n and m are natural numbers.

Exponent Law for Dividing Powers

To divide powers with the same base, write the base and subtract the exponents.
$a^n \div a^m = a^{n-m}$, where n and m are natural numbers, and $n > m$, and $a \neq 0$.

Discuss

Why do we include "$a \neq 0$" in the exponent law for dividing powers?

Example 1

Write each product as a single power. Then evaluate.

a) $2^3 \times 2^2$

b) $(-3)^4 \times (-3)$

A single power is one base with one exponent.

Solution

a) $2^3 \times 2^2 = 2^{3+2}$
$\qquad = 2^5$
$\qquad = 32$

b) $(-3)^4 \times (-3) = (-3)^4 \times (-3)^1$
$\qquad = (-3)^{4+1}$
$\qquad = (-3)^5$
$\qquad = -243$

When no exponent is written, it is understood the exponent is 1.

Example 2

Write each quotient as a single power. Then evaluate.

a) $2^3 \div 2^2$

b) $(-3)^4 \div (-3)$

Solution

a) $2^3 \div 2^2 = \dfrac{2^3}{2^2}$
$\qquad = 2^{3-2}$
$\qquad = 2^1$
$\qquad = 2$

b) $(-3)^4 \div (-3)^1 = \dfrac{(-3)^4}{(-3)^1}$
$\qquad = (-3)^{4-1}$
$\qquad = (-3)^3$
$\qquad = -27$

Example 3

Write each expression as a single power. Evaluate to 3 decimal places, where necessary.

a) $(3.2)^5 \times (3.2)^4$ **b)** $\dfrac{(-4.8)^5}{(-4.8)^2}$ **c)** $\dfrac{8^{200}}{8^{199}}$

Solution

a) $(3.2)^5(3.2)^4 = 3.2^{5+4}$ Use a calculator.
$$= 3.2^9$$
$$\doteq 35\,184.372$$

```
(3.2)^9
        35184.37209
```

b) $\dfrac{(-4.8)^5}{(-4.8)^2} = (-4.8)^{5-2}$ Use a calculator.
$$= (-4.8)^3$$
$$= -110.592$$

```
(-4.8)^3
        -110.592
```

c) $\dfrac{8^{200}}{8^{199}} = 8^{200-199}$
$$= 8^1$$
$$= 8$$

In *Example 3* part c, we used exponent laws (instead of a calculator) to calculate large numbers mentally.

2.2   Exercises

1. Write each product as a single power.

  a) $2^5 \times 2^4$ **b)** $3^2 \times 3^5$ **c)** $10^2 \times 10^9$

  d) $12^8 \times 12^3$ **e)** $7^2 \times 7^4$ **f)** $8^3 \times 8^5$

2. Write each quotient as a single power.

  a) $2^5 \div 2^4$ **b)** $3^5 \div 3^2$ **c)** $10^9 \div 10^2$

  d) $12^8 \div 12^3$ **e)** $7^4 \div 7^3$ **f)** $8^5 \div 8^3$

3. Write each expression as a single power. Do not evaluate.

  a) $3^4 \times 3^6$ **b)** $7^4 \times 7^7$ **c)** $(-5)^{16} \times (-5)^9$

  d) $\dfrac{1.5^{18}}{1.5^6}$ **e)** $\dfrac{(-6)^8}{(-6)^2}$ **f)** $\dfrac{(-2.3)^7}{(-2.3)^3}$

4. Write each expression as a single power. Do not evaluate.

a) $3^8 \div 3^3$ **b)** $2^{16} \div 2^7$ **c)** $(-8)^{20} \div (-8)^5$

d) $2.1^5 \times 2.1^5$ **e)** $(-8)^5 \times (-8)$ **f)** $(-1.7)^4 \times (-1.7)^3$

5. Write each product as a single power. Evaluate. Round to 3 decimal places where necessary.

a) $3^3 \times 3^5$ **b)** $(-2.1)^2 \times (-2.1)^5$ **c)** $(-5)^3 \times (-5)^2$

d) $(-8.6) \times (-8.6)$ **e)** 4.6×4.6^6 **f)** $(-1.25)^4 \times (-1.25)^4$

6. Write each quotient as a single power. Evaluate. Round to 3 decimal places where necessary.

a) $9^4 \div 9^2$ **b)** $(-1)^8 \div (-1)^5$ **c)** $(-8.7)^7 \div (-8.7)^4$

d) $(-0.2)^{10} \div (-0.2)^8$ **e)** $6.84^6 \div 6.84^2$ **f)** $(-9)^8 \div (-9)^4$

7. Knowledge/Understanding Write each expression as a single power. Then evaluate.

a) $3^3 \times 3^2$ **b)** $9^4 \div 9^2$ **c)** $(-8)^7 \div (-8)^4$

d) $(-2.3) \times (-2.3)^3$ **e)** $2^2 \times 2^2 \times 2^2$ **f)** $(7.1)^5 \div (7.1)^3$

8. Evaluate to 3 decimal places.

a) $(4.6)^2 \times (4.6)^4$ **b)** $(-1.7)^5 \div (-1.7)^2$ **c)** $(8.3)^7 \div (8.3)^4$

d) $(-3.7)^4 \times (-3.7)^3$ **e)** $0.2^4 \div 0.2$ **f)** 0.1×0.1^2

9. Communication

a) A rectangular wheat field is 10^5 m long and 10^3 m wide. Explain how to find its area.

b) Another rectangular field is $10\,000$ m wide. Its area is 10^9 m^2. Explain how to find its length.

10. Application The tallest tree in the world is about 10^2 m tall. The highest mountain is about 10^4 m. About how many times as high as the tree is the mountain? Does this make sense? Explain.

11. a) Write each expression as a single power.

    i) $6^5 \times 6^2$ **ii)** $6^2 \times 6^5$ **iii)** $6^7 \div 6^2$ **iv)** $6^7 \div 6^5$

    v) $(-7)^8 \div (-7)^5$ **vi)** $(-7)^8 \div (-7)^3$ **vii)** $(-7)^3 \times (-7)^5$ **viii)** $(-7)^5 \times (-7)^3$

b) Explain what your results from part a show about the relationship between multiplying and dividing powers.

12. **a)** List the powers of 2 to 2^8. Evaluate each power.

   b) Use your answers from part a. Evaluate each expression by multiplying or dividing powers.

   i) 16×16 **ii)** 32×4 **iii)** $256 \div 8$ **iv)** $128 \div 32$

13. **a)** Earth's diameter is about 10^7 m. The diameter of the largest known star is 10^{12} m. About how many times as great as the diameter of Earth is the diameter of the largest star?

   b) Astronomers estimate that there are about 10^{11} galaxies in the universe. Each galaxy contains about 10^{11} stars. About how many stars are in the universe?

14. **Thinking/Inquiry/Problem Solving** A telephone tree is used to send messages. The person at the top of the tree calls 2 people. Each person calls 2 more people. Suppose it takes 1 min to call someone. The photographs show the process. The message is relayed until the bottom row has 256 people. How long does this take?

C 15. Write each expression as a single power. Then evaluate.

   a) $\dfrac{10^5 \times 10^2}{10^3}$ **b)** $\dfrac{2^7 \times 2^3}{2^4}$ **c)** $\dfrac{3^{12}}{3 \times 3^6}$

   d) $\dfrac{(-5)^9 \times (-5)}{(-5)^4}$ **e)** $\dfrac{6^7 \times 6^{11}}{6^8 \times 6^2}$ **f)** $\dfrac{(-1)^{10}}{(-1)^5 \times (-1)}$

An expression such as $(2^4)^3$ is a power of a power.

$(2^4)^3$ means $2^4 \times 2^4 \times 2^4$.

So, $(2^4)^3 = 2^4 \times 2^4 \times 2^4$

$= 2^{4+4+4}$

$= 2^{12}$

The exponent of 2^{12} is the product of the exponents in the expression $(2^4)^3$.

That is, $(2^4)^3 = 2^{4 \times 3}$

$= 2^{12}$

We use this result to write an exponent law for a power of a power.

TAKE NOTE

Exponent Law for a Power of a Power

$(a^m)^n = a^{mn}$, where m and n are integers

We can use this exponent law to simplify expressions with powers.

Example 1

Write as a power with a single exponent.

a) $(4^2)^5$　　　　　　　**b)** $(2^3)^2$　　　　　　　**c)** $(m^3)^3$

Solution

a) $(4^2)^5 = 4^{2 \times 5}$　　　　**b)** $(2^3)^2 = 2^{3 \times 2}$　　　　**c)** $(m^3)^3 = m^{3 \times 3}$

$= 4^{10}$　　　　　　　　　　$= 2^6$　　　　　　　　　　$= m^9$

Example 2

Write as a single power, then evaluate.

a) $(2^2)^4$　　　　　　　　　　　　**b)** $(3^2)^2$

Solution

a) $(2^2)^4 = 2^{2 \times 4}$　　　　　　**b)** $(3^2)^2 = 3^{2 \times 2}$

$= 2^8$　　Use a calculator.　　　　$= 3^4$　　Use a calculator.

$= 256$　　　　　　　　　　　　　$= 81$

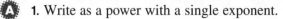
A 1. Write as a power with a single exponent.

a) $(2)^2$ b) $(2^2)^2$ c) $(2^3)^2$ d) $(2^4)^2$

e) $(2^5)^2$ f) $(2^6)^2$ g) $(2^7)^2$ h) $(2^8)^2$

✓ 2. Write as a power with a single exponent.

a) (2^2) b) $(2^2)^2$ c) $(2^2)^3$ d) $(2^2)^4$

e) $(2^2)^5$ f) $(2^2)^6$ g) $(2^2)^7$ h) $(2^2)^8$

3. What do you notice about the results of exercises 1 and 2? Explain the results.

✓ 4. Write as a power with a single exponent.

a) $(a^2)^4$ b) $(b^3)^5$ c) $(c^7)^2$ d) $(d^4)^3$

B 5. **Knowledge/Understanding** Write as a single power, then evaluate.

a) $(10^2)^3$ b) $(3^2)^2$ c) $(4^3)^2$ d) $(10^4)^2$

6. Write as a single power, then evaluate.

a) $(5^2)^2$ b) $(4^2)^4$ c) $(2^{-3})^2$ d) $(6^{-1})^2$

7. Use a calculator. Evaluate each expression in two different ways:

i) Complete the operations in brackets first. Then evaluate.

ii) Use the exponent laws first. Then evaluate.

Compare the results. Confirm they are equal.

a) $(3^2)^4$ b) $[(-2)^6]^2$

✓ 8. Express as a single power. Use the power of a power law. Then use the law for multiplying powers. Do not evaluate.

a) $(3^2)^3 \times (3^4)^2$ b) $(7^3)^2 \times (7^8)^2$

c) $(8^{-5}) \times (8^3)^{-4}$ d) $(29^{-6})^2 \times (29^3)^4$

✓ 9. Express as a single power. Use the power of a power law. Then use the law for dividing powers. Do not evaluate.

a) $\dfrac{(6^5)^2}{(6^2)^3}$ b) $\dfrac{(15^3)^4}{(15^5)^2}$

c) $\dfrac{(4^{-2})^{-3}}{(4^{-6})^{-2}}$ d) $\dfrac{(101^{-8})^{-4}}{(101^{-7})^{-5}}$

Use this table of powers of 2 to complete exercises 10 and 11.

$2^{25} = 33\,554\,432$	$2^8 = 256$
$2^{24} = 16\,777\,216$	$2^7 = 128$
$2^{23} = 8\,388\,608$	$2^6 = 64$
$2^{22} = 4\,194\,304$	$2^5 = 32$
$2^{21} = 2\,097\,152$	$2^4 = 16$
$2^{20} = 1\,048\,576$	$2^3 = 8$
$2^{19} = 524\,288$	$2^2 = 4$
$2^{18} = 262\,144$	$2^1 = 2$
$2^{17} = 131\,072$	$2^0 = 1$
$2^{16} = 65\,536$	$2^{-1} = 0.5$
$2^{15} = 32\,768$	$2^{-2} = 0.25$
$2^{14} = 16\,384$	$2^{-3} = 0.125$
$2^{13} = 8192$	$2^{-4} = 0.0625$
$2^{12} = 4096$	$2^{-5} = 0.031\,25$
$2^{11} = 2048$	$2^{-6} = 0.015\,625$
$2^{10} = 1024$	$2^{-7} = 0.007\,812\,5$
$2^9 = 512$	$2^{-8} = 0.003\,906\,25$

✓ **10. Application** Use the powers in the table. Find each answer without using a calculator.

a) 128×256 b) 4096×512 c) $\dfrac{65\,536}{2048}$

d) $\dfrac{8192}{1024}$ e) 64^3 f) 4^7

11. Use the powers in the table. Find each answer without using a calculator.

a) 0.125×0.0625 b) $131\,072 \times 0.007\,812\,5$ c) $\dfrac{16\,384}{0.031\,25}$

d) $\dfrac{0.015\,625}{0.031\,25}$ e) 0.25^3 f) 0.125^{-2}

✓ **12. Communication** Explain why you add the exponents when you write $2^4 \times 2^3$ as a power, and why you multiply the exponents when you write $(2^4)^3$ as a power.

2.4 Zero and Negative Exponents

Suppose we apply the exponent law to $2^3 \div 2^3$: $2^{3-3} = 2^0$

Suppose we apply the exponent law to $2^2 \div 2^5$: $2^{2-5} = 2^{-3}$

The power 2^3 means $2 \times 2 \times 2$, but we cannot explain powers such as 2^0 and 2^{-3} in this way. We cannot multiply 0 twos together. We cannot multiply -3 twos together.

To understand powers such as 2^0 and 2^{-3}, we look at number patterns.

INVESTIGATION

Descending Powers

1. Copy this table. Evaluate each power down to 2^1.
   Write your answers in the *Number* column.
   What pattern do you see?

2. Continue the pattern from exercise 1 to complete the *Number* column. Write these numbers as fractions.

3. Write the denominator of each fraction as a power of 2. What do you notice?

4. Use the pattern in your results from exercise 3.

   a) Write 2^{-5} as a fraction.

   b) Write 2^{-6} as a fraction.

   c) Express each fraction in parts a and b as a power of 2.

Power	Number
2^4	
2^3	
2^2	
2^1	
2^0	
2^{-1}	
2^{-2}	
2^{-3}	
2^{-4}	

5. Copy each table. Use the method of exercises 1 to 3 to complete each table.

a)

Power	Number
3^4	
3^3	
3^2	
3^1	
3^0	
3^{-1}	
3^{-2}	
3^{-3}	
3^{-4}	

b)

Power	Number
10^4	
10^3	
10^2	
10^1	
10^0	
10^{-1}	
10^{-2}	
10^{-3}	
10^{-4}	

6. Use the patterns in your results from exercise 5. Write each power as a fraction.

   a) 3^{-5} **b)** 3^{-6} **c)** 10^{-5} **d)** 10^{-6}

7. Write each power as a number.

   a) 2^{0} **b)** 3^{0} **c)** 10^{0}

We can generalize the *Investigation* results as follows:

TAKE NOTE

Zero Exponent

x^{0} is equal to 1: that is, $x^{0} = 1$ $(x \neq 0)$

Negative Integer Exponent

x^{-n} is the reciprocal of x^{n}: that is, $x^{-n} = \dfrac{1}{x^{n}}$ $(x \neq 0$ and n is an integer)

Similarly, $\dfrac{1}{x^{n}} = x^{-n}$ $(x \neq 0$ and n is an integer)

We can use these definitions to evaluate a power with any integer exponent.

Example

Evaluate each power.

   a) 5^{-2} **b)** $(-3)^{-1}$ **c)** $\dfrac{1}{5^{-2}}$

Solution

a) $5^{-2} = \dfrac{1}{5^{2}}$ **b)** $(-3)^{-1} = \dfrac{1}{(-3)^{1}}$ **c)** $\dfrac{1}{5^{-2}} = \dfrac{5^{2}}{1}$

         $= \dfrac{1}{25}$ $= \dfrac{1}{-3}$ $= 25$

                                   $= -\dfrac{1}{3}$

Discuss

How are the powers in parts a and c related?

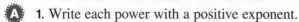

A **1.** Write each power with a positive exponent.

  a) 2^{-7} **b)** 3^{-2} **c)** 4^{-1} **d)** 5^{-8} **e)** 2^{-9} **f)** 10^{-3}

2. Write each power with a positive exponent.

  a) $\dfrac{1}{3^{-3}}$ **b)** $\dfrac{1}{4^{-1}}$ **c)** $\dfrac{1}{2^{-7}}$ **d)** $\dfrac{1}{10^{-6}}$ **e)** $\dfrac{1}{9^{-8}}$ **f)** $\dfrac{1}{5^{-5}}$

B **3.** Write each power with a positive exponent. Then evaluate.

  a) 3^{-1} **b)** 2^{-2} **c)** 7^{-1} **d)** 10^{-5} **e)** 3^{-3} **f)** 6^{-2}

4. Write each power with a positive exponent. Then evaluate.

  a) $\dfrac{1}{2^{-1}}$ **b)** $\dfrac{1}{3^{-2}}$ **c)** $\dfrac{1}{5^{-2}}$ **d)** $\dfrac{1}{2^{-3}}$ **e)** $\dfrac{-1}{4^{-2}}$ **f)** $\dfrac{-1}{10^{-4}}$

5. Use a calculator to evaluate each power.

  a) 0.2^{-1} **b)** 0.25^{-2} **c)** 0.5^{-3} **d)** $(-2)^0$ **e)** 1.5^{-1} **f)** $(-1.2)^{-2}$

6. a) Evaluate each power.

  i) 6^0 **ii)** $(-3)^0$ **iii)** 1.8^0 **iv)** 5.6^0 **v)** $(-0.8)^0$ **vi)** $(-10)^0$

  b) Look at the results of part a. Write a rule for evaluating a power when the exponent is 0.

7. Use a calculator to evaluate each power. Round to 6 decimal places where necessary.

  a) 4^{-5} **b)** 5^{-4} **c)** $(-5)^{-6}$ **d)** $(-6)^{-3}$ **e)** 1.2^{-10}

8. Knowledge/Understanding Evaluate each power. Round to 4 decimal places where necessary.

  a) 3^{-5} **b)** $\dfrac{1}{4^{-2}}$ **c)** $(0.35)^{-3}$ **d)** 9^0 **e)** 7^{-2} **f)** $(-1.5)^0$

9. Evaluate.

  a) 10^3 **b)** 10^2 **c)** 10^1 **d)** 10^0

  e) 10^{-1} **f)** 10^{-2} **g)** 10^{-3} **h)** 10^{-4}

10. Communication Evaluate. How are the powers in each pair similar? How are they different?

  a) 4^3 and 4^{-3} **b)** 4^3 and -4^{-3} **c)** $(-4)^3$ and -4^{-3}

11. Thinking/Inquiry/Problem Solving Is a power with a negative exponent always negative? Is it always positive? Or, is it sometimes negative and sometimes positive? Explain. Look at the exercises you have completed to help you.

12. Application There is only one integer n so that $n^n = \dfrac{1}{4}$. This integer is negative. What is the integer? Justify your answer.

13. Scientists grow bacteria in a culture for medical research. This table shows how the number of a typical bacterium doubles every hour.

Time	Elapsed time after noon, (h)	Number of bacteria
noon	0	1000×2^0
1:00 P.M.	1	1000×2^1
2:00 P.M.	2	1000×2^2
3:00 P.M.	3	1000×2^3

a) Evaluate the powers in the table to find the number of bacteria at each time.

i) noon ii) 1:00 P.M.

iii) 2:00 P.M. iv) 3:00 P.M.

b) The number of bacteria after n hours is 1000×2^n, where n is the elapsed time in hours. Find the number of bacteria for each elapsed time.

i) 3 h ii) 6 h iii) 9 h iv) 12 h

c) An hour before noon, the value of n is -1. Evaluate each expression to find the number of bacteria each number of hours before noon.

i) For 1 h before noon, the number of bacteria is 1000×2^{-1}.

ii) For 2 h before noon, the number of bacteria is 1000×2^{-2}.

iii) For 3 h before noon, the number of bacteria is 1000×2^{-3}.

d) How many bacteria are in the culture for each number of hours before noon? Round to the nearest whole number, if necessary.

i) 3 h ii) 4 h iii) 6 h iv) 8 h

14. Consider a square with side length 2 units. Its area is 2^2 units^2. Imagine cutting the square in half, then repeatedly cutting the remaining region in half. The area of each region, in square units, is shown.

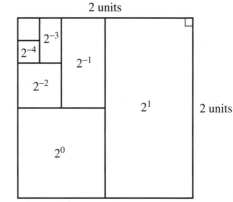

a) Explain why the areas are 2^2, 2^1, 2^0, 2^{-1}, 2^{-2}, 2^{-3}, 2^{-4}, and so on.

b) Suppose we label the regions in part a from 1 to 7. We can write the areas of the regions in a table.

Region	1	2	3	4	5	6	7
Area (square units)	2^2	2^1	2^0	2^{-1}	2^{-2}	2^{-3}	2^{-4}

Use a whole sheet of grid paper. Graph the data in the table. Describe the graph.

2.5　Scientific Notation

We can use scientific notation to express very large numbers and very small numbers.

Scientific Notation

To write a number in scientific notation, write it as the product of:
a number between 1 and 10, and a power of 10.

There are about 120 000 000 000 stars in our galaxy, the Milky Way.

The zeros in this very large number are placeholders. They show the position of the decimal point. The decimal point at the end of the number is not shown. To express the number of stars in our galaxy using scientific notation, we write:

$$120\,000\,000\,000 = 1.2 \times 100\,000\,000\,000$$
$$= 1.2 \times 10^{11}$$

The number of stars in our galaxy is about 1.2×10^{11}.

Hydrogen is the most abundant element in the universe. The mass of a hydrogen atom is about 0.000 000 000 000 000 000 000 001 67 g.

The zeros in this very small number are placeholders. They show the position of the decimal point. To express the mass of a hydrogen atom using scientific notation, we write:

$0.000\,000\,000\,000\,000\,000\,000\,001\,67$
$= 1.67 \times 0.000\,000\,000\,000\,000\,000\,000\,001$
$= 1.67 \times 10^{-24}$

The mass of a hydrogen atom is about 1.67×10^{-24} g.

> 120 000 000 000
> The true place of the decimal is 11 right, so 10^{11}.
> 1.2 is between 1 and 10.
> 10^{11} is a power of 10.

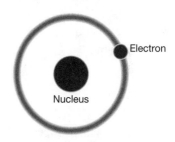

Electron

Nucleus

Diagram of a hydrogen atom

> 0.000 000 000 000 000 000 000 001 67
> The true place of the decimal is 24 left, so 10^{-24}.
> 1.67 is between 1 and 10.
> 10^{-24} is a power of 10.

Example 1

Write in scientific notation.

a) 1 350 000   **b)** 0.002 796

Solution

a) 1 350 000

Place the decimal point to the right of the first non-zero digit.
1.350 000

The true position of the decimal point is 6 places to the right,
so multiply 1.35 by 10^6.
$1 350 000 = 1.35 \times 10^6$

b) 0.002 796

Place the decimal point to the right of the first non-zero digit.
0 002.796

The true position of the decimal point is 3 places to the left,
so multiply 2.796 by 10^{-3}.
$0.002 796 = 2.796 \times 10^{-3}$

Discuss

In parts a and b, how did we know which power of 10 to use?
How did we know whether the exponent was positive or negative?

We can reverse the process of *Example 1* to write a number in scientific notation in standard form.

Example 2

Write in standard form.

a) 2.376×10^9 **b)** 1.48×10^{-7}

Solution

a) 2.376×10^9

To multiply 2.376 by 10^9, move the decimal point 9 places to the right.
Write zeros as place holders.
$2.376 \times 10^9 = 2\ 376,000,000.$
$2.376 \times 10^9 = 2\ 376\ 000\ 000$

b) 1.48×10^{-7}

To multiply 1.48 by 10^{-7}, move the decimal point 7 places to the left.
Write zeros as place holders.

$1.48 \times 10^{-7} = 0.\underset{\smile\smile\smile}{000\,000\,1}48$

$1.48 \times 10^{-7} = 0.000\,000\,148$

Discuss

When writing a number in scientific notation in standard form, how do you know which way to move the decimal point?

To calculate with numbers in scientific notation, we can use the exponent key on a calculator to input a power of 10.

For the TI-30X IIS calculator, press (2nd) (x^{-1}) for EE. For a different calculator, check its manual.

Example 3

Simplify. Check whether the answers are reasonable.

a) $(3.3 \times 10^5) \times (6.0 \times 10^{24})$

b) $\dfrac{2.1 \times 10^7}{1.9 \times 10^{-30}}$

Solution

a) $(3.3 \times 10^5) \times (6.0 \times 10^{24})$

Press: 3.3 (2nd) (x^{-1}) 5 (×) 6 (2nd) (x^{-1}) 24 (ENTER =)

$(3.3 \times 10^5) \times (6.0 \times 10^{24}) = 1.98 \times 10^{30}$

Check.

$$3.3 \times 10^5 \times 6.0 \times 10^{24} \doteq 3 \times 6 \times 10^{5+24}$$
$$= 18 \times 10^{29}$$
$$= 1.8 \times 10^1 \times 10^{29}$$
$$= 1.8 \times 10^{30}$$

The answer is reasonable.

> `3.3E5*6E24`
>
> `1.98`ₓ₁₀`30`

b) $\dfrac{2.1 \times 10^7}{1.9 \times 10^{-30}}$

Press: 2.1 (2nd) (x^{-1}) 7 (÷) 1.9 (2nd) (x^{-1}) ((-)) 30 (ENTER =)

$\dfrac{2.1 \times 10^7}{1.9 \times 10^{-30}} = 1.1053 \times 10^{37}$

> `2.1E7/1.9E-30`
>
> `1.105263158`ₓ₁₀`37`

Check.

$$\frac{2.1 \times 10^7}{1.9 \times 10^{-30}} \doteq \frac{2 \times 10^7}{2 \times 10^{-30}}$$
$$= \frac{2}{2} \times \frac{10^7}{10^{-30}}$$
$$= 1 \times 10^{7-(-30)}$$
$$= 1 \times 10^{37}$$

The answer is reasonable.

A **1.** Write each exponent.

a) $6\,300\,000 = 6.3 \times 10^{\square}$ b) $0.000\,481 = 4.81 \times 10^{\square}$

c) $70\,000 = 7.0 \times 10^{\square}$ d) $0.000\,000\,029 = 2.9 \times 10^{\square}$

e) $941\,000\,000 = 9.41 \times 10^{\square}$ f) $0.000\,09 = 9.0 \times 10^{\square}$

2. Write in scientific notation.

a) $300\,000\,000$ b) $30\,000\,000$ c) $3\,000\,000$ d) $300\,000$

e) $30\,000$ f) 3000 g) 300 h) 30

3. Write in scientific notation.

a) 0.4 b) 0.04 c) 0.004 d) 0.0004

e) $0.000\,04$ f) $0.000\,004$ g) $0.000\,000\,4$ h) $0.000\,000\,04$

4. Write in standard form.

a) 5.0×10^8 b) 5.0×10^7 c) 5.0×10^6 d) 5.0×10^5

e) 5.0×10^4 f) 5.0×10^3 g) 5.0×10^2 h) 5.0×10^1

5. Write in standard form.

a) 6.3×10^{-1} b) 6.3×10^{-2} c) 6.3×10^{-3} d) 6.3×10^{-4}

e) 6.3×10^{-5} f) 6.3×10^{-6} g) 6.3×10^{-7} h) 6.3×10^{-8}

B **6.** Write in scientific notation.

a) $450\,000$ b) 201 c) 9300 d) 37

e) $58\,000$ f) $579\,000$ g) $60\,000$ h) $1\,010\,000$

7. Write in scientific notation.

a) 0.0029 b) $0.000\,002\,5$ c) $0.000\,018$ d) 0.54

e) $0.000\,004\,8$ f) 0.007 g) $0.000\,51$ h) $0.000\,000\,99$

8. Communication Can every number can be written in scientific notation? Explain.

9. Complete this table.

		Standard Form	Scientific Notation
a)	Temperature of the sun's interior	$1\,300\,000°C$	
b)	Thickness of a piece of paper	$0.000\,01$ m	
c)	Mass of an electron		9.2×10^{-28} g
d)	Estimated age of Earth	$4\,500\,000\,000$ years	
e)	Diameter of a hydrogen atom	$0.000\,000\,005$ cm	
f)	Land area of Earth		1.5×10^8 km^2

10. Scientific calculators display results differently. What do you think each display means?

a) Calculator 1

i)

2.5^{12}

ii)

6.25^{-10}

b) Calculator 2

i)

3.125E-16

ii)

4E24

c) Calculator 3

i)

4.33333E22

ii)

5.E-40

11. When asked to express 1500 in scientific notation, Kimi replied 15×10^2. Why is this not correct?

12. Knowledge/Understanding Write in scientific notation.

    a) 1200   **b)** 270 000   **c)** 400   **d)** 0.24

    e) 0.0007   **f)** 0.000 014 8   **g)** 13 600   **h)** 0.000 018 8

    i) 18×10^2 **j)** 142×10^5 **k)** 16×10^{-2} **l)** 236×10^{-6}

13. Write in standard form.

    a) 1.8×10^5 **b)** 2.9×10^4 **c)** 3.3×10^7 **d)** 4.4×10^9

    e) 1.6×10^{-1} **f)** 8.4×10^{-2} **g)** 2.24×10^{-4} **h)** 1.88×10^{-5}

    i) 2.41×10^{-10} **j)** 1.87×10^6 **k)** 3.02×10^{-3} **l)** 2.16×10^{-1}

14. Simplify.

    a) $(1.4 \times 10^{10}) \times (3.71 \times 10^{14})$ **b)** $(3.62 \times 10^{-23}) \times (5.9 \times 10^6)$

    c) $(1.2 \times 10^{-13}) \times (4.0 \times 10^9)$ **d)** $(7.12 \times 10^{-21}) \times (5.6 \times 10^8)$

15. Simplify.

    a) $(3.0 \times 10^7) \times (4.0 \times 10^8)$ **b)** $(9.8 \times 10^{11}) \times (1.3 \times 10^4)$

    c) $(2.4 \times 10^{-9}) \times (5.6 \times 10^8)$ **d)** $(4.15 \times 10^{-26}) \times (3.2 \times 10^{-9})$

✓ **16.** Write each number in scientific notation.

    a) 5 thousand   **b)** 5 hundred thousand

    c) 5 million   **d)** 5 billion

✓ **17.** Simplify. Check whether the answers are reasonable.

    a) $(5.9 \times 10^5) \times (4.7 \times 10^{-8})$ **b)** $(3.53 \times 10^9) \div (8.0 \times 10^{-5})$

    c) $(2.4 \text{ million}) \times (6.5 \text{ million})$ **d)** $1 \div (5 \text{ billion})$

18. Simplify. Check whether the answers are reasonable.

a) $\dfrac{3.72 \times 10^{10}}{1.47 \times 10^{8}}$ b) $\dfrac{9.0 \times 10^{-2}}{3.3 \times 10^{7}}$ c) $\dfrac{2.43 \times 10^{-7}}{2.3 \times 10^{-4}}$ d) $\dfrac{2.55 \times 10^{-9}}{3.0 \times 10^{15}}$

19. Application A TV program about sea otters made these statements:

- 1 cm^2 of a sea otter's fur contains about 20 000 hairs.

- A sea otter has about 8 billion hairs.

a) Write the two numbers in scientific notation.

b) Calculate the area of a sea otter's body, in square centimetres.

c) Express your answer to part b in square metres. Does the result seem reasonable? Explain.

20. a) All matter is made of atoms. Atoms are so small that 6.022×10^{23} gold atoms have a mass of about 200 g. Write 6.022×10^{23} in standard form.

b) Diatoms are a primary source of food in the sea. A diatom measures about 0.0005 mm across. Write this measurement in scientific notation.

c) The mass of Earth is about 6.0×10^{24} kg. The mass of the sun is about 3.3×10^{5} times the mass of Earth. Calculate the mass of the sun.

d) Write a question that involves scientific notation. Answer your question. Trade questions with a classmate. Then compare answers.

21. Thinking/Inquiry/Problem Solving One *light-year* is the distance light travels in 1 year. The speed of light is 3×10^{8} m/s. How far is 1 light-year in kilometres?

distance = speed × time

m/s is metres per second.

22. Express each number in this news item in scientific notation.

A new fingerprinting method uses gold particles to bind to the proteins every finger leaves behind. The amount of protein is tiny—only one billionth of a gram per print. The gold particles are about two thousandths of a millimetre in diameter.

1. Write each power as a product. Then evaluate.

   a) $\left(\frac{7}{10}\right)^2$
   b) $\left(-\frac{3}{8}\right)^4$
   c) $\left(\frac{5}{6}\right)^5$
   d) $\left(-\frac{2}{11}\right)^3$

2. Evaluate each power. Round to 3 decimal places where necessary.

   a) $(-10)^5$
   b) 2.5^7
   c) 9^6
   d) $\left(-\frac{2}{3}\right)^7$
   e) $\left(\frac{6}{7}\right)^2$

3. Write as a single power, then evaluate. Round to 3 decimal places where necessary.

   a) $4^3 \times 4$
   b) $(-7)^6 \div (-7)^5$
   c) $(5.1)^2 \times (5.1)^6$
   d) $(-5.4)^9 \div (-5.4)^7$

4. Write as a single power, then evaluate. Round to 3 decimal places where necessary.

   a) $(2^3)^2$
   b) $(7^2)^2$
   c) $(1.6^{-4})^{-2}$
   d) $[(-2.1)^7]^0$

5. Write each power with a positive exponent.

   a) 7^{-5}
   b) $\frac{1}{6^{-3}}$
   c) $\frac{1}{2^{-9}}$
   d) 8^{-6}
   e) $\frac{1}{7^{-4}}$

6. Evaluate each power. Round to 6 decimal places where necessary.

   a) $(-5)^{-6}$
   b) 1.7^{-5}
   c) $(-2.5)^{-2}$
   d) $(-7.2)^0$
   e) 6^{-3}

7. Write in scientific notation.

   a) $130\,000$
   b) $0.000\,29$
   c) 45×10^5
   d) 992×10^{-4}

8. Write in standard form.

   a) 7.5×10^5
   b) 8.0×10^{-3}
   c) 1.02×10^6
   d) 9.23×10^{-7}

9. Simplify.

   a) $(4.7 \times 10^6) \times (3.12 \times 10^5)$
   b) $(6.0 \times 10^{-4}) \times (8.3 \times 10^{-7})$
   c) $\frac{2.5 \times 10^7}{3.0 \times 10^4}$
   d) $\frac{8.21 \times 10^{-5}}{1.7 \times 10^6}$

Preparation for Ontario Testing

10. A mass of about 200 g of gold contains 6.022×10^{23} atoms.
    What is the number of atoms in 1 g of gold?

    a) 3.011×10^{-21}

    b) 3.011×10^{21}

    c) 1.2044×10^{-26}

    d) 1.2044×10^{26}

Graphing Squares

Consider squares with side lengths that increase by 1 cm.

1. Copy and continue the table for squares with side lengths up to 15 cm.

Side length x, (cm)	Area y, (cm²)
0	0
1	1
2	4
3	9

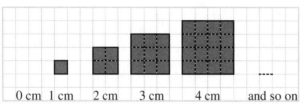

0 cm 1 cm 2 cm 3 cm 4 cm and so on

2. Use the table. Find the area of a square with each side length.

   a) 5 cm   b) 11 cm   c) 14 cm

3. Use the table. Find the side length of a square with each area.

   a) 36 cm²   b) 81 cm²   c) 25 cm²

4. Can you use the table to find the area of a square with side length 4.5 cm? Explain.

5. Can you use the table to find the side length of a square with area 120 cm². Explain.

6. Graph the data in exercise 1. Draw the graph as large as possible. Plot *Area (cm²)* vertically and *Side length (cm)* horizontally.

7. Should you connect the points with a smooth curve? Explain.

8. Use the graph. Estimate the side length of a square with each area.

   a) 30 cm²   b) 57 cm²   c) 183 cm²

9. Use the graph. Estimate the area of a square with each side length.

   a) 7.5 cm   b) 9.5 cm   c) 12.25 cm

10. The equation for the graph is $y = x^2$. Look at each pair of numbers in the table.

    a) How is the second number related to the first number?

    b) How is the first number related to the second number?

When we square a number, we multiply it by itself:

$$5^2 = 5 \times 5 \qquad\qquad (-5)^2 = (-5) \times (-5)$$
$$= 25 \qquad\qquad\qquad\qquad = 25$$

Since $5 \times 5 = 25$, we say that 5 is a square root of 25. We write $\sqrt{25} = 5$.

Since $(-5) \times (-5) = 25$, another square root of 25 is −5.

A square root is a number that produces a given number when mulitplied by itself.

All positive numbers have square roots.

A *perfect square* is a number whose square roots are integers. For example, 64 is a perfect square because its square roots are 8 and −8.

Using the radical sign, $\sqrt{}$, means only the positive square root.

So, the square roots of 64 are 8 and −8. But $\sqrt{64}$ is 8.

Example 1

Find the square roots of each perfect square.

a) 49   **b)** 100   **c)** 1

Solution

a) Since $7 \times 7 = 49$ and $(-7) \times (-7) = 49$, the square roots of 49 are 7 and −7.

b) Since $10 \times 10 = 100$ and $(-10) \times (-10) = 100$, the square roots of 100 are 10 and −10.

c) Since $1 \times 1 = 1$ and $(-1) \times (-1) = 1$, the square roots of 1 are 1 and −1.

We can use a calculator to determine the square root of a number that is not a perfect square. For the TI-30X IIS calculator, press [2nd] [x^2] for $\sqrt{}$.

Example 2

Calculate each square root to 3 decimal places.

a) $\sqrt{40}$ **b)** $\sqrt{0.6}$

Solution

a) $\sqrt{40}$ Press: [2nd] [x^2] 40 [ )] [ENTER =]

$\sqrt{40} \doteq 6.325$

> $\sqrt{(40)}$
>
> 6.32455532

b) $\sqrt{0.6}$ Press: [2nd] [x^2] 0.6 [ )] [ENTER =]

$\sqrt{0.6} \doteq 0.775$

> $\sqrt{(0.6)}$
>
> 0.774596669

A **1.** What is the square of each number?

a) 4　　　b) 8　　　c) 1　　　d) 9　　　e) 14

2. Use the completed table from the *Investigation*. What is the area of a square with each side length?

a) 6 cm　　b) 0 cm　　c) 10 cm　　d) 7 cm

3. Use the completed table from the *Investigation*. What is the side length of a square with each area?

a) 4 cm^2　　b) 1 cm^2　　c) 25 cm^2　　d) 9 cm^2

B **4.** What are the two square roots of each number?

a) 4　　　b) 9　　　c) 49　　　d) 81　　　e) 1

5. What are the two square roots of each number?

a) 64　　　b) 25　　　c) 100　　　d) 16　　　e) 36

6. Find the square roots of each number to 1 decimal place. To check your answers, compare the results with those you obtained in exercise 4.

a) 5　　　b) 10　　　c) 50　　　d) 75　　　e) 2

7. Find the square roots of each number to 1 decimal place. To check your answers, compare the results with those you obtained in exercise 5.

a) 60　　　b) 30　　　c) 95　　　d) 15　　　e) 40

8. Evaluate.

a) $\sqrt{16}$　　b) $\sqrt{4}$　　c) $\sqrt{64}$　　d) $\sqrt{36}$　　e) $\sqrt{100}$

9. Evaluate.

a) $\sqrt{9}$　　b) $\sqrt{49}$　　c) $\sqrt{81}$　　d) $\sqrt{1}$　　e) $\sqrt{25}$

10. Why are there 2 square roots for each answer in exercises 4 and 5? Why is there one square root for each answer in exercises 8 and 9?

11. Knowledge/Understanding Use a calculator. Evaluate to 1 decimal place.

a) $\sqrt{76}$　　b) $\sqrt{86}$　　c) $\sqrt{117}$　　d) $\sqrt{140}$　　e) $\sqrt{45}$　　f) $\sqrt{105}$

12. Evaluate.

a) $\sqrt{144}$　　　b) $\sqrt{14\,400}$　　　c) $\sqrt{1\,440\,000}$

d) $\sqrt{1.44}$　　　e) $\sqrt{0.0144}$　　　f) $\sqrt{0.000\,144}$

13. Find the area of the square with each side length.

a) 3.2 cm　　　b) 10.8 m　　　c) 0.1 cm　　　d) 300 m

14. Find the side length of the square with each area. Round to 1 decimal place where necessary.

a) 400 cm²   **b)** 0.25 m²   **c)** 90 cm²

d) 150 cm²   **e)** 300 cm²   **f)** 25 000 m²

✓ **15. Application** A square garden has area 230 m².

a) How long is each side of the garden, to the nearest centimetre?

b) How much fencing is needed to enclose the garden?

16. a) Find the side length of each square to the nearest unit.

     i) The Great Pyramid in Egypt has a square base that covers 52 441 m².

     ii) The outer walls of the Hanging Gardens of Babylon enclosed a square with an area of 8121 km².

     iii) The area of the base of the Eiffel Tower is 10 282 m².

b) Measure the side lengths of a square object. Calculate the area. Trade areas with a classmate, and calculate the side lengths.

✓ **17. Communication** Explain the difference between the square root of a number and the square of a number. Use a diagram, examples, and words in your explanation.

18. a) Use a calculator to find each square root.

     i) $\sqrt{3\,000\,000}$ **ii)** $\sqrt{30\,000}$ **iii)** $\sqrt{300}$

     iv) $\sqrt{3}$ **v)** $\sqrt{0.03}$ **vi)** $\sqrt{0.0003}$

b) Look at the results in part a. Explain the pattern.

19. Thinking/Inquiry/Problem Solving A square has one vertex at (0, 0) and an area of 49 square units. Draw the 4 possible squares on a grid. Name the coordinates of the other 3 vertices of each square.

20. What happens when you try to use a calculator to find the square root of a negative integer such as −3? Why do you think this happens?

2.7　The Pythagorean Theorem

The Pythagorean Theorem relates the areas of the squares on the sides of
a right triangle. Centuries ago, different civilizations knew this property
of right triangles.

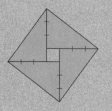

Egypt, 2000 B.C.E.

The Egyptians may have used a knotted rope with
triangle side lengths of 3, 4, and 5 units to design
the pyramids.

Babylonia, 1700 B.C.E.

Clay tablets show that the Babylonians
knew how to calculate the length of the
diagonal of a square.

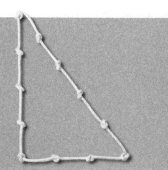

Greece, 540 B.C.E.

The Pythagorean Theorem is named after the
Greek philosopher, Pythagoras. He was the
first to prove that this theorem applies to all
right triangles.

China, 200 B.C.E.

About the time of the Han period, the Chinese
text Chòu-peï contained a discussion of the
Pythagorean Theorem based on this diagram.

In a right triangle, the side opposite the right angle is the *hypotenuse*.
The two shorter sides are the *legs*.

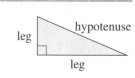

The Pythagorean Theorem

In a right triangle, the area of the square on the hypotenuse is equal to the sum of the areas of the squares on the other two sides.

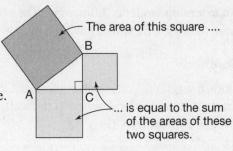

The area of this square ....

... is equal to the sum of the areas of these two squares.

The side opposite the right angle is the hypotenuse. The two shorter sides are the legs.

The hypotenuse is the longest side.

For the right triangle shown:

- Area of square on AB = Area of square on BC + Area of square on AC
- That is, $AB^2 = BC^2 + AC^2$

We can use Pythagorean Theorem to calculate the length of a side of a right triangle if we know the lengths of the other 2 sides.

Example 1

Calculate the length of the hypotenuse, h, in this right triangle.

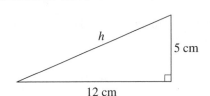

Solution

Use the Pythagorean Theorem.

$h^2 = 12^2 + 5^2$
$\quad = 144 + 25$
$\quad = 169$
$h = \sqrt{169}$
$h = 13$

The hypotenuse is 13 cm long.

Discuss

Why is only the positive square root of 169 reasonable for the side length of a triangle?

Example 2

An extension ladder is 7.0 m long. The bottom of the ladder is 2.0 m from the base of a wall. How high up the wall does the ladder reach?

Solution

Draw a diagram. Let w metres represent the height that the ladder reaches up the wall.
Use the Pythagorean Theorem.

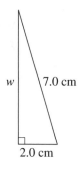

w 7.0 cm

2.0 cm

$w^2 + 2^2 = 7^2$
$w^2 + 4 = 49$
$w^2 = 49 - 4$
$w^2 = 45$
$w = \sqrt{45}$
$w \doteq 6.7082$

The ladder reaches about 6.7 m up the wall.

Discuss

Why is only the positive square root used here?

The Pythagorean Theorem can be used on a coordinate grid because the grid defines right angles.

Example 3

A line segment joins the points P(−1, 3) and Q(4, 6). Calculate the length of PQ to 1 decimal place.

Solution

Plot P and Q on a grid.
Draw a right triangle with PQ as the hypotenuse.
Count squares to find the lengths of the legs.
They are 5 units and 3 units.

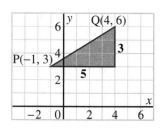

Use the Pythagorean Theorem.

$PQ^2 = 5^2 + 3^2$
$= 25 + 9$
$= 34$
$PQ = \sqrt{34}$
$PQ \doteq 5.8310$

Line segment PQ is about 5.8 units long.

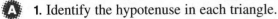
A   **1.** Identify the hypotenuse in each triangle.

✓

a) 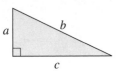   **b)** 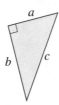   **c)**   **d)**

✓   **2.** Calculate the length of each hypotenuse, *h*.

a) 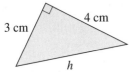   **b)** 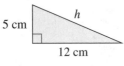   **c)**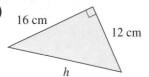

3. Calculate the length of each longer leg, *l*.

a)   **b)** 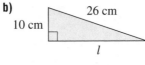   **c)**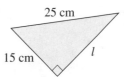

4. Calculate the length of each shorter leg, *s*.

a) 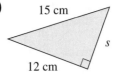   **b)** 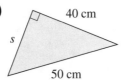   **c)**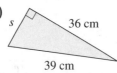

B   **5.** Calculate the length of the third side of each triangle. Give each answer to 1
✓   decimal place.

a) 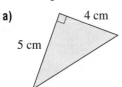   **b)** 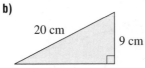   **c)**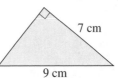

d)   **e)** 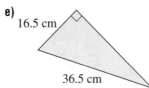   **f)**

6. Calculate the length of each line segment. The grid has 1-cm squares.

a)
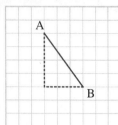

b)
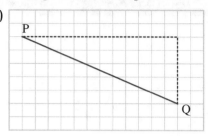

✓ **7. Knowledge/Understanding** Calculate the length of the third side of each triangle. Round to 1 decimal place.

a)
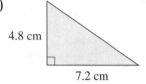

b)
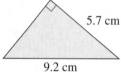

c)
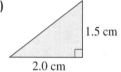

d)
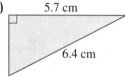

8. Calculate the length of a diagonal of each rectangle. Give each length to 1 decimal place where necessary.

a)

5 cm
5 cm

b)
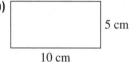
5 cm
10 cm

c)
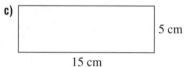
5 cm
15 cm

9. For each diagram, calculate the distance between S and T.

a)
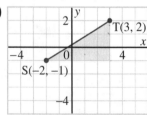

b)
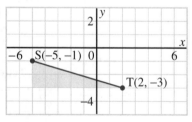

10. Calculate the length of each line segment.

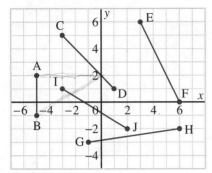

11. Plot each pair of points. Calculate the distance between them. Estimate to check.

a) A(1, 3), B(5, 5)   **b)** C(6, 0), D(8, 2)   **c)** E(–3, 2), F(1, –3)

d) G(–4, 2), H(–1, 3)   **e)** J(–1, –4), K(2, –1)   **f)** L(–3, 1), M(0, –1)

12. Communication A triangle has vertices J(–3, 2), K(2, 3), and L(4, –1).

a) Explain how to calculate the side lengths of the triangle in units.

b) Follow your explanation. Make any changes to your explanation that you think would help someone use it.

c) Follow explanations by a few classmates to calculate the side lengths. Describe what you learned by using their explanations.

d) Describe the role of the Pythagorean Theorem in your explanation for calculating the side lengths.

13. A rectangle has vertices P(–3, –2), Q(1, 2), R(3, 0), and S(–1, –4).

a) Draw the rectangle on grid paper. Calculate its length and width.

b) Calculate its area.

c) Calculate the lengths of its diagonals.

✓ **14. Application** The dimensions of a computer screen are 28 cm by 21 cm. The size of the screen is the length of its diagonal.

a) What is size of this screen?

b) What are advantages of using the Pythagorean Theorem instead of measuring to determine the size?

15. a) Calculate the length of a diagonal of each rectangle to the nearest unit. You might draw diagrams to help you visualize the figures.

  i) A volleyball court is 18 m long and 9 m wide.

  ii) Each side length of a baseball diamond is 2743 cm.

  iii) A basketball court is 28 m long and 15 m wide.

  iv) A hockey rink is about 30 m wide and 60 m long.

b) Choose a sport from part a. Explain whether the length of the diagonal seems reasonable.

16. a) Measure the length, width, and height of a cardboard box.

b) Calculate the length of the diagonal of each face of the box.

c) Calculate the length of the body diagonal.

d) Check part c by measuring the body diagonal as shown in the photograph. Compare the value for the body diagonal you got from using the Pythagorean Theorem to the value you got from measuring.

e) Suppose you wanted to put a metal rod in the box. What is the length of the longest rod that would fit? Explain how you know.

17. Thinking/Inquiry/Problem Solving A 5-m ladder is placed against a wall. The base of the ladder is 3 m from the wall. The top of the ladder is then lowered 2 m. How far is the base of the ladder from the wall?

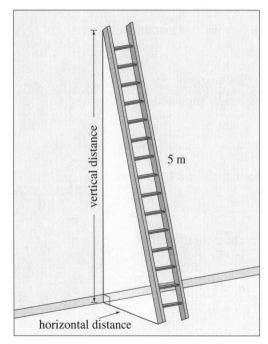

2.8 How Thick Is the Pile of Paper?

On page 45, you considered this situation: a piece of paper is folded in half as many times as possible.

You will need a sheet of blank paper and a ruler.

1. Fold the paper in half, forming 2 layers of paper.
   Fold it in half again, forming 4 layers.
   Continue to fold in half as long as you can.

2. Copy this table. Record your results.
   Extend the table at least as far as the
   maximum number of folds you were
   able to make.

Number of folds	Number of layers
0	1
1	
2	
3	

3. As you fold, the pile of paper
   becomes thicker. At some point,
   it will be about 1 mm thick.

   a) How many layers of paper
      are there when the pile is
      about 1 mm thick?

   b) Use the result of part a.
      Estimate the thickness
      of the sheet of paper
      you started with.

4. Suppose you could fold the
   paper 10 times.

   a) How many layers of paper
      would there be?

   b) About how thick would the
      pile of paper be?

5. Suppose you could fold the paper 50 times.

a) How many layers of paper would there be?

b) About how thick would the pile of paper be?
Express your answer in the most appropriate unit of measurement.

c) Compare your answer in part b with the measures in the chart that follows. Which measure is closest to the thickness of the pile of paper that is folded 50 times?

Height of an adult	2 m
Height of a 2-storey house	10 m
Height of a 10-storey apartment building	50 m
Height of the CN Tower	550 m
Height of jet aircraft in flight	12 000 m
Height of the space shuttle in orbit	200 km
Distance to the moon	380 000 km
Distance to the sun	150 000 000 km

6. As you fold, the area of paper on the top layer becomes smaller.

a) Measure the length and the width of the unfolded piece of paper in millimetres.

b) Calculate the area of the paper in square millimetres.

c) Add another column to your table for the area of the top layer. Write your answer from part a in the first row. Calculate the area of the top layer for each number of folds. Enter the results in the new column.

Number of folds, f	Number of layers, l	Area of top layer, a (mm^2)
0	1	
1		
2		
3		

7. Suppose you could fold the paper 10 times. What would the area of the top layer be?

8. Suppose you could fold the paper 50 times.

   a) What would the area of the top layer be?

   b) Compare your answer in part b with the areas in the chart below. Which area is closest to the area of the top layer of the pile of paper that is folded 50 times?

Area of one face of a sugar cube	100 mm^2
Area of this circle: •	1 mm^2
Area of the dot in this letter: i	0.01 mm^2
Area of a pollen grain	0.001 mm^2
Area of a pit in a CD track	10^{-5} mm^2

9. Your table in exercise 6 is a mathematical model. It represents the number of layers and the area of the top layer when the piece of paper is folded over and over again. List any assumptions for this model.

10. Use the data in the first 2 columns of your table in exercise 6.

   a) Draw a graph of the number of layers, l, against the number of folds, f. Plot f horizontally and l vertically.

   b) Should the points be joined? Explain.

   c) Is the relation linear or non-linear? Explain.

   d) Describe how the number of layers changes as the number of folds increases.

11. Use the data in the 1st and 3rd columns of your table in exercise 6.

   a) Draw a graph of the area of the top layer, a, against the number of folds, f.

   b) Should the points be joined? Explain.

   c) Is the relation linear or non-linear? Explain.

   d) Describe how the area of the top layer changes as the number of folds increases.

12. **Communication** Write about this experiment. Explain what you did and what you found out. Include the tables of values and graphs in your explanation.

Products of Rational Numbers

- Rational numbers can be written as fractions or decimals; for example, $\frac{1}{2}$, $-\frac{5}{3}$, $0.\overline{3}$, -8, ...
- The product of positive rational numbers is positive. $(+) \times (+) \times (+) = +$
- The product of an even number of negative rational numbers is positive.
  $(-) \times (-) \times (-) \times (-) = +$
- The product of an odd number of negative rational numbers is negative.
  $(-) \times (-) \times (-) = -$

Exponent Laws

- Multiplying powers: $a^n \times a^m = a^{n+m}$, n and m are intergers.
- Dividing powers: $a^n \div a^m = a^{n-m}$, n and m are intergers.

$$5^6 \times 5^2 = 5^{6+2}$$
$$= 5^8$$

$$5^6 \div 5^2 = 5^{6-2}$$
$$= 5^4$$

Power of a Power

- $(a^m)^n = a^{mn}$, m and n are intergers.

$$(5^2)^3 = 5^{2 \times 3}$$
$$= 5^6$$

Zero Exponent

- $a^0 = 1$ $(a \neq 0)$

Negative Integer Exponent

- $a^{-n} = \frac{1}{a^n}$ ($a \neq 0$ and n is an integer.)
- $\frac{1}{a^n} = a^{-n}$ ($a \neq 0$ and n is an integer.)

$$5^{-1} = \frac{1}{5}$$

$$\frac{1}{5} = 5^{-1}$$

Scientific Notation

- To write a number in scientific notation,
  write it as the product of: a number between
  1 and 10 and a power of 10.

$$53\,000 = 5.3 \times 10^4$$
$$0.0041 = 4.1 \times 10^{-3}$$

Squares and Square Roots

- All positive numbers have square roots.
- When taking the square root, consider positive and negative values.
- The radical sign, $\sqrt{\ }$, means evaluate only the positive square root.

The Pythagorean Theorem

- $h^2 = l^2 + s^2$

2.1 **1.** Write each power as a product. Then evaluate.

a) $(1.4)^3$ b) $(-8)^5$ c) $\left(-\dfrac{5}{8}\right)^2$ d) $(-2.6)^4$

2. Evaluate. Round to 3 decimal places where necessary.

a) $(-1.8)^3$ b) 4^2 c) $(2.4)^4$

d) $(-0.9)^3$ e) $\left(\dfrac{7}{2}\right)^2$ f) $\left(-\dfrac{4}{5}\right)^1$

3. Evaluate mentally.

a) 10^4 b) 10^6 c) 10^2 d) 10^9

4. Evaluate.

a) The Solar System has 3^2 planets.   b) Each year has 2^2 seasons.

5. Make up a statement similar to exercise 4. Trade statements with classmates and evaluate the powers.

6. Evaluate.

a) $\left(-\dfrac{1}{2}\right)^3$ b) $\left(-\dfrac{2}{4}\right)^3$ c) $\left(-\dfrac{6}{12}\right)^3$ d) $\left(-\dfrac{5}{10}\right)^3$

7. Evaluate.

a) $\left(-\dfrac{15}{20}\right)^4$ b) $\left(-\dfrac{3}{4}\right)^4$ c) $\left(-\dfrac{75}{100}\right)^4$ d) $\left(-\dfrac{6}{8}\right)^4$

2.2 **8.** Write each product as a single power.

a) $3^5 \times 3^2$ b) $(-2)^4 \times (-2)^3$ c) $2^3 \times 2^5$ d) $(-15)^3 \times (-15)^2$

9. Write each quotient as a single power.

a) $4^5 \div 4^3$ b) $3^8 \div 3^6$ c) $\dfrac{12^9}{12^8}$ d) $\dfrac{16^3}{16^2}$

10. Write each product as a single power. Evaluate. Round to 3 decimal places where necessary.

a) $(-1)^2 \times (-1)^2$ b) $3.2^3 \times 3.2^5$ c) $(-0.8)^1 \times (-0.8)^1$

d) $6.25^2 \times 6.25^3$ e) $10^3 \times 10^4$ f) $(-1.5)^2 \times (-1.5)$

11. Write each quotient as a single power. Evaluate. Round to 3 decimal places where necessary.

a) $8^7 \div 8^3$ b) $(-7)^6 \div (-7)^5$ c) $(-1.6)^5 \div (-1.6)^2$

d) $(-5.4)^9 \div (-5.4)^7$ e) $(-0.9)^8 \div (-0.9)^4$ f) $1.25^5 \div 1.25^4$

2.3 **12.** Write as a single power. Do not evaluate.

a) $(3^2)^5$ b) $(3^5)^4$ c) $(3^{-2})^3$ d) $(3^2)^0$

13. Write as a single power.

a) $(m^3)^5$ **b)** $(m^2)^6$ **c)** $(m^{-5})^{-1}$ **d)** $(m^{-2})^3$

14. Write as a single power, then evaluate.

a) $(2^2)^3$ **b)** $(-4^2)^2$ **c)** $(-5^7)^0$ **d)** $(3^{-2})^{-3}$

2.4 **15.** Write each power with a positive exponent.

a) 5^{-3} **b)** $\dfrac{1}{4^{-2}}$ **c)** 6^{-4} **d)** $\dfrac{1}{10^{-3}}$ **e)** 2^{-5} **f)** $\dfrac{1}{3^{-6}}$

16. Use a calculator to evaluate each power. Round to 4 decimal places where necessary.

a) 4^{-5} **b)** $(-6)^{-3}$ **c)** 1.8^{-1} **d)** $(-3.4)^{-2}$ **e)** 5^{-4} **f)** $(-2.4)^{-3}$

17. Evaluate each power.

a) $(-5)^0$ **b)** 2^0 **c)** 4.7^0 **d)** $(-9.5)^0$ **e)** $(-1.1)^0$ **f)** 5.6^0

2.5 **18.** Write in scientific notation.

a) 64 000 **b)** 0.0045 **c)** 0.000 006

d) 7 250 000 000 **e)** 4×10^5 **f)** 800×10^{-4}

19. Write in standard form.

a) 4.8×10^8 **b)** 7.31×10^{-4} **c)** 3.0×10^{-6}

d) 1.07×10^2 **e)** 6.1×10^{-9} **f)** 8.02×10^{-5}

20. When you write a number in scientific notation, explain how you know whether the exponent is positive or negative.

21. Simplify. Check whether the answers are reasonable.

a) $(3.2 \times 10^4) \times (1.0 \times 10^{-6})$ **b)** $(8.14 \times 10^2) \times (9.5 \times 10^8)$

c) $(6.03 \times 10^{-5}) \times (4.6 \times 10^{-1})$ **d)** $(3.8 \times 10^{-7}) \times (7.1 \times 10^3)$

22. Simplify.

a) $\dfrac{7.1 \times 10^{-4}}{8.0 \times 10^6}$ **b)** $\dfrac{1.0 \times 10^{-1}}{3.48 \times 10^{-5}}$

23. One grain of grass pollen has an estimated mass of 0.000 000 005 g. Write this mass in scientific notation.

24. Every atom contains electrons and protons. Write each mass in standard form.

a) An electron has a mass of 9.11×10^{-28} g.

b) A proton has a mass of 1.67×10^{-24} g.

2.6 **25.** What are the square roots of each number?

a) 64 **b)** 4 **c)** 36 **d)** 144 **e)** 1

26. Evaluate.

a) $\sqrt{9}$ b) $\sqrt{16}$ c) $\sqrt{100}$

d) $\sqrt{25}$ e) $\sqrt{121}$ f) $\sqrt{10\,000}$

27. Find the square roots of each number. Round to 1 decimal place.

a) 80 b) 25 c) 98

d) 150 e) 83 f) 210

28. Evaluate. Round to 1 decimal place.

a) $\sqrt{20}$ b) $\sqrt{65}$ c) $\sqrt{180}$ d) $\sqrt{1256}$ e) $\sqrt{948}$

29. a) Find the perimeter of a square with area 49 cm^2.

b) Find the approximate perimeter of a square with area 150 cm^2.

2.7 **30.** Calculate the length of the third side of each triangle to 1 decimal place.

a)

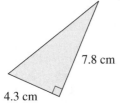

7.8 cm

4.3 cm

b)

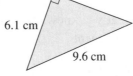

6.1 cm

9.6 cm

31. Calculate the length of a diagonal of each rectangle to 1 decimal place.

a)

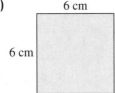

6 cm

6 cm

b)

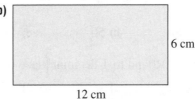

6 cm

12 cm

32. Plot each pair of points. Calculate the distance between them.

a) L(2, 4), M(−3, 1) b) J(0, −5), K(−6, −8) c) E(−2, 6), F(6, 3)

33. a) Is the hypotenuse always the longest side of a right triangle? How do you know?

b) Explain how you can use your answer for part a to check calculations with the Pythagorean Theorem.

1. Evaluate each power. Round to 4 decimal places where necessary.

   a) 7^4　　　b) $(-1.2)^{-5}$　　c) $(-8.6)^0$　　d) 12^{-2}　　e) $\left(\dfrac{3}{5}\right)^6$　　f) 10^0

2. **Knowledge/Understanding** Write each expression as a power. Evaluate each power. Round to 3 decimal places where necessary.

   a) $8^3 \times 8^2$　　　　b) $(-1.4)^8 \div (-1.4)^3$　　c) $5^6 \div 5^2$　　　d) $(-10)^6 \times (-10)^5$

3. Write in scientific notation.

   a) $201\,000$　　　b) 0.0009　　　c) $735\,200$　　　d) $0.000\,007\,8$

4. Write in standard form.

   a) 9.0×10^{-6}　　b) 3.4×10^8　　c) 1.65×10^9　　d) 8.22×10^{-4}

5. **Communication** Explain what you know about a number in scientific notation from the sign of its exponent.

6. Simplify. State in scientific notation.

   a) $(3.8 \times 10^{-4}) \times (2.0 \times 10^3)$　　　b) $\dfrac{1.0 \times 10^2}{4.53 \times 10^{-3}}$

7. Find the square roots of each number. Round to 1 decimal place where necessary.

   a) 15　　　b) 100　　　c) 50　　　d) 1　　　e) 82

8. Find each square root. Round to 1 decimal place where necessary.

   a) $\sqrt{64}$　　b) $\sqrt{42}$　　c) $\sqrt{120}$　　d) $\sqrt{81}$　　e) $\sqrt{6}$

9. Calculate the length of the third side of each triangle. Round to 1 decimal place.

   a)

   6.4 cm

   3.2 cm

   b)

   8.5 cm

   2.7 cm

10. **Application** A triangle has side lengths 3.6 m, 4.8 m, and 6.0 m.

    a) If the triangle were a right triangle, which side would be the hypotenuse? Why?

    b) Is the triangle a right triangle? Why?

11. **Thinking/Inquiry/Problem Solving** Suppose the length and width of a rectangle are doubled. Predict what would happen to the lengths of its diagonals. Explain why your prediction is reasonable. Use the Pythagorean Theorem to show whether your prediction is true for two examples.

1. The area of a rectangle is given by the formula, $A = lw$.
   A scientist looking at bacteria under a microscope noticed
   a rectangular cluster of bacteria.

   2.8×10^{-5} cm

   1.6×10^{-5} cm

   Find the approximate area of the
   rectangle. Show your work.

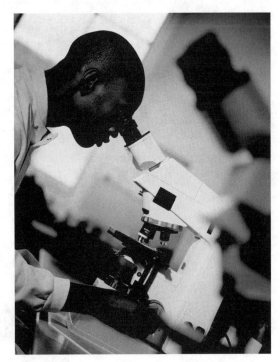

2. Javier simplified $2^3 \times 2^4$ as: $2^3 \times 2^4 = 2^{12}$
   His friend, Miriam, correctly told Javier to add the exponents as shown:
   $2^3 \times 2^4 = 2^7$
   "But why add?" Javier asked. "It says to multiply."

   Explain why adding the exponents is correct.

3

Algebra

By the end of this chapter, you will:

- Expand and simplify expressions.
- Use algebra to solve equations.
- Use equations to solve problems. Compare using equations with other methods to solve the same problem.
- Manipulate first-degree polynomials to solve equations.
- Communicate solutions to problems, and justify your reasoning in solving problems.

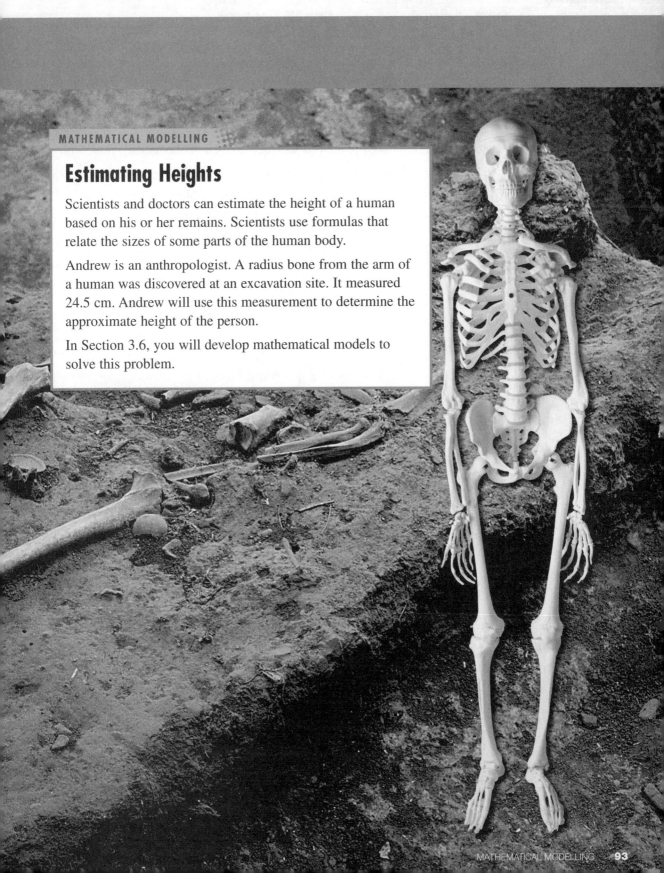

Estimating Heights

Scientists and doctors can estimate the height of a human based on his or her remains. Scientists use formulas that relate the sizes of some parts of the human body.

Andrew is an anthropologist. A radius bone from the arm of a human was discovered at an excavation site. It measured 24.5 cm. Andrew will use this measurement to determine the approximate height of the person.

In Section 3.6, you will develop mathematical models to solve this problem.

Necessary Skills

Solving Equations by Inspection

Recall that an equation is a way to write a word sentence about a mathematical situation.

For example, $x + 3 = 5$ is read "A number plus 3 equals 5."

To solve an equation means to find the value of the variable that makes the equation true.

The solution of the equation $x + 3 = 5$ is $x = 2$, because $2 + 3 = 5$.

Example

Solve.

a) $10 + a = 14$ **b)** $c - 3 = 8$ **c)** $3m = 18$ **d)** $\frac{n}{2} = 5$

Solution

a) $10 + a = 14$

What number, added to 10, makes 14?
Since $10 + 4 = 14$, the solution is $a = 4$.

b) $c - 3 = 8$

From what number do we subtract 3
to get 8? Since $11 - 3 = 8$, the solution
is $c = 11$.

c) $3m = 18$

What do we multiply 3 by, to get 18?
Since $3 \times 6 = 18$, the solution is $m = 6$.

d) $\frac{n}{2} = 5$

What number do we divide by 2 to get 5?
Since $\frac{10}{2} = 5$, the solution is $n = 10$.

Exercises

1. Solve.

   a) $x + 5 = 12$ **b)** $3 + m = 8$ **c)** $15 = a + 9$ **d)** $21 = 14 + n$

   e) $x - 5 = 12$ **f)** $10 - m = 8$ **g)** $15 = a - 9$ **h)** $12 = 14 - n$

2. Solve.

   a) $2a = 16$ **b)** $3n = 24$ **c)** $30 = 6x$ **d)** $42 = 7m$

   e) $\frac{n}{2} = 3$ **f)** $\frac{x}{3} = 5$ **g)** $8 = \frac{m}{4}$ **h)** $1 = \frac{a}{9}$

Writing Simple Equations

We can use algebra to write a word sentence as an equation.

Example

Write an equation to represent each sentence.

a) Three more than a number is 12.

b) A number decreased by two is six.

c) Six times a number is 24.

d) A number divided by four is five.

Solution

a) Three more than a number is 12.
Let the number be n.
Then, three more than the number is
$n + 3$; this equals 12.
So, the equation is $n + 3 = 12$.

b) A number decreased by two is six.
Let the number be x.
Then, the number decreased by two
is $x - 2$; this equals 6.
So, the equation is $x - 2 = 6$.

c) Six times a number is 24.
Let the number be y.
Then, six times the number is $6y$;
this equals 24.
So, the equation is $6y = 24$.

d) A number divided by four is five.
Let the number be m.
Then, the number divided by four is $\frac{m}{4}$;
this equals 5.
So, the equation is $\frac{m}{4} = 5$.

Exercises

1. Write an equation to represent each sentence.

   a) Two more than a number is nine.   **b)** Five less than a number is 11.
   c) A number subtracted from 12 is six.   **d)** Eight more than a number is 20.

2. Solve each equation from exercise 1.

3. Write an equation to represent each sentence.

   a) Five times a number is 20.   **b)** A number divided by three is 12.
   c) A number times four is 28.   **d)** Two divided into a number is seven.

4. Solve each equation from exercise 3.

3.1 Representing Variables and Expressions

The area of this rectangular garden can be calculated in two ways.

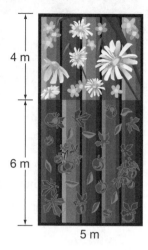

4 m

6 m

5 m

Method 1:

Total area = width × length
$$= 5(4 + 6)$$
$$= 5(10)$$
$$= 50$$

Method 2:

Total area = area with flowers + area with vegetables
$$= 5 \times 4 + 5 \times 6$$
$$= 20 + 30$$
$$= 50$$

For both methods, the area is 50 m².

$$5(4 + 6) = 5 \times 4 + 5 \times 6$$

In arithmetic, we write equations such as: $5(4 + 6) = 5 \times 4 + 5 \times 6$

In algebra, we use variables to write the equation: $a(b + c) = ab + ac$.
This equation is called the *distributive law*.

TAKE NOTE

Distributive Law

$a(b + c) = ab + ac$

$a(b - c) = ab - ac$ where a, b, and c are any real numbers

We can use algebra tiles to represent algebraic expressions.

This tile is a 1-tile.
It represents one unit, or 1.

To represent the opposite,
which is −1, flip the tile.

This tile below is a variable tile. It represents
a variable. For example, if you are using s,
you can call this tile an s-tile.

To represent the opposite of s, which
is $-s$, flip the tile.

To represent the expression $s + 4$ with algebra tiles, use one s-tile and four 1-tiles.

To represent $2w + 10$, use two w-tiles and ten 1-tiles.

To represent $2(w + 5)$, form two equal groups of tiles. Each group contains one w-tile and five 1-tiles.

The algebra tiles demonstrate an example of the distributive law: $2(w + 5) = 2w + 10$
When we write an expression without brackets, we *expand* it.

Algebra Tiles and the Distributive Law

1. What expression does each set of algebra tiles represent?

a)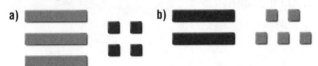

b)

2. Use algebra tiles to represent each expression.

a) $2x + 1$ **b)** $3y - 5$

3. For each expression, use algebra tiles to represent the equal groups. Then use the tiles to write the expression without brackets. That is, expand the expression.

a) $2(x + 4)$ **b)** $3(-2c - 1)$

4. How can you expand each expression in exercise 3 without using tiles?

5. Try your method from exercise 4 with these expressions. Check with tiles.

a) $3(s - 1)$ **b)** $2(-3t + 2)$

6. a) Use algebra tiles to represent $(-w - 2)$.

  b) To represent the opposite, flip the tile. Since $-(-w - 2)$ is the opposite of $(-w - 2)$, flip the tiles to represent $-(-w - 2)$. Use the tiles to expand $-(-w - 2)$.

  c) What do you notice about the expressions in part b?

7. a) Use algebra tiles to represent equal groups for $2(2m - 4)$.

  b) Flip the tiles to represent $-2(2m - 4)$. Use the tiles to expand $-2(2m - 4)$.

  c) What do you notice about the expressions in part b?

8. Explain how you can expand an expression that has a negative sign before the brackets.

9. Try your method from exercise 8 with these expressions. Check with tiles.

a) $-4(n + 1)$ **b)** $-3(-2q + 5)$

Example 1

a) Use algebra tiles to represent the expression $5 - 2x$.

b) Use algebra tiles to represent the expression $-(5 - 2x)$.

Solution

a) $5 - 2x$

Use five 1-tiles and two flipped x-tiles.

b) $-(5 - 2x)$

Just as $-x$ represents the opposite of x, so $-(5 - 2x)$ represents the opposite of $5 - 2x$.
Use tiles to represent $5 - 2x$. Then flip the tiles.
$-(5 - 2x) = -5 + 2x$, or $2x - 5$

Discuss

How is expanding $-(5 - 2x)$ the same as multiplying 5 by -1 and multiplying $-2x$ by -1?

Example 2

Use algebra tiles to represent each expression. Use the result to expand the expression.

a) $2(3x - 4)$ **b)** $-3(p - 3)$

Solution

a)

Think ...
     2 equal groups of tiles

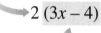

Each group has three x-tiles and four flipped 1-tiles.

In all, there are six x-tiles and eight flipped 1-tiles.
So, $2(3x - 4) = 6x - 8$

b)

> *Think ...*
>
> 3 equal groups of tiles
>
>
>
> $-3\ (p-3)$

Each group has one p-tile and three flipped 1-tiles.

The negative sign in front of the brackets means flip all the tiles.

In all, there are three flipped p-tiles and nine 1-tiles.
So, $-3(p-3) = -3p + 9$

Instead of using algebra tiles, we can use the distributive law to expand an expression.

Example 3

Expand using the distributive law.

a) $6(3n + 4)$

b) $-3(4b - 7)$

Solution

a) $6(3n + 4) = 6(3n) + 6(4)$
$= 18n + 24$

b) $-3(4b - 7) = -3(4b) - 3(-7)$
$= -12b + 21$

3.1   Exercises

A

1. Write two different expressions for the total area of the gardens.

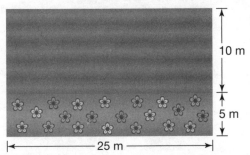

2. Use the distributive law to expand.

a) $3(5 + 7)$ b) $6(19 - 9)$ c) $5(-4 + 6)$

d) $6(2 + 7 + 1)$ e) $3(2 - 1 + 9)$ f) $5(-4 - 5 + 2)$

3. Use the distributive law to expand.

a) $-(2x + 1)$ b) $-(2x - 1)$ c) $-(-2x + 1)$

d) $-(-2x - 1)$ e) $-(1 + 2x)$ f) $-(1 - 2x)$

4. Expand.

a) $4(8 + 3m)$ b) $-4(8 + 3m)$ c) $4(-8 + 3m)$

d) $4(8 - 3m)$ e) $4(3m + 8)$ f) $-4(3m + 8)$

5. What expression does each group of algebra tiles represent?

a)    b)

c) 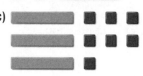   d)

6. Suppose you flipped all the tiles in exercise 5. What expression would each group of algebra tiles represent?

B **7.** Expand using the distributive law.

a) $3(5 + 8)$ b) $5(6 - 4)$ c) $11(5 - 7)$ d) $-6(8 - 4)$

e) $12(5 - 6)$ f) $-4(7 - 9)$ g) $13(1 + h)$ h) $8(11 - d)$

8. Expand using the distributive law.

a) $5(4 + 10 + 2)$ b) $4(11 - 5 - 2)$ c) $9(4 + 5 - 8)$ d) $-8(9 - 2 + 8)$

9. Use algebra tiles to represent each expression.

a) $3a + 5$ b) $-4c - 6$ c) $-2e + 4$ d) $-1 - 6g$

e) $4q + 7$ f) $-6 - 3k$ g) $7 - 2t$ h) $-3 + 5s$

10. Use algebra tiles to represent each expression.

a) $4z - 6$ b) $-3 + 2a$ c) $-3x + 5$ d) $-7 - k$

e) $8 + 6c$ f) $-p - 4$ g) $6x + 1$ h) $-7 - 4t$

11. Communication Which expression is equivalent to $3(2y - 5)$? Explain your choice.

a) $2y - 15$ b) $6y - 15$ c) $2y + 15$ d) $6y - 5$

12. a) Knowledge/Understanding Use algebra tiles to represent each expression. Use the tiles to write the expression without brackets.

   i) $5(k + 1)$ **ii)** $2(3 - 2w)$ **iii)** $4(2m + 1)$ **iv)** $-1(4 + 5y)$

   v) $-3(2 - p)$ **vi)** $3(1 - 3b)$ **vii)** $-2(4t - 5)$ **viii)** $-4(2s + 2)$

b) Write a rule for determining whether a term is positive or negative after expanding. Check whether your rule works for 3 expressions in part a.

 13. Only two expressions in each set are equal. Which are they? Use algebra tiles to justify your answer.

   a) $3x + 2$ $3x - 2$ $2 + 3x$ $2 - 3x$

   b) $-4g + 5$ $-5g + 4$ $-5g - 4$ $4 - 5g$

   c) $2j - 7$ $7 - 2j$ $-7 - 2j$ $-2j + 7$

   d) $-5b + 3$ $-3 - 5b$ $-5 + 3b$ $-5b - 3$

14. Which of the following expressions is equal to $5(m + 3) - 16$? Explain.

   a) $5(m + 3 - 16)$ **b)** $5m + 15 - 16$ **c)** $5m + 15 - 80$

15. Application Expand using the distributive law.

   a) $3(x + 2y - 7)$ **b)** $-2(a - 5b + 2)$ **c)** $-(6m - 7n)$

   d) $4(9p + q - 9r)$ **e)** $5(x + 6y - 4)$ **f)** $3(7c - 9 + d)$

16. Thinking/Inquiry/Problem Solving
A rectangular garden is made up of smaller gardens as shown.

  a) Write as many different expressions as you can think of to represent the total area of the garden.

  b) How can you use the distributive law to find the total area of the garden?

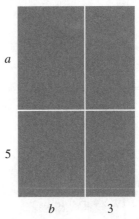

17. Thinking/Inquiry/Problem Solving Decide whether each statement is always true, sometimes true, or never true. Justify your answers.

  a) A 1-tile is positive and a flipped 1-tile is negative.

  b) A variable tile is positive and a flipped variable tile is negative.

  c) The variable x is positive and $-x$ is negative.

In arithmetic, we add, subtract, multiply, and divide numbers.

In algebra, we add, subtract, multiply, and divide algebraic expressions.

The terms represented by variable tiles are *variable* terms. The terms represented by 1-tiles are *constant* terms.

When we add or subtract expressions using algebra tiles, we use the *Zero Principle*.

TAKE NOTE

The Zero Principle

A 1-tile plus a flipped 1-tile have the sum 0.
Any two opposite tiles have the sum 0.

So, we can add or remove pairs of opposite tiles without changing the value of an expression.

We see: or

We think:
The sum of each pair is 0.

We use the Zero Principle when we combine groups of tiles. For example, these groups of tiles represent $4x$, $-2x$, and 5, respectively.

We use the Zero Principle to remove two pairs of opposite tiles. Two variable tiles and five 1-tiles remain. We cannot combine the variable tiles and 1-tiles since they are not the same type.

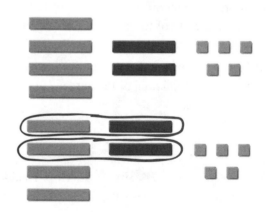

Like terms contain the same variable. For example, $4x$ and $-2x$ are like terms. 7 and -3 are like terms. Since they contain no variables they are *constant* terms. Like terms can be combined to *simplify* an expression.

We write: $4x - 2x + 5 = 2x + 5$

TAKE NOTE

The terms $4x$ and $-2x$ are *like* terms because they contain the same variable. Similarly, 7 and -3 are like terms. They contain no variables. The terms $2x$ and 5 are not like terms, so they cannot be combined.

When we combine like terms, we simplify the expression.

Example 1

a) Use algebra tiles to simplify the expression $4a + 3 + 2a - 4$.

b) What is the value of this expression for each value of a?
   i) $a = 8$ ii) $a = -2$

Solution

a)

Think ...

four a-tiles

and two a-tiles

three 1-tiles

and four flipped 1-tiles

$$4a + 3 + 2a - 4$$

Group similar tiles together.
Use the Zero Principle to cancel.
Count remaining tiles.

From the tiles, $4a + 3 + 2a - 4 = 6a - 1$

b) i) When $a = 8$, the value of the expression $6a - 1$ is: $6(8) - 1 = 48 - 1$
$$= 47$$

ii) When $a = -2$, the value of the expression $6a - 1$ is: $6(-2) - 1 = -12 - 1$
$$= -13$$

We could simplify the expression in *Example 1* without using algebra tiles. We do this in *Example 2*.

Example 2

Simplify the expression $4a + 3 + 2a - 4$ by combining like terms.

Solution

$$4a + 3 + 2a - 4 = 4a + 2a + 3 - 4 \qquad \text{Rearrange to group like terms.}$$
$$= 6a - 1 \qquad\qquad\quad\;\; \text{Note: the sign of the term moves with the term.}$$

In *Example 2*, we combined the variable terms $4a$ and $2a$. In the term $4a$, 4 is the *coefficient*. In the term $2a$, 2 is the coefficient. In both terms, a is the variable.

Example 3

Use algebra tiles to combine like terms: $2(x + 2) - 3(2 - x)$

Solution

Think ...

Combine two groups of these tiles ...   ... and flip three groups of these tiles.

$$2(x + 2) \;-\; 3(2 - x)$$

two x-tiles and four 1-tiles   Flip six 1-tiles and three flipped x-tiles.

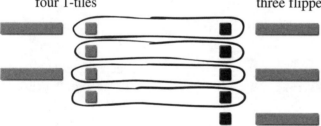

From the tiles, $2(x + 2) - 3(2 - x) = 5x - 2$

Discuss

What is the coefficient of the variable term in $5x - 2$?

When we do not use algebra tiles, we use the distributive law.

Example 4

Simplify the expression $2(x + 2) - 3(2 - x)$.

Solution

$$2(x + 2) - 3(2 - x) = 2(x) + 2(2) - 3(2) - 3(-x)$$
$$= 2x + 4 - 6 + 3x$$
$$= 2x + 3x + 4 - 6$$
$$= 5x - 2$$

Discuss

Why does it make sense to have the same results in *Examples 3* and *4*?

3.2   Exercises

A   **1.** Which are like terms?

   a) $5x$, $-2x$ **b)** $3a$, 7 **c)** $2x$, -1 **d)** 4, 8

   e) $2x$, $3y$ **f)** $-5c$, c **g)** $-x$, $4x$ **h)** 3, $3s$

   i) $8k$, $-4k$, 3 **j)** $9p$, -4, $7p$ **k)** $2s$, $2t$, $2u$ **l)** -82, $6w$, $-8v$

2. There are 5 pairs of like terms. Find all 5 pairs.

   $2x$ $-3y$ $5w$ $-y$ 3 $-x$ $5z$ $4w$ -1 $-2z$

3. Find the like terms for $4a$.

   7 $2a$ $-x$ -4 a $-4b$ $-2a$ 0 $3z$

4. Find the like terms for 9.

   $9x$ 5 -9 0 $9a$ $-3y$ -1 $2a$ 4

5. Identify the constant terms.

   3 $2b$ -8 0 x $-8y$ 10 -1 $5k$

6. Identify the variable terms.

   4 $-s$ $2y$ $7m$ $-3a$ -6 $4x$ 2 n

B   **7.** Combine like terms. Write an expression for each using x.

   a) 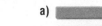   **b)**    **c)**

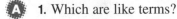

8. Combine like terms.

a) $5a - 5a$ b) $8 + 8$ c) $-2x + 2x$

d) $7 - 7$ e) $-1 + 1$ f) $-3b - 3b$

 9. Find the value of each expression.

a) $4(-2) + 1$ b) $3(4) - 3$ c) $7(-1) - 2$

10. Use algebra tiles to combine like terms.

a) $6s + 3s$ b) $4v - 2v$ c) $-5b + 2b + 4b$

d) $7p - p + 3p$ e) $-6c - 2c - c$ f) $6t + 5 + 2t$

 11. Simplify. Use algebra tiles if you like.

a) $5 - 2a - 3a$ b) $11n - 12n + 6$ c) $9 - 4d + 3d$

d) $4u - 6 + u + 3$ e) $-k + 2k - 3k + 4k$ f) $-6q - 2q + q - 7$

12. Simplify. Use algebra tiles if you like.

a) $3x + 4x - 3x$ b) $-3a + 2a - a$ c) $-8 + 5c - 3c$

d) $3k - 2 - k + 1$ e) $5(2b + 1) + 3b$ f) $-4u + 1 - 2(2 + 3u)$

13. Use the Zero Principle to simplify mentally. Write only the result.

a) $6x - 6x + 2$ b) $-7 + s + 7$ c) $2d - d - d$

d) $3a - 2 + 1 + 1$ e) $4y - 3 - 4y + y$ f) $8f + 2 - 8f$

14. Explain your method from exercise 13. Write an expression you can simplify mentally using the Zero Principle.

15. Expand. Then combine like terms. Find the value when $x = 0$.

a) $3(x - 2) + 4$ b) $-x - 5 + 2(1 + 3x)$ c) $-3 + 4(1 - x) + 5x$

d) $-8(-x - 1) - 3x - 5$ e) $2(x + 3) - (5 - x)$ f) $-3(2 + 3x) + 8x - 3$

16. Knowledge/Understanding Simplify each expression. Find its value when $x = 1$.

a) $-7x + 12 - 2x$ b) $8x + 3 - 11x - 7$ c) $10(x - 5) + 7x - 2$

d) $9 + 3x - (8x - 12)$ e) $5x + 3(4x - 2) - 12$ f) $2(3x + 2) + 4(2 + x)$

 17. Simplify each expression. Find its value when $x = -3$.

a) $4x + 2x - 2$ b) $5x - 6x - 2$ c) $11x - 5 - 7x - 4$

d) $9 + 3x - (8x - 12)$ e) $2x + 3(4x - 2)$ f) $-8(3 - 2x) - 7 - 6x$

18. Simplify each expression. Find its value when the variable has the given value.

a) $4a + 7a - 3$ for $a = 3$ b) $-3m + 21 + 7m$ for $m = -7$

c) $15(s + 2) - s$ for $s = 0$ d) $20x - 3 - 6x$ for $x = 2$

19. Simplify each expression. Find its value when: **i)** $x = 7$ **ii)** $x = -2$

a) $9x - 5 - 6x + 4$

b) $8x - 2 - 6x - 6$

c) $-3(x - 1) - (2x - 3)$

d) $5x - 3(x - 4)$

e) $-(x - 2) + 4(3 - x)$

f) $7(1 - x) - 2(3x - 2)$

 20. Communication In exercise 19, we could find the value of each expression when $x = 7$ and when $x = -2$ without simplifying. Why do we simplify first?

21. Simplify.

a) $7a + 3a + 2(a - 5)$

b) $-(3m + 2) - 3(1 + 4m)$

c) $20s - 7 + 5(3 - s)$

d) $4x - 3 - (x - 1)$

e) $4(5p - 4) - 1 - 3(6p - 2)$

f) $-32g + 5(2 - 3g) + (-3)$

22. Simplify.

a) $m - 2 + 5(m - 2)$

b) $2(a + 3) - 1 - 3a - (2a - 5)$

c) $3x - 2 + 7(1 - x) - 7$

d) $2s - 1 - 4(s - 2) + 3(s + 1)$

e) $7(-2d - 4) - 6d - 8$

f) $5(q - 7) - (q + 4)$

23. Thinking/Inquiry/Problem Solving

a) If possible, simplify each expression. If it is not possible, explain why.

   i) $2 + 3x + 0$ **ii)** $-7v + v + 2 + 1$ **iii)** $64v$

b) In your opinion, which expression is simpler? Give a reason for your opinion.

   i) $7(x - 4)$ **ii)** $7x - 28$

c) Without using the words "simple," "simpler," or "simplest," explain what the word "simplify" means.

24. Application Write an expression for the perimeter of each rectangle. Simplify the expression.

a)

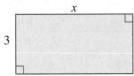

b)

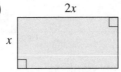

On page 94, you solved equations by inspection. To solve by inspection, you look at an equation and calculate the solution. Some equations cannot be easily solved this way. They must be solved algebraically.

To solve an equation algebraically:

- Collect like terms: variable terms on one side of the equation and constant terms on the other side.
- Simplify each side of the equation.
- Isolate the variable. Divide each side of the equation by the coefficient of the variable term.

Example 1

Solve algebraically.

$12 + k = 4 - 3k$

Solution

$12 + k = 4 - 3k$	Collect the k-terms on the left side.
$12 + k + 3k = 4 - 3k + 3k$	To use the Zero Principle, add $3k$ to each side.
$12 + 4k = 4$	Collect the constant terms on the right side.
$12 + 4k - 12 = 4 - 12$	Subtract 12 from each side.
$4k = -8$	Isolate the variable.
$\dfrac{4k}{4} = \dfrac{8}{4}$	Divide each side by the coefficient, 4.
$k = -2$	

To check the solution of an equation you have solved:

- Substitute the solution for the variable in each side of the **original** equation.
- Simplify each side of the equation. If the results are the same, the solution is correct.

Example 2

Solve algebraically. Check the solution.

$3x - 17 = 28$

Solution

$$3x - 17 = 28$$
$$3x - 17 + 17 = 28 + 17 \qquad \text{Add 17 to each side.}$$
$$3x = 45$$
$$\frac{3x}{3} = \frac{45}{3} \qquad \text{Divide each side by 3.}$$
$$x = 15$$

Check.

Substitute $x = 15$ in each side of the original equation: $3x - 17 = 28$

Left side $= 3x - 17$ Right side $= 28$
$$= 3(15) - 17$$
$$= 45 - 17$$
$$= 28$$

Since both sides are equal, $x = 15$ is correct.

Discuss

Describe the steps for substituting a solution in an equation to check.

We can use an equation to model a situation and solve a related problem.

Example 3

Nasmin has $15 and saves $4 per week. Her savings, N dollars, after w weeks can be modelled by the equation $N = 15 + 4w$.

Mayumi has $24 and saves $3 per week. Her savings, M dollars, after w weeks can be modelled by the equation $M = 24 + 3w$.

a) How much will each girl have after 5 weeks?

b) Who will be the first to have $55 for a computer game?

Solution

a) To find how much each girl will have after 5 weeks, substitute $w = 5$, then solve.

For Nasmin: $N = 15 + 4w$
$$= 15 + 4(5)$$
$$= 15 + 20$$
$$= 35$$

Nasmin will have $35 after 5 weeks.

For Mayumi: $M = 24 + 3w$
$$= 24 + 3(5)$$
$$= 24 + 15$$
$$= 39$$

Mayumi will have $39 after 5 weeks.

b) To find how long before each girl has $55, substitute $N = 55$ and $M = 55$, then solve for w.

For Nasmin: $N = 15 + 4w$
$$55 = 15 + 4w$$
$$55 - 15 = 15 + 4w - 15 \qquad \text{Subtract 15 from each side.}$$
$$40 = 4w$$
$$\frac{40}{4} = \frac{4w}{4} \qquad \text{Divide each side by 4.}$$
$$10 = w$$

Nasmin will have $55 after 10 weeks.

For Mayumi: $M = 24 + 3w$
$$55 = 24 + 3w$$
$$55 - 24 = 24 + 3w - 24 \qquad \text{Subtract 24 from each side.}$$
$$31 = 3w$$
$$\frac{31}{3} = \frac{3w}{3} \qquad \text{Divide each side by 3.}$$
$$10.3 \doteq w \qquad \text{Use a calculator.}$$

Mayumi will have $55 after 11 weeks.
Nasmin will have $55 first.

Discuss

Why is Mayumi's time not rounded down to 10 weeks?

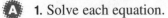
A **1.** Solve each equation.

a) $a + 2 = 5$ **b)** $v - 1 = 4$ **c)** $7 - c = -1$ **d)** $6 + b = 0$

e) $5 = n - 3$ **f)** $8 = 15 - s$ **g)** $j + 2 = -3$ **h)** $x + 5 = 9$

2. Solve each equation.

a) $3t = 27$ **b)** $4k = -20$ **c)** $-6 = 3b$ **d)** $-5s = 35$

3. Solve each equation.

a) $5j = 15$ **b)** $4p = -20$ **c)** $-3s = 9$ **d)** $c - 5 = -2$

e) $15 - p = 12$ **f)** $a + 6 = 8$ **g)** $-2v = -10$ **h)** $t - 4 = 1$

4. Check whether the solution $x = -3$ is correct for each equation.

a) $9x = 27$ **b)** $4 + x = 1$ **c)** $3x + 5 = -4$ **d)** $7x = -21$

e) $2x - 3 = 3$ **f)** $-9 = 3 + 4x$ **g)** $-x = -3$ **h)** $6 - x = 3$

5. Solve. Check by substituting.

a) $4v = 12$ **b)** $j + 27 = 30$ **c)** $24 - p = 20$ **d)** $-4c = -28$

e) $q + 7 = 11$ **f)** $36 = -4h$ **g)** $-5g = 3$ **h)** $c - 5 = 6$

B **6. Knowledge/Understanding** Solve each equation.

a) $4x = -28$ **b)** $3a - 1 = 20$ **c)** $12 + 5y = -13$

d) $7p + 14 = 0$ **e)** $8z - 42 = 2z$ **f)** $3f = 12f + 21$

7. Solve each equation.

a) $-3 + x = -4x - 43$ **b)** $12m - 25 = 4m + 7$ **c)** $2e - 6 = -5 - 4e$

d) $24 - 4c = 15 - c$ **e)** $6b - 8 = 4 - 3b$ **f)** $-5b + 9 = 3b - 15$

8. Solve each equation. Check the solution.

a) $7 = 23 - 4x$ **b)** $3a - 10 = 10$ **c)** $8 - 2z = 5 + 3z$

d) $4m + 9 = 2m$ **e)** $12x + 17 = 10 - 2x$ **f)** $5 - 3k = -4$

9. Solve each equation. Check each solution.

a) $5x + 4 = 40$ **b)** $9 - 2a = a + 5$ **c)** $2 - 4x = 1 - x$

d) $3 + 7c = 2c - 3$ **e)** $2 = 9a - 3$ **f)** $5 - 6n = 2n + 5$

10. Lester has $53 in savings. Each week he saves $16. His total savings are modelled by the equation $S = 53 + 16n$, where S is his savings in dollars, and n is the number of weeks.

a) To determine how much money Lester will have after 3 weeks, substitute $n = 3$. Calculate S.

b) Lester wants to buy a pair of in-line skates for $165, including taxes. To find how many weeks it will take him to save $165, substitute $S = \$165$. Solve for n.

11. Callum drove at an average speed of 90 km/h. The distance Callum drove can be modelled by the equation $d = 90t$, where d kilometres is the distance driven and t hours is the length of time.

a) How far had Callum travelled after each length of time?
   i) 1 h   ii) 3 h   iii) 5 h   iv) 6 h

b) How many hours had Callum driven to travel each distance?
   i) 180 km   ii) 225 km   iii) 360 km   iv) 315 km

c) What assumptions did you make in parts a and b? How reasonable do you think these assumptions are?

12. The cost, C dollars, to produce a school yearbook is modelled by the equation $C = 8000 + 9n$, where n is the number of yearbooks printed.

a) What does each term on the right side of the equation represent?

b) The yearbook committee has a budget of $10 000. Calculate the number of yearbooks produced for $10 000. Substitute $C = 10\,000$, then solve for n.

c) How many yearbooks are produced for $20 000?

13. Application Volcanoes and geysers illustrate that Earth's interior is very hot. The equation $T = 10d + 20$ is used to estimate the temperature, T degrees Celsius, at a depth of d kilometres.

a) What does each term on the right side of the equation represent?

b) To estimate the depth where the temperature is 50°C, substitute $T = 50$, then solve for d.

c) Estimate the depth for each temperature.

   i) 60°C   **ii)** 90°C   **iii)** 80°C   **iv)** 70°C

d) At what depth is the temperature 100°C?

e) Order the depths in parts b to d from least to greatest. Explain whether this order is reasonable for the given temperatures.

14. Thinking/Inquiry/Problem Solving

a) A rectangular field is 135 m long and requires 450 m of fencing to enclose it. Calculate the width of the field.

b) Another field is 45 m wide and requires 380 m of fencing. How long is the field?

c) Explain how you calculated each length in parts a and b.

15. Communication Suppose a classmate phones you for help to solve this equation: $3x + 7 = x - 5$. Explain how you would solve the equation over the phone.

16. One side of a rectangle is 6 cm. The perimeter of the rectangle is numerically equal to its area.

a) What do you think "numerically equal" means?

b) Find the lengths of the other sides of the rectangle.

c) Verify your answer by calculating the perimeter and area of the rectangle.

3.4　Simplifying Equations before Solving

In Section 3.3, we solved equations by collecting like terms. In this section, we will use the distributive law to simplify equations, before solving.

Example 1

Solve.

a) $2(3m - 4) = 10$

b) $9 = -4(2t - 7)$

Solution

a)
$$2(3m - 4) = 10 \qquad \text{Use the distributive law.}$$
$$2(3m) - 2(4) = 10$$
$$6m - 8 = 10$$

$$6m - 8 + 8 = 10 + 8 \qquad \text{Add 8 to each side.}$$
$$6m = 18$$

$$\frac{6m}{6} = \frac{18}{6} \qquad \text{Divide each side by 6.}$$
$$m = 3$$

b)
$$9 = -4(2t - 7) \qquad \text{Use the distributive law.}$$
$$9 = -4(2t) - 4(-7)$$
$$9 = -8t + 28$$

$$9 - 28 = -8t + 28 - 28 \qquad \text{Subtract 28 from each side.}$$
$$-19 = -8t$$

$$\frac{-19}{-8} = \frac{-8t}{-8} \qquad \text{Divide each side by } -8.$$
$$\frac{-19}{-8} = t$$
$$t = \frac{19}{8}, \text{ or } 2.375$$

Discuss

How could you check each solution?

Example 2

Solve $3(a - 3) + 4a + 7 = 5a - 3$.
Check the solution.

Solution

$3(a - 3) + 4a + 7 = 5a - 3$ Use the distributive law.
$3a - 9 + 4a + 7 = 5a - 3$
$7a - 2 = 5a - 3$

$7a - 2 + 2 = 5a - 3 + 2$ Add 2 to each side.
$7a = 5a - 1$

$7a - 5a = 5a - 1 - 5a$ Subtract $5a$ from each side.
$2a = -1$

$\dfrac{2a}{2} = \dfrac{-1}{2}$ Divide each side by 2.

$a = -\dfrac{1}{2}$

Check.
Substitute $a = -\dfrac{1}{2}$ in each side of the equation.

Left side $= 3(a - 3) + 4a + 7$ Right side $= 5a - 3$

$\quad = 3\left(-\dfrac{1}{2} - 3\right) + 4\left(-\dfrac{1}{2}\right) + 7$ $= 5\left(-\dfrac{1}{2}\right) - 3$

$\quad = 3\left(-\dfrac{1}{2} - \dfrac{6}{2}\right) - 2 + 7$ $= -\dfrac{5}{2} - 3$

$\quad = 3\left(-\dfrac{7}{2}\right) + 5$ $= -\dfrac{5}{2} - \dfrac{6}{2}$

$\quad = -\dfrac{21}{2} + \dfrac{10}{2}$ $= -\dfrac{11}{2}$

$\quad = -\dfrac{11}{2}$

Or use a calculator.

Left side

Press: 3 ((−) 1 A% 2 − 3
) + 4 ((−) 1 A%
2) + 7 ENTER

```
3(-1⌐2-3)+4(-1⌐2)+7
            -5u1/2
```

Right side

Press: 5 ((−) 1 A% 2)
− 3 ENTER

```
5(-1⌐2)-3
            -5u1/2
```

Since both sides are equal, $a = -\dfrac{1}{2}$ is correct.

Discuss

What happens if you substitute $a = -0.5$ in each side of the equation? Why?

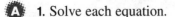
A **1.** Solve each equation.

a) $4b - 8b = 24$
b) $-27 = -9t + 6t + 3$
c) $13 + 4q = -2q + 12 + q$

d) $24 - 6j = 36$
e) $7 + 7k = 2k - 8$
f) $6s - 30 = 24$

2. Solve.

a) $4x + 6x = -20$
b) $50 = 8x - x + 1$

c) $3x - 2 + x = 5 + 7x - 3$
d) $3x + x = 6 - x$

3. Solve. Check each solution.

a) $5c + 2c + 6 = 34$
b) $4y - 7y = 18$

c) $12 = 2x - 7x - 8$
d) $-10 = -n + 2 - 2n$

4. Solve.

a) $2(x + 1) = 4$
b) $3(x + 1) = 6$
c) $4(x + 1) = 8$

d) $5(x + 1) = 10$
e) $6(x + 1) = 12$
f) $7(x + 1) = 14$

5. Solve.

a) $-2(x + 1) = 4$
b) $-3(x + 1) = 6$
c) $-4(x + 1) = 8$

d) $-5(x + 1) = 10$
e) $-6(x + 1) = 12$
f) $-7(x + 1) = 14$

6. Solve.

a) $4 = 2(x - 1)$
b) $6 = 3(x - 1)$
c) $8 = 4(x - 1)$

d) $10 = 5(x - 1)$
e) $12 = 6(x - 1)$
f) $14 = 7(x - 1)$

B **7.** Solve.

a) $2(x - 4) = 10$
b) $5(x - 6) = -15$
c) $2(4 - 3m) = 13$

d) $-3(n + 2) = 12$
e) $7 = -2(-3 - y)$
f) $3(2t + 6) = 0$

8. Knowledge/Understanding Solve. Check each solution.

a) $7x - 3x + 5 = 7$
b) $6 = 4x - x + 9$

c) $3(n + 2) = 21$
d) $-(3d + 4) = 5(2 - d)$

9. Solve each equation.

a) $9x - 1 - 7x - 4 = 5x$
b) $3(1 - 2y) + y = 2$
c) $4 = 6 - 2(x + 1)$

d) $-3(2 - a) - a = 1$
e) $-2(3n - 1) + 2n = 4$
f) $2(p + 1) = 3(p - 1)$

10. Communication When checking a solution, is it better to substitute the solution in the original equation? Why should each side be simplified separately when checking? Use an example in your explanation.

11. **Application** Keyboarding speed, S, is measured in words per minute. It is calculated using the equation $5S = w - 10e$, where w is the number of words typed in 5 min and e is the number of errors.

a) Marti typed 275 words in 5 min and made 8 errors. Substitute $w = 275$ and $e = 8$. What was her speed?

b) In keyboarding, a word is 5 characters. So, the number of words typed is $\frac{\text{the number of characters}}{5}$. Boris typed 1250 characters in 5 min. He had a speed of 40 words/min. Substitute for w and S. How many errors did he make?

c) Jake made 3 errors in 5 min and had a speed of 30 words/min. How many words did he type?

✓ 12. **Thinking/Inquiry/Problem Solving** A store hires students to replace employees who are on vacation. A student worked for 7 h, 3 h, 6 h, and 5 h at an hourly rate and received a $20 bonus. The amount earned was $188.

a) Write an equation that can be used to solve for the hourly rate.

b) Find the hourly rate.

c) Use your general knowledge to explain whether your solution is reasonable.

C 13. In the 1970s, Canada started using the Celsius scale for temperature instead of the Fahrenheit scale. An approximate rule for converting Celsius to Fahrenheit is "Double the temperature in degrees Celsius then add 30." This rule is modelled by the equation $F = 2C + 30$, where F is a temperature in degrees Fahrenheit and C is a temperature in degrees Celsius.

a) Use the equation to estimate each temperature in degrees Fahrenheit.

   i) 6°C   **ii)** 28°C   **iii)** 0°C   **iv)** −20°C

b) Use the equation to estimate each temperature in degrees Celsius.

   i) −5°F   **ii)** 80°F   **iii)** −30°F   **iv)** 54°F

c) Use the thermometer at the right to estimate each temperature from parts a and b.

d) Compare the advantages of using an equation to model the relationship between Fahrenheit and Celsius temperatures with the advantages of reading a thermometer. Explain why both methods result in estimated temperatures.

1. Use the distributive law to expand.

   a) $4(3 + 2)$

   b) $-5(-2 + 1)$

   c) $-(-6 - 4)$

   d) $5(2 - 3y)$

   e) $-(6j + 2)$

   f) $-7(-3 - 4p)$

2. Combine like terms.

   a) $5a - a + 4$

   b) $6k - 3 + 1 - 2k$

   c) $7 + 2 - 4b + 1 - b$

3. Simplify each expression. Find its value when $x = -2$.

   a) $2x - 7 + 1 - 3x$

   b) $4x - x + 2 + 5$

   c) $-8 - 5x + 3 - 2x + x$

   d) $1 - 4x + 2(3x - 1)$

   e) $4(6 - x) + 4$

   f) $3x - 4(2x - 4) - 2$

4. Solve.

   a) $8x = -24$

   b) $7 + a = -2$

   c) $b - 3 = 0$

   d) $n - 1 = 5$

   e) $42 = -6z$

   f) $2c = -1$

5. Solve. Check each solution.

   a) $2m + 1 = -3$

   b) $k + 9 = 2k$

   c) $1 - 4y = 13$

   d) $7 = 4 - 3b$

   e) $8 - j = j + 4$

   f) $-3p + 2 = -p + 6$

6. Solve.

   a) $8 = 2(x + 4)$

   b) $-(x + 1) = 15$

   c) $4(x - 3) = -1$

   d) $3(2 + x) = -3$

   e) $16 = -2(x - 4)$

   f) $-5(x - 2) = 0$

7. Solve. Check each solution.

   a) $2(g - 6) = -4$

   b) $5(x - 3) = 1 + x$

   c) $-2(3 - c) = -3(2c + 1)$

   d) $a + 3 = 2(a - 1)$

8. The total earnings, E dollars, a bike courier earns is made up of a daily flat rate of $25, plus $8 per delivery, where d represents the number of deliveries. Which equation represents this relationship?

   a) $E = 25d + 8$

   b) $E = 25 + 8d$

   c) $E = d(25 + 8)$

   d) $E = 25 + 8$

Suppose this pattern of figures continues. One figure will have 20 blue squares.
How many green squares will it have?

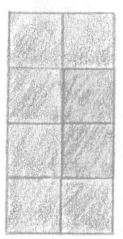  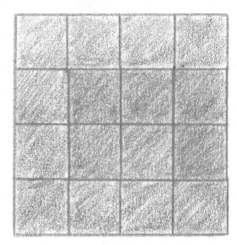

To solve this problem, we could continue to draw all the figures until we reach
the figure with 20 blue squares. This could be tedious.
Another way is to write an equation that relates the number of blue and green
squares in each figure.

In each figure, there are 4 more blue squares than green squares.
Let g represent the number of green squares.
Let b represent the number of blue squares.
The number of blue squares is 4 more than the number of green squares: $b = 4 + g$

For 20 blue squares, $b = 20$; so, substitute $b = 20$.
The equation becomes $20 = 4 + g$.
Solve this equation: $20 - 4 = g$
$$g = 16$$

There will be 16 green squares in the figure with 20 blue squares.

We can solve a problem in many ways. One method is to model the situation
with an equation. To use an equation:

• Use a variable to represent the unknown quantity.

• Express any other unknown quantities in terms of this variable, if possible.

• Write an equation, then solve it.

• State the answer to the problem.

• Check the answer by substituting it in the problem. Also check that the solution is reasonable.

Example

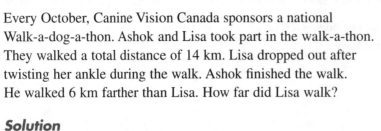

Every October, Canine Vision Canada sponsors a national Walk-a-dog-a-thon. Ashok and Lisa took part in the walk-a-thon. They walked a total distance of 14 km. Lisa dropped out after twisting her ankle during the walk. Ashok finished the walk. He walked 6 km farther than Lisa. How far did Lisa walk?

Solution

Let x kilometres represent the distance Lisa walked.
Since Ashok walked 6 km farther than Lisa, the distance Ashok walked is $(x + 6)$ kilometres.
The total distance they walked is 14 km. So,
Distance Lisa walked + Distance Ashok walked = 14

$$x + (x + 6) = 14$$
$$2x + 6 = 14 \qquad \text{Solve this equation.}$$
$$2x + 6 - 6 = 14 - 6$$
$$2x = 8$$
$$\frac{2x}{2} = \frac{8}{2}$$
$$x = 4$$

Lisa walked 4 km.

Check.
Ashok walked 4 km + 6 km = 10 km.
The total distance was 4 km + 10 km = 14 km.
The solution is correct.

Discuss

What other way could you check the solution?

3.5 Exercises

B **1. Knowledge/Understanding** Suppose a person earns e dollars per hour. Write an expression for each amount.

a) the amount earned for 1 hour plus a bonus of $5

b) the amount earned for 3 h

c) the amount earned for 1 hour less a deduction of $3

d) the amount earned for 2 h plus $10 commission

e) the amount earned for 5 h less $5 spent on transportation

2. Ravi is 8 years older than Natasha. Let Natasha's age be a years.

a) The expression for Ravi's age is ☐ years.

b) The expression for the sum of Ravi's and Natasha's ages is ☐ years.

c) The sum of their ages is 42. Find their ages.

3. The ages of Kirsten and Victor total 27 years. Let y years represent Kirsten's age.

a) The expression for Victor's age is ☐ years.

b) The expression for twice Kirsten's age is ☐ years.

c) Victor's age plus twice Kirsten's age is 43. Find Kirsten's and Victor's ages.

4. The combined mass of a dog and a cat is 28 kg. Let the cat's mass be m kilograms.

a) The expression for the dog's mass is ☐ kilograms.

b) The expression for three times the cat's mass is ☐ kilograms.

c) The dog is three times as heavy as the cat. Find the mass of the dog and of the cat.

5. Lesley's mass is 7.5 kg less than her twin brother Shelby's. Let s kilograms represent Shelby's mass.

a) Lesley's mass is ☐ kilograms.

b) The sum of their masses is ☐ kilograms.

c) The sum of their masses is 116.5 kg. Find the mass of Lesley and of Shelby.

6. Let n represent the number of fish in Linda's aquarium.

a) i) John's aquarium has 3 more fish than Linda's. Write an expression for the number of fish in John's aquarium.

ii) Suppose John's aquarium has 11 fish. Write an equation. Use it to find the number of fish in Linda's aquarium.

b) i) Adriana's aquarium has twice as many fish as Linda's. Write an expression for the number of fish in Adriana's aquarium.

ii) Suppose Adriana's aquarium has 24 fish. Write an equation. Use it to find the number of fish in Linda's aquarium.

c) i) Brett's aquarium has one-third as many fish as Linda's. Write an expression for the number of fish in Brett's aquarium.

ii) Suppose Brett's aquarium has 9 fish. Write an equation. Use it to find the number of fish in Linda's aquarium.

7. Members of the school band sold chocolate bars to raise money. Livio sold twice as many bars as Shaun. They sold a total of 48 bars. How many did each boy sell?

✓ 8. **Thinking/Inquiry/Problem Solving** Find two consecutive numbers with the sum 273.

9. Marisa and Sandy ran as far as they could in 30 min. Sandy ran 2 km farther than Marisa. They ran a total distance of 9 km. How far did each run?

✓ 10. **Communication** Jaquie and her brother Michel entered a weekend fishing derby. The mass of fish Jaquie caught was four times the mass of Michel's catch. Their total catch was 25 kg. Explain how to use an equation to find the mass of fish each person caught.

11. A package deal for skis and boots costs $225. The skis cost $60 more than the boots. How much do the skis cost?

✓ 12. **Application** A movie and popcorn cost $14. The movie costs $5 more than the popcorn.

a) Model this relationship with an equation to find the cost of the movie.

b) Explain how you could reason out the solution from part a to find the cost of the movie. Why does your reasoning make sense?

c) Suppose the movie cost $7 more than the popcorn. Use your method from part a or b to find the cost of the movie.

d) Suppose the movie cost $3 more than the popcorn. Use the costs from parts b and c to explain what the cost of the movie would be.

e) Choose a solution strategy you used for this exercise and explain an advantage of it.

13. Zelma used 500 cm of trim to frame a banner. The banner is 22 cm wide. How long can it be?

22 cm

14. A cord with a length of 118 cm is cut into two pieces. One piece is 18 cm longer than the other. How long are the pieces?

15. An airplane travels eight times as fast as a car. The difference in their speeds is 420 km/h. How fast does each vehicle travel?

3.6 Estimating Heights

On page 93, you considered the following problem.

A radius bone from the lower arm of a human was discovered at an excavation site. It measured 24.5 cm. Andrew's task is to use this measurement to determine the approximate height of the person. How can he solve this problem?

In this section, you will consider some models for solving this problem.

Using a Measuring Model

Work with a partner. You will need a tape measure or metre stick.

1. It is impossible to measure your radius bone because you are not a skeleton. So, we measure the lower arm instead. To measure the lower arm, place your hand flat against a wall. Your partner will measure from your wrist to the tip of your elbow. Record the length in the table.

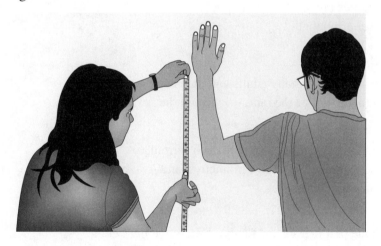

2. Measure and record your heights, in centimetres.

3. Combine your data with those of other students in your group or class. Record the data in a table.

Females		Males	
Length of Lower Arm (cm)	Height (cm)	Length of Lower Arm (cm)	Height (cm)

4. Does your data include a lower arm length of 24.5 cm? If so, what might be the answer to the problem? If not, explain how you might use your data to approximate the answer.

Using a Graphical Model

You will need two sheets of grid paper; one for the female data, and the other for the male data. Construct each graph using the following steps.

5. **a)** Draw axes on a grid. Label *Height* (*cm*) vertically.
Label *Length of lower arm* (*cm*) horizontally.

   b) Determine a scale for the graph. Label the origin 0.
Use the same scale for both axes. Write a title for your graph.

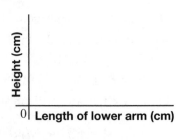

   c) Plot the data.
   i) What do you notice about the points on your graph?
   ii) Draw the best straight line through the points.

   d) Look at the line. What happens to the height as the length of the lower arm increases?

   e) What is the relationship between a person's height and the length of their lower arm? Explain.

   f) How can you use your graph to solve Andrew's problem?

   g) Suppose you know a person's height. How could you use the graph to determine her or his lower arm length?

Using an Algebraic Model

Scientists have taken measurements from many adults and then used the data to find a relationship between the length of the radius bone and the height for females and males.

The formulas for females and males are given below. In each formula, r represents the length of a person's radius bone, in centimetres, and h is the person's approximate height, in centimetres.

Female: $h = 3.34r + 81.2$ Male: $h = 3.27r + 85.9$

6. **a)** A female has a radius bone that measures 21.6 cm. Determine her height. Will a male have the same height? Justify your answer.

   b) Use the algebraic model to solve Andrew's problem. Estimate the height of the person if the radius bone is from a female and if the radius bone is from a male.

   c) **i)** Choose a lower arm length from the female data you collected. Substitute this value into the formula for females. What value do you get for the height?
   ii) Compare this number with the height measurement recorded in your table. Are they the same?

   d) Repeat part c for a lower arm length from the male data.

7. **Communication** You have considered 3 models: measuring, graphical, and algebraic. Which model would you choose to solve a problem similar to Andrew's? Justify your choice.

CHAPTER 3

MATHEMATICS TOOLKIT

Distributive Law

- $a(b + c) = ab + ac$
- $a(b - c) = ab - ac$ where a, b, and c are any real numbers

Terms

- A variable term contains a variable, for example, $2x$ and $-x$.
- A constant term does not contain a variable, for example, 7 and -3.
- Like terms contain the same variable and can be combined.

The Zero Principle

- Any two opposite terms have the sum 0.

Solving Equations

- Collect like terms with variable terms on one side of the equation and constant terms on the other side.
- Simplify each side.
- Divide each side by the coefficient of the variable term.

Algebraic Modelling

- Use a variable to represent the unknown quantity.
- Express other unknown quantities in terms of the variable.
- Write, then solve, an equation.
- State the answer.

3.1

1. Which two expressions in each set are equal? Use the distributive law to justify your answers.

a) $7x - 5$ $-(7x + 5)$ $5 - 7x$ $-7x - 5$

b) $-(4y - 1)$ $-4y - 1$ $-4y + 1$ $-(-4y + 1)$

c) $-3(b - 6)$ $-3b - 18$ $3b - 18$ $3(b - 6)$

d) $-7(2s + 7)$ $-7(2s - 7)$ $-14s + 49$ $14s - 49$

2. Use the distributive law to expand.

a) $5(1 + 6)$ b) $-9(4 - 7)$ c) $-4(-2 - 10)$

d) $3(-5 + 9)$ e) $-(3 + 5 - 6)$ f) $8(-1 + 8 - 4)$

3. Expand.

a) $4(q + 4)$ b) $-3(-d + 5)$ c) $2(2x + 9)$

d) $-5(6 - 5a)$ e) $-8(-3s - 6)$ f) $-7(1 - 7r)$

3.2 **4. Combine like terms.**

a) $8y + 2y$ b) $2 + 4a - 3$ c) $s - 1 - 2s + 3$

d) $2x + 7 + 3x - 5$ e) $3m - 12 - 7m + 2$ f) $-3(2q - 5) + 8q - 9$

5. Simplify.

a) $4y - 11 - 9y + 16$ b) $5t - 2(3 + 9t)$ c) $-2(4m - 7) - 13$

d) $5(2x - 3) + 10 - 3x$ e) $-3 - x + 2(5x - 4)$ f) $7(2x - 3) - 5 - 2x$

6. Simplify. Find each value when $x = 4$.

a) $5x + 2x + 1$ b) $8x - 3 + 4x + 9$ c) $2x - 7 - 6x + 3$

d) $x - 4x + 3x - x$ e) $-3(x + 2) - 4x$ f) $2x + 11 - 4(3x + 7)$

7. Simplify. Find each value when $x = -3$.

a) $8 + 3x - 2x$ b) $5x + x - 1 + 3$ c) $-2 + x - 4 + 2x$

d) $3x - 2 + 4(x - 5)$ e) $4 - 5x - (x + 2)$ f) $-3(4x + 1) - (-7x - 5)$

3.3 **8. Solve.**

a) $6c = -6$ b) $m + 2 = 0$ c) $y - 1 = 4$

d) $2 = 5 + t$ e) $p - 3 = 10$ f) $9g = 81$

g) $5 - u = 4$ h) $-32 = 4w$ i) $5h = -1$

9. Solve.

a) $3x + 2 = 8$ b) $2x - 3 = 1$ c) $7 - 4x = -5$

d) $3x + 4 = 2x - 3$ e) $2x - 5 = 6x + 7$ f) $3x - 1 = 5x - 9$

g) $12 + 4x = 5x + 8$ h) $-3x + 4 = -5x + 10$ i) $-7 - 3x = 8 + 2x$

10. Solve each equation. Check each solution.

a) $2x + 7 = 17$ b) $3 - 2x = 15$ c) $-40 = -4 + 4x$

d) $3x - 2 = 5x + 8$ e) $7 - 5x = 6 + x$ f) $-11 + 6x = -6x + 13$

3.4 **11. Solve.**

a) $2(x + 1) = 4$ b) $-(x - 2) = -3$ c) $-2(x + 3) = -8$

d) $6 = 3(x - 1)$ e) $4(x + 4) = 8$ f) $9 = -3(x - 5)$

g) $-(x - 1) = -1$ h) $3 = 2(x + 2)$ i) $3(x - 2) = -4$

12. Solve each equation.

a) $3(a + 2) = 2$ **b)** $-(g - 1) = 7$ **c)** $2(n - 4) = 0$

d) $-2(k + 3) = -3$ **e)** $4(2b + 1) = 9b$ **f)** $5(j - 2) = -3$

g) $3 = 4(y + 2)$ **h)** $-2 = -(3x - 1)$ **i)** $0 = 3(-r + 1)$

13. Solve each equation. Check each solution.

a) $2(x + 1) = 3(x - 2)$ **b)** $5(2x - 3) = 10$

c) $4(-2 - x) = -5(2x + 4)$ **d)** $-2(1 - x) = 3(2 - x)$

3.5 **14.** The difference between two masses is 5 kg. Let m kilograms represent the lighter mass.

a) An expression for the heavier mass is ☐ kilograms.

b) An expression for twice the lighter mass is ☐ kilograms.

c) The heavier mass plus twice the lighter mass is 20 kg. Find the masses.

15. For two consecutive numbers, the sum of the smaller number plus twice the larger number is 38. What are the numbers?

16. a) The length of a rectangle is 3 cm greater than the width. Let w centimetres represent the width. Write an expression for the length.

b) Write an expression for the length plus the width.

c) Write an expression for the perimeter.

d) The perimeter is 18 cm. Use this measure and the expression in part c to write an equation.

e) Solve the equation to find the width.

f) What is the length of the rectangle?

g) Sketch the rectangle and check your solution.

17. The length of a rectangle is 5 cm longer than the width. The perimeter is 54 cm. What are the dimensions of the rectangle?

18. An apple orchard sells baskets of Macintosh and Delicious apples. The orchard has 8 times as many baskets of Macintosh apples as Delicious apples. The orchard has a total of 153 baskets of apples. How many baskets of each type are there?

1. Expand.

   a) $2(j - 5)$ **b)** $-(4m + 1)$ **c)** $-3(6 - 2g)$

   d) $5(3a - 3)$ **e)** $-4(-2 + 7s)$ **f)** $6(5r - 4)$

2. **Knowledge/Understanding** Simplify.

   a) $4b + b - 2$ **b)** $6 - 3d + 2 + d$ **c)** $-n + 5 - 2n + 3n$

   d) $6(f - 3) + 1$ **e)** $-(4 - 3e) - 5 + e$ **f)** $1 + 2(t + 3) - 3(t - 4)$

3. Solve. Check each solution.

   a) $x + 4 = -2$ **b)** $8 - k = 9$ **c)** $-3h = 30$

   d) $2f - 7 = 5$ **e)** $6 + 3y = -8 + 2y$ **f)** $1 + 4j = 2j - 9$

4. Solve.

   a) $2(x - 3) = 6$ **b)** $7 = -(x + 1)$

   c) $5x = 2x + 3(2x + 1)$ **d)** $-2(x - 5) = x - 2$

5. Solve.

   a) $-x + 4(x - 1) = 4x$ **b)** $1 + x = 5(x - 3)$

   c) $4 - (x + 4) = -1$ **d)** $4(x + 2) = 6 - 2(2x + 1)$

6. **Communication** Explain why substituting a solution in the original equation provides a method of checking whether the solution for an equation is correct. Use an equation from one of these exercises to illustrate your answer.

7. **Thinking/Inquiry/Problem Solving** Write two different equations that have the solution $x = -1$. Solve each equation to check.

8. Gerri earned $20 more cutting lawns on Tuesday than on Monday. She earned a total of $140 on these two days. Write then solve an equation to find how much Gerri earned each day.

9. **Application** The perimeter of a rectangle is 40 cm. The difference between the lengths of the longer and shorter sides is 6 cm. Write then solve an equation to find the lengths of the sides. Illustrate your solution with a diagram and explain why it is reasonable.

1.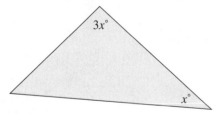

1

2

3

4

After looking at the diagrams above, Anya realized that there is a pattern that can be modelled by the equation, $s = 4d - 1$ where s is the number of small squares, and d is the diagram number.

If the pattern is continued, which diagram number would have 91 squares? Show your work.

2. In this triangle, the largest angle is three times greater than the smallest. The other angle is two times greater than the smallest.

$3x°$

$x°$

Doug wanted to know the measure of each angle. He started his solution as shown in the above diagram. His friend, Mark, reminded him that the angles in a triangle have to add to 180°.

Complete Doug's solution to find the measure of each angle in the triangle. Show your work.

1. a) A car is travelling at a constant speed on a highway. The driver increases the speed to pass another car, then returns to the original speed. Which graph best describes this motion? Explain.

i)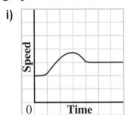

ii)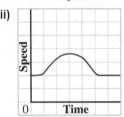

iii)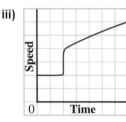

b) Choose a graph from part a that does not describe the motion of the car. Describe a situation the graph could represent.

2. Describe a situation each graph below could represent. State the labels of each axis.

a)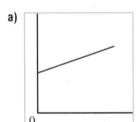

b)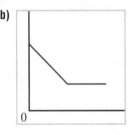

c)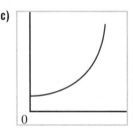

3. a) Copy the table of values. Use the formula $A = \pi r^2$ to complete it.

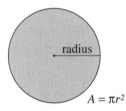

radius

$A = \pi r^2$

Circle radius (cm)	1	2	3	4	5	6
Circle area (cm²)						

b) Graph the data.

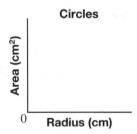

Circles

Area (cm²)

0   Radius (cm)

c) Describe patterns in the table of values. Relate the patterns to the graph.

d) Is the relation linear or non-linear? Explain how you know.

4. A laser printer can print 4 pages of text per minute.

    a) At this rate, how many pages could it print in 5 min?

    b) How long would it take to print a 50-page report?

5. Express as a single power.

    a) $4^1 \times 4^5$ **b)** $(-5)^3 \times (-5)^2$ **c)** $(-3)^4 \times (-3)^5$ **d)** $2^6 \times 2^3$

    e) $(-1)^6 \div (-1)^3$ **f)** $6^7 \div 6^4$ **g)** $\dfrac{4^8}{4^3}$ **h)** $\dfrac{7^5}{7^2}$

6. Evaluate each power.

    a) 5^0 **b)** 3^{-5} **c)** $(-5)^{-1}$ **d)** $(-3)^{-5}$ **e)** 3^0

7. Write in scientific notation.

    a) $2\,000\,000$ **b)** 0.005 **c)** $527\,000$ **d)** $0.000\,431$

    e) $0.000\,002\,5$ **f)** $700\,120\,000$ **g)** $19\,000$ **h)** $0.000\,000\,16$

8. Evaluate.

    a) $\sqrt{16}$ **b)** $\sqrt{4}$ **c)** $\sqrt{49}$ **d)** $\sqrt{64}$ **e)** $\sqrt{144}$

9. Find the square roots of each number. Round to 1 decimal place where necessary.

    a) 25   **b)** 256   **c)** 169   **d)** 90   **e)** 5

10. The bottom of an 8.0-m ladder is 2.0 m from the base of a building. How high up the building does the ladder reach? Round to the nearest tenth of a metre.

11. Each day Naj walks home from school around a field (shown in blue). One day he decides to walk through the field instead of around it (shown in red). Which route is longer? How much longer?

house

1 km

1.5 km

sidewalk

school

12. Expand using the distributive law.

    a) $3(2x + 7)$ **b)** $-5(4 + 3n)$ **c)** $12(4s - 5)$

    d) $-2(4b - 3)$ **e)** $-(6p + 10)$ **f)** $-6(-3c - 5)$

13. Simplify each expression. Evaluate each expression for the given value.

    a) $5t + 2t - 1 - t$ for $t = 1$

    b) $3(4a - 2) - (a + 3)$ for $a = 5$

    c) $4 + 2(x - 1) - 6x$ for $x = -3$

14. Solve each equation.

    a) $8x = -2$ **b)** $4(a - 10) = 15$ **c)** $2 - y = 16$

    d) $8m + 27 = 3$ **e)** $3(b - 1) = 4$ **f)** $-(3m + 2) = 1$

CHAPTER

By the end of this chapter, you will:

- Construct tables of values, graphs, and formulas to represent linear relations.

- Relate straight lines to linear relations and curves to non-linear relations.

- Use a table of values to determine whether a relation is linear or non-linear.

- Compare equations of straight lines and non-linear relations.

- Identify practical situations involving slopes, then calculate the slopes.

- Find the slope of a line segment using the formula: slope $= \dfrac{\text{rise}}{\text{run}}$

- Plot points on a coordinate grid.

- Graph lines by hand and with graphing calculators.

- Communicate solutions with clear reasons.

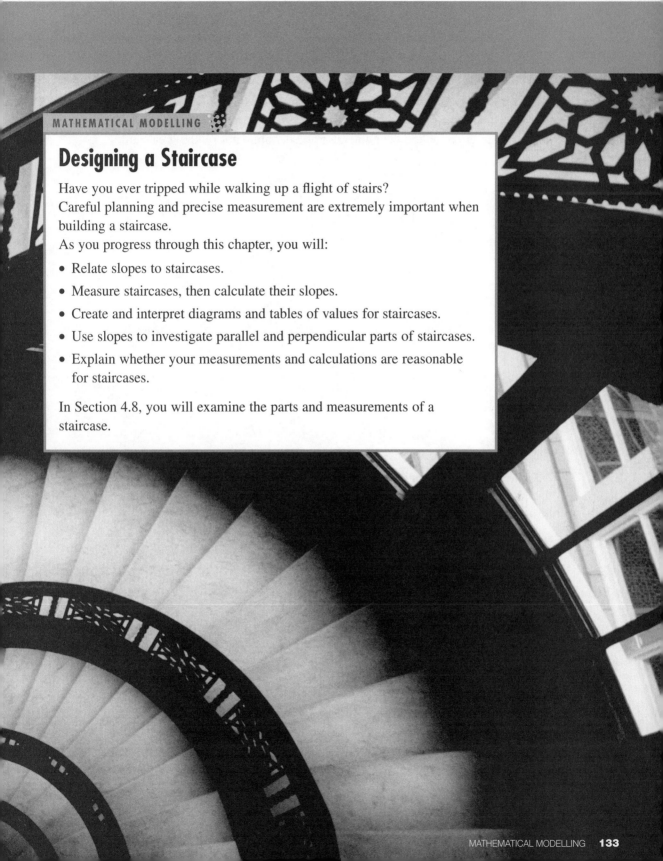

Designing a Staircase

Have you ever tripped while walking up a flight of stairs?
Careful planning and precise measurement are extremely important when building a staircase.

As you progress through this chapter, you will:

- Relate slopes to staircases.

- Measure staircases, then calculate their slopes.

- Create and interpret diagrams and tables of values for staircases.

- Use slopes to investigate parallel and perpendicular parts of staircases.

- Explain whether your measurements and calculations are reasonable for staircases.

In Section 4.8, you will examine the parts and measurements of a staircase.

Necessary Skills

Simplifying Fractions and Reciprocals

To simplify a fraction, divide the numerator and denominator by the greatest common factor.

Example 1

Simplify.

a) $\dfrac{8}{-4}$

b) $\dfrac{-24}{18}$

Solution

a) $\dfrac{8}{-4} = \dfrac{2}{-1}$ Divide numerator and denominator by 4.

$= -2$ $2 \div (-1) = -2$

b) $\dfrac{-24}{18} = \dfrac{-4}{3}$ Divide numerator and. denominator by 6.

$= -\dfrac{4}{3}$

To write the reciprocal of a fraction, turn it upside down.

Example 2

a) Write the reciprocal of $\dfrac{2}{3}$.

b) Write the reciprocal of –4.

Solution

a) The reciprocal of $\dfrac{2}{3}$ is $\dfrac{3}{2}$.

b) Write –4 as $-\dfrac{4}{1}$.

The reciprocal is $-\dfrac{1}{4}$.

Exercises

1. Simplify.

a) $\dfrac{-4}{2}$
b) $\dfrac{3}{-1}$
c) $\dfrac{12}{6}$
d) $\dfrac{10}{-5}$
e) $\dfrac{8}{4}$
f) $\dfrac{-9}{3}$

2. Write each reciprocal.

a) $\dfrac{4}{7}$
b) $-\dfrac{1}{6}$
c) $\dfrac{4}{3}$
d) –4
e) 1
f) $\dfrac{-5}{8}$

3. Write each reciprocal. If possible, simplify first.

a) –2
b) $\dfrac{1}{5}$
c) $\dfrac{-5}{10}$
d) $\dfrac{8}{12}$

e) 5
f) $\dfrac{-1}{4}$
g) $\dfrac{3}{9}$
h) $\dfrac{8}{-10}$

Order of Operations

The order of operations for whole numbers also applies to integers.

Do the operations within brackets.

Simplify numbers with exponents.

Multiply and divide from left to right.

Add and subtract from left to right.

Brackets

Exponents

Division

Multiplication $\quad>\quad$ In the order that they occur, from left to right

Addition

Subtraction $\quad>\quad$ In the order that they occur, from left to right

Example

Simplify.

a) $10 + 3(-4)$ 　　　　 b) $3(5) - 4$ 　　　　 c) $5(-1) + (-2)^2$

Solution

a) $\begin{aligned} 10 + 3(-4) &= 10 - 12 \\ &= -2 \end{aligned}$ 　　　 First multiply: $3(-4)$

b) $\begin{aligned} 3(5) - 4 &= 15 - 4 \\ &= 11 \end{aligned}$ 　　　 First multiply: $3(5)$

c) $\begin{aligned} 5(-1) + (-2)^2 &= 5(-1) + (4) \\ &= -5 + 4 \\ &= -1 \end{aligned}$ 　　 Calculate: $\begin{aligned}(-2)^2 &= (-2)(-2) \\ &= 4\end{aligned}$ 　　 Next multiply: $5(-1)$

Exercises

1. Simplify.

　a) $3 + (-2)(4)$ 　　　　 b) $3 - (-2)(4)$ 　　　　 c) $-3 + (-2)(4)$

　d) $3 - (-2)(-4)$ 　　　　 e) $-3 - (-2)(-4)$ 　　　　 f) $-3 - (2)(4)$

2. Simplify.

　a) $5(-1) + 7$ 　　　　 b) $(-3)(2) - 10$ 　　　　 c) $(-1)(-4) + 2$

　d) $(4)(-3) + 22$ 　　　　 e) $(-2)^2 + 3(-3)$ 　　　　 f) $8(-2) - (-3)^2$

The slant or incline of a roof is its *slope*.

For any incline, we can measure two distances — the rise and the run.

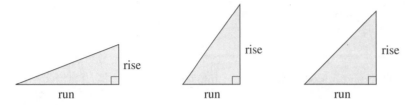

The rise and the run determine the slope of the incline.

The Slope of a Roof

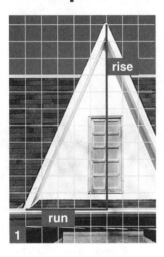

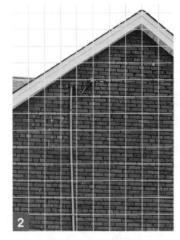

1. a) Which roof looks steepest?

   b) Which roof looks the least steep?

   c) List the roofs from steepest to least steep.

2. Picture 1, above, shows the rise and run of the first roof.

   a) Copy this table. Count the squares on the grids to complete the 2nd and 3rd columns.

   b) Record $\frac{rise}{run}$ for each roof to complete the 4th column.

Roof	rise	run	$\frac{rise}{run}$	$\frac{rise}{run}$ as a decimal
1				
2				
3				

c) Divide the rise by the run. In the 5th column, write each result as
a decimal to the nearest tenth.

d) Order the numbers in the 5th column from greatest to least.

3. Compare the order of the numbers in exercise 2d with the order of the
roofs in exercise 1c. What do you notice?

From the *Investigation*, you should have found that the greater the slope, the
steeper the line. The same is true for a line or line segment.

The slope of a line indicates how steep it is.

TAKE NOTE

Slope

Slope $= \dfrac{\text{rise}}{\text{run}}$

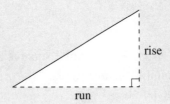

Example 1

Find the slope of each line segment.

a)

b)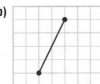

Solution

a)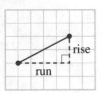

The rise is 2. The run is 4.

Slope $= \dfrac{\text{rise}}{\text{run}}$

$= \dfrac{2}{4}$

$= \dfrac{1}{2}$

b)

The rise is 4. The run is 2.

$$\text{Slope} = \frac{\text{rise}}{\text{run}}$$

$$= \frac{4}{2}$$

$$= 2$$

Discuss

Which line segment is steeper? How do you know?

Example 2

On grid paper, draw a line segment with each slope.

a) $\frac{3}{5}$ **b)** 4

Solution

a) Slope $= \frac{3}{5}$

Mark any point. The rise is 3, so count 3 squares up.
The run is 5. Then count 5 squares right.
Mark a point. Join the points.

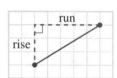

b) Slope $= 4$ or $\frac{4}{1}$

Mark any point. The rise is 4 so count 4 squares up.
The run is 1. Then count 1 square right.
Mark a point. Join the points.

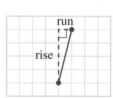

Example 3

Each diagram shows the rise and run of a wave. Scientists have found that a wave breaks when its slope is greater than $\frac{2}{7}$. Find out whether each wave would break.

a)

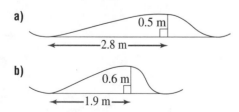

b)

Solution

Find the slope of each wave.

a) $\text{Slope} = \dfrac{\text{rise}}{\text{run}}$

$\qquad = \dfrac{0.5}{2.8}$

$\qquad \doteq 0.179$

b) $\text{Slope} = \dfrac{\text{rise}}{\text{run}}$

$\qquad = \dfrac{0.6}{1.9}$

$\qquad \doteq 0.316$

Compare each slope to $\dfrac{2}{7}$.

$\qquad \dfrac{2}{7} \doteq 0.286$

In part a, the slope is less than $\dfrac{2}{7}$ $(0.179 < 0.286)$, so the wave does not break.

In part b, the slope is greater than $\dfrac{2}{7}$ $(0.316 > 0.286)$, so the wave does break.

4.1   Exercises

 A **1.** Identify the rise and run for each slope.

a) $\dfrac{5}{9}$ **b)** $\dfrac{1}{8}$ **c)** 4

d) $\dfrac{7}{3}$ **e)** 1 **f)** $\dfrac{2}{3}$

 2. Sketch a roof with each slope. Label the rise and run in each sketch.

a) $\dfrac{2}{7}$ **b)** $\dfrac{8}{3}$ **c)** $\dfrac{1}{5}$

3. Write each slope as a fraction in simplest form or as an integer.

a) $\dfrac{3}{9}$ **b)** $\dfrac{9}{3}$ **c)** $\dfrac{8}{12}$ **d)** $\dfrac{4}{6}$

> To simplify a slope, divide the rise and run by the same factor.

 4. Knowledge/Understanding Calculate each slope.

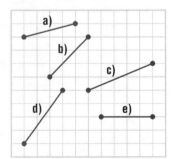

5. On grid paper, draw a line segment with each slope.

a) 1 **b)** 2 **c)** 3 **d)** $\dfrac{1}{2}$

e) $\dfrac{1}{3}$ **f)** $\dfrac{1}{4}$ **g)** $\dfrac{2}{3}$ **h)** $\dfrac{5}{2}$

✓ **6.** Simplify to find out which slopes are equal.

a) $\frac{6}{18}$ **b)** $\frac{15}{5}$ **c)** $\frac{12}{8}$ **d)** $\frac{1}{3}$ **e)** $\frac{8}{12}$ **f)** $\frac{10}{5}$

✓ **7.** Find the slope of AB in each diagram.

a)

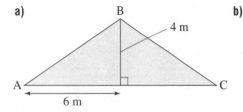

b)

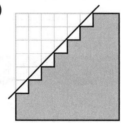

8. Each staircase has a board placed along it. Find the rise, run, and slope for each staircase.

a)

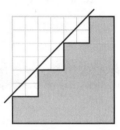

b)

9. Copy each staircase on grid paper. Draw the board that would lie on the staircase. What is the slope of each staircase?

a)

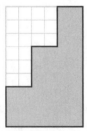

b)

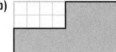

c)

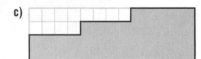

10. a) Pick a staircase in your home or school. Measure its rise and run.

b) Calculate the slope of the staircase.

c) Compare your results with those of your classmates. Discuss similarities and differences.

11. Application This drawing represents the side view of part of a roller coaster. The side of each grid square represents 1 m.

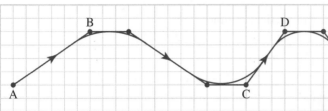

a) Find the height of each hill.

b) Which hill has a steeper climb? How do you know?

c) Explain how two roller-coaster hills can have the same height but not the same steepness.

d) How would the steepness affect the roller coaster's speed?

12. A section of a roller-coaster track rises 25 m over a horizontal distance of 15 m. What is the slope of this section of the track?

13. Communication Explain how the slope of a segment is defined by its rise and run. Include sketches of:

- a slope greater than 1
- a slope equal to 1
- a slope between 0 and 1

14. Thinking/Inquiry/Problem Solving
Draw line segments to show your answers.

a) Suppose the rise of a line segment remains the same, but the run increases. What happens to the slope?

b) Suppose the rise of a line segment decreases, but the run remains the same. Does the slope increase or decrease?

c) Suppose both the rise and run of a line segment are doubled. What happens to the slope? How do you know?

You have worked with both horizontal and vertical number lines.

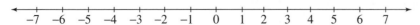

When a vertical number line and a horizontal number line intersect at right angles and at the point zero on each line, they form axes on a *coordinate plane*.

The number lines intersect at the *origin*, which we label zero.
The horizontal axis is labelled *x*. The vertical axis is labelled *y*.

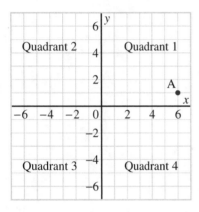

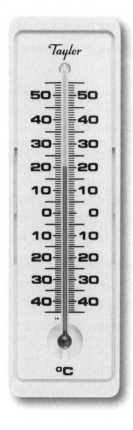

The axes divide the coordinate plane into four sections. These sections are known as *quadrants*. Any point in the plane can be described by its coordinates.

The coordinates of point A are (6, 1). The *x*-coordinate is 6. It represents the distance and direction from zero along the horizontal number line.

The *y*-coordinate is 1. It represents the distance and direction from zero along the vertical number line.

The two coordinates together, (6, 1), are an *ordered pair*.

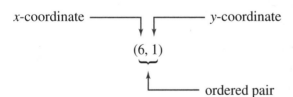

To plot the point B(−5, −3), begin at the origin.
Move 5 units left, then 3 units down.
Mark the point B.

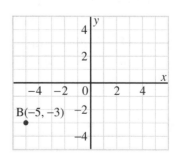

Example

Plot and label each point.

a) A(−3, 2) **b)** B(0, 4) **c)** C(−1, 0) **d)** D(4, −2)

Solution

To plot each point, we can begin at its *x*-coordinate on the *x*-axis.

a) To plot A(−3, 2), begin at −3 on the *x*-axis, then move up 2 units. Label point A.

b) To plot B(0, 4), begin at 0, then move up 4 units. Label point B.

c) To plot C(−1, 0), begin at −1 on the *x*-axis. Since the *y*-coordinate is 0, we do not move up or down. Label point C at −1 on the *x*-axis.

d) To plot D(4, −2), begin at 4 on the *x*-axis, then move down 2 units. Label point D.

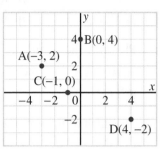

4.2   Exercises

1. Name the coordinates of each point.

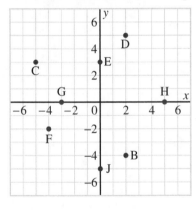

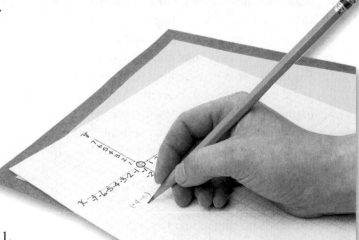

2. The points below are from exercise 1.
Name the quadrant in which each point lies.

  a) C   **b)** F   **c)** D   **d)** B

3. Plot only the points with a positive *x*-coordinate.

  a) A(6, −2)   **b)** B(−4, 7)   **c)** C(4, 5)   **d)** D(1, −1)

  e) E(0, −5)   **f)** F(0, 0)   **g)** G(8, 0)   **h)** H(0, 6)

4. Plot only the points that lie on the *y*-axis.

  a) I(0, 3)   **b)** J(−6, 0)   **c)** K(0, −2)   **d)** L(1, −1)

  e) M(0, −5)   **f)** N(0, 0)   **g)** P(8, 0)   **h)** Q(0, 6)

5. Plot only the points that lie on the *x*-axis.

    a) R(–7, 0)   **b)** S(2, 0)   **c)** T(0, 0)   **d)** U(0, 4)

    e) V(–2, 2)   **f)** W(0, –4)   **g)** X(–2, 0)   **h)** Y(0, –7)

6. Plot only the points in quadrant 2.

    a) A(4, –2)   **b)** B(–4, –2)   **c)** C(–4, 2)   **d)** D(4, 2)

    e) E(–5, –1)   **f)** F(–5, 1)   **g)** G(5, 1)   **h)** H(5, –1)

7. a) Which of these points lie in quadrant 3?

    F(8, –3), G(–6, –7), H(7, 1), I(0, –9), J(–8, 6),
    K(–7, –9), L(–4, 6), M(8, –9), N(–10, 10)

  b) How are all the points in quadrant 3 similar?

8. Plot each set of points to form a figure.

    a) Square ABCD: A(1, 1), B(1, 5), C(–3, 5), D(–3, 1)

    b) Parallelogram JKLM: J(1, –3), K(5, 1), L(8, 1), M(4, –3)

    c) Quadrilateral PQRS: P(–3, 0), Q(–6, –2), R(4, –4), S(10, 0)

9. Activity: Battleship Play with a partner. Draw axes for 2 coordinate planes. Ensure each plane has values up to 10 and –10 along the *x*- and *y*-axes, respectively. Draw five ships anywhere on one coordinate plane. The ships occupy 6 coordinates, 5 coordinates, 4 coordinates, 3 coordinates, and 2 coordinates, respectively. Your partner will also draw five ships on one coordinate plane. You will try to locate the positions of your partner's ships. Start by naming coordinates, for example (2, –4). If that coordinate locates one of your partner's ships, she/he will reply "hit." If there is no ship in that location, she/he will reply "miss." Your partner will state coordinates to locate your ships. Take turns until all of one person's ships have been hit.

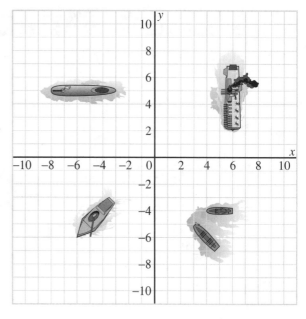

Use the second coordinate plane to mark coordinates you have asked your partner about. Mark each hit with a checkmark, each miss with an X. This is your tracking sheet.

10. **Knowledge/Understanding** Plot these points. Join them in order. What figure do you see?

(2, 1), (5, 5), (1, 2), (0, 5), (−1, 2), (−5, 5), (−2, 1), (−5, 0), (−2, −1), (−5, −5), (−1, −2), (0, −5), (1, −2), (5, −5), (2, −1), (5, 0)

11. **a)** Plot these points. Join them in order. What figure do you see?

(0, 0), (0, 1), (−2, 1), (−2, 2), (−4, 2), (−4, 3), (−6, 3), (−6, 4), (−8, 4), (−8, 5)

b) Continue the pattern in part a for 5 more points. Record the coordinates for these points.

12. What are the coordinates of the point that is on both the *x*-axis and the *y*-axis? What is this point called?

13. **Communication** For each line or quadrant, explain what all the points have in common.

a) on the *x*-axis **b)** on the *y*-axis **c)** in quadrant 1 **d)** in quadrant 4

14. **Application** Draw a design on the coordinate plane. Make sure each vertex is at an intersection of grid lines. List the coordinates of the vertices. Exchange coordinates with a partner. Draw the design from your partner's coordinates. Compare designs with those of your partner.

15. For each list:

a) (−3, 5)	**b)** (−3, −5)	**c)** (−3, 9)
(−2, 4)	(−2, −3)	(−2, 4)
(−1, 3)	(−1, −1)	(−1, 1)
(0, 2)	(0, 1)	(0, 0)
(1, 1)	(1, 3)	(1, 1)
(2, 0)	(2, 5)	(2, 4)
(3, −1)	(3, 7)	(3, 9)

i) Plot the points on a grid.
ii) Describe the geometric pattern.
iii) Write the coordinates of two other points that fit the pattern.

16. **Thinking/Inquiry/Problem Solving** The points S(2, 2) and T(−2, 2) are two vertices of a square. What are the possible coordinates of the other two vertices? Find as many answers to this question as you can.

In Section 4.1, all the line segments had positive slopes.
That is, all the segments rose to the right.

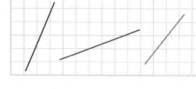

When a line segment falls to the right,
it has a negative slope.

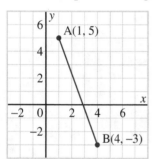

The rise is –5.
The run is 4.
The slope is $\frac{-5}{4}$ or $-\frac{5}{4}$.

We can now find the slope of a line segment on the coordinate plane.

Example 1

Find the slope of line segment AB.

Solution

Count squares vertically from A to B.
The rise is 8 down, or –8.
Count squares horizontally from A to B.
The run is 3 right, or 3.

$$\text{Slope of AB} = \frac{\text{rise}}{\text{run}}$$

$$= \frac{-8}{3}$$

$$= -\frac{8}{3}$$

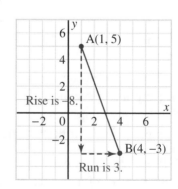

Discuss

What other way could you draw the rise and the run in this diagram?
Find the slope using this new rise and run.

Example 2

Find the slope of each line segment.

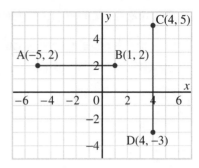

Solution

Since there is no change vertically from A to B, the rise is 0.

Count squares horizontally from A to B. The run is 6 right, or 6.

Slope of AB $= \dfrac{\text{rise}}{\text{run}}$

$\phantom{\text{Slope of AB }} = \dfrac{0}{6}$

$\phantom{\text{Slope of AB }} = 0$

Count vertically from C to D. The rise is 8 down, or −8.

Since there is no change horizontally from C to D, the run is 0.

Slope of CD $= \dfrac{\text{rise}}{\text{run}}$

$\phantom{\text{Slope of CD }} = \dfrac{-8}{0}$

The denominator is 0, and division by 0 is not defined.

The slope of CD is *undefined*.

Example 2 shows that a horizontal line segment has slope 0, and a vertical line segment has a slope that is undefined.

TAKE NOTE

Slopes of Line Segments

A line segment that *rises* to the right has a *positive* slope.	A line segment that *falls* to the right has a *negative* slope.	The slope of a horizontal line segment is zero.	The slope of a vertical line segment is undefined.
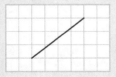	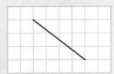		

Example 3

This diagram represents a side view of a water coaster.

Find the slope of each segment.

a) AB   **b)** BC

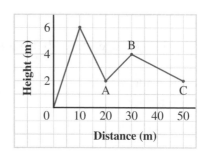

Solution

a) Line segment AB has endpoints A(20, 2) and B(30, 4).

$$\text{Slope of AB} = \frac{\text{rise}}{\text{run}}$$

$$= \frac{2}{10}$$

$$= \frac{1}{5}$$

The slope of AB is $\frac{1}{5}$.

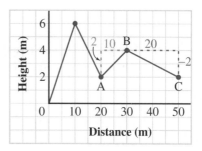

b) Line segment BC has endpoints B(30, 4) and C(50, 2).

$$\text{Slope of BC} = \frac{\text{rise}}{\text{run}}$$

$$= \frac{-2}{20}$$

$$= -\frac{1}{10}$$

The slope of BC is $-\frac{1}{10}$.

1. Find the slope of each line segment.

a)

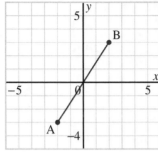

b)

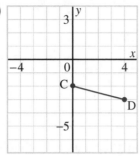

c)

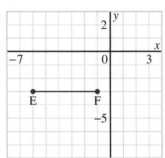

d)

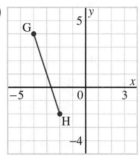

2. Simplify each slope.

a) $\dfrac{8}{-2}$ **b)** $\dfrac{6}{10}$ **c)** $\dfrac{-4}{6}$

d) $\dfrac{3}{-12}$ **e)** $\dfrac{-8}{6}$ **f)** $\dfrac{5}{10}$

3. a) Which line segments have negative slopes?

b) How are all the line segments with negative slopes similar?

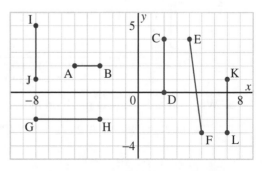

4. a) Which line segments have undefined slopes?

b) How are all the line segments with undefined slopes similar?

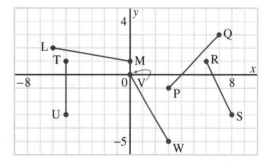

5. Find the slope of each line segment.

a)

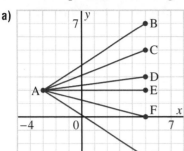

b)

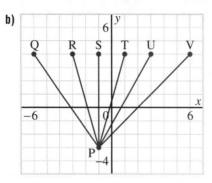

B **6.** Graph each pair of points on a separate grid. Find the slope of AB.

✓

    a) A(−7, 4), B(−3, 3)   **b)** A(3, 6), B(3, 1)   **c)** A(1, −5), B(4, −1)

    d) A(−3, −4), B(1, −7)   **e)** A(0, 0), B(4, −6)   **f)** A(−8, −4), B(−8, 2)

✓ **7. Knowledge/Understanding** For each pair of endpoints:

    a) A(−2, 7), B(6, −4)   **b)** C(3, −5), D(8, 10)

    c) G(−3, 7), H(−3, −7)   **d)** L(2, −7), M(7, −7)

    i) Graph the line segment.

    ii) State whether the line segment rises to the right, falls to the right, is horizontal, or is vertical.

    iii) Find the slope. State whether it is positive, negative, or neither.

    iv) What do you know about the direction of a line segment and its slope?

8. Each set of points represents a triangle. Graph each triangle. Find the slope of each side.

    a) A(5, −1), B(0, 4), C(−2, −5)   **b)** R(−3, 4), S(6, 7), T(2, −3)

9. Communication How are line segments with positive slopes different from line segments with negative slopes? Explain using a diagram.

✓ **10.** This diagram represents a side view of a railway track on a mountain.

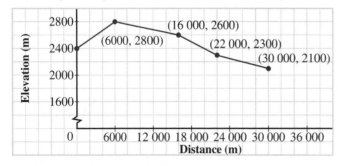

    a) Why is there a zigzag mark on the vertical axis?

    b) What is the slope of each section of the track?

11. **Application** This diagram represents a side view of a water coaster. The slope of each segment is given. Find the coordinates of each point A to F.

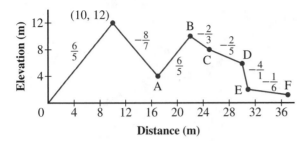

12. a) Draw a line segment with each slope. Find the coordinates of the endpoints of each segment.

    i) 3   ii) −5   iii) $\frac{3}{5}$ iv) $-\frac{5}{3}$ v) −3   vi) 5

    b) Which is the steepest line segment in part a?

    c) Compare your line segments with those of your classmates. Explain any differences.

13. A staircase has three main parts.

    The run or *tread* is the horizontal part of a step.

    The rise or *riser* is the vertical part of a step.

    The *stringers* are the sloping boards running diagonally between floors. The stringers support the staircase.

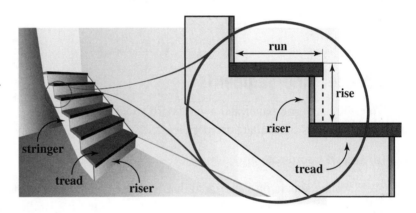

    a) Sketch a staircase on a coordinate plane.

    b) What is the slope of the staircase you sketched in part a?

    c) Compare the slope of the staircase you sketched with those of a few classmates. Explain which staircases might be easier to use.

14. **Thinking/Inquiry/Problem Solving** Use a coordinate plane.

    a) If possible, draw a triangle so that all 3 sides have positive slopes.

    b) If possible, draw a quadrilateral so that 3 sides have positive slopes.

    c) If possible, draw a quadrilateral so that all 4 sides have positive slopes.

    d) For any of parts a to c that you could not draw, explain why. If you drew examples for all 3 parts, explain how you did it.

Lines in the same plane that do not intersect are *parallel lines*.

These lines
are parallel.

What parallel line segments can you see in the picture above right?

Parallel Line Segments

You will need grid paper and a cardboard square.
Opposite sides of a square are parallel.

1. Draw a coordinate grid.

2. Place the square on the grid so that one side goes through 2 points where grid lines meet. Draw line segments along two parallel sides of the square.

3. Label the line segments AB and DE.

4. Find the slopes of AB and DE.

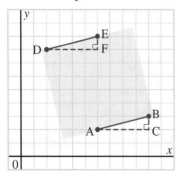

5. Move the square. Repeat exercises 2 to 4 to draw a different pair of parallel line segments.

6. Repeat exercise 5 two more times. Include vertical and horizontal line segments.

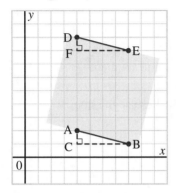 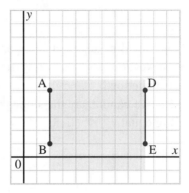 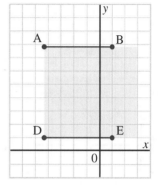

7. For each pair of parallel line segments, what do you notice about the slopes of AB and DE?

8. Write a statement about the slopes of parallel line segments.

The *Investigation* shows that the slopes of parallel line segments are equal.

In this diagram, line segments AB and CD are parallel.

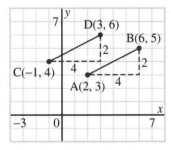

Slope of AB $= \dfrac{2}{4}$ Slope of CD $= \dfrac{2}{4}$

$\qquad\quad = \dfrac{1}{2}$ $\qquad\quad = \dfrac{1}{2}$

This example illustrates a fundamental property of slope: equal slopes indicate parallel lines.

Parallel Line Segments

If the slopes of two line segments are equal, the segments are parallel.

If two line segments are parallel but not vertical, their slopes are equal.

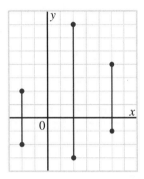

Vertical line segments are parallel.
However, the slope of a vertical line segment is undefined.
So, we cannot say the slopes of these segments are equal.

Example 1

Here are the endpoints of pairs of line segments.
Which line segments are parallel? How do you know?

a) W(−3, 3), S(2, 0) and T(−1, −1), Z(7, −7)

b) L(−4, 3), M(−1, 3) and P(0, −2), Q(4, −2)

Solution

a) Graph WS and TZ.

$$\text{Slope of WS} = \frac{\text{rise}}{\text{run}} \qquad \text{Slope of TZ} = \frac{\text{rise}}{\text{run}}$$

$$= \frac{-3}{5} \qquad\qquad\qquad = \frac{-6}{8}$$

$$= -\frac{3}{5} \qquad\qquad\qquad = -\frac{3}{4}$$

The slopes are not equal, so WS and TZ are not parallel.

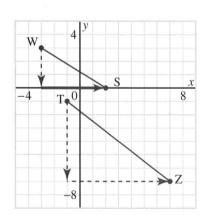

b) Graph LM and PQ.

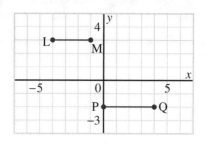

Slope of LM = $\frac{\text{rise}}{\text{run}}$ Slope of PQ = $\frac{\text{rise}}{\text{run}}$

$\qquad = \frac{0}{3}$ $\qquad\qquad\qquad = \frac{0}{4}$

$\qquad = 0$ $\qquad\qquad\qquad = 0$

The slopes are equal, so LM and PQ are parallel.

Discuss

Explain how you know the lines are parallel as soon as you graph them.

Example 2

A quadrilateral has vertices A(0, −6), B(2, −1), C(−1, 5), and D(−3, 0). Is the quadrilateral a parallelogram? Explain.

> A parallelogram is a quadrilateral with opposite sides parallel.

Solution

Graph the quadrilateral.

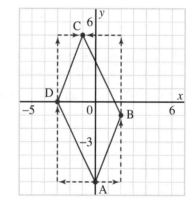

Slope of AB = $\frac{\text{rise}}{\text{run}}$ Slope of DC = $\frac{\text{rise}}{\text{run}}$

$\qquad = \frac{5}{2}$ $\qquad\qquad\qquad = \frac{5}{2}$

The slopes of AB and DC are equal, so line segments AB and DC are parallel.

Slope of AD = $\frac{\text{rise}}{\text{run}}$ Slope of BC = $\frac{\text{rise}}{\text{run}}$

$\qquad = \frac{6}{-3}$ $\qquad\qquad\qquad = \frac{6}{-3}$

$\qquad = -2$ $\qquad\qquad\qquad = -2$

The slopes of AD and BC are equal, so line segments AD and BC are parallel.

Since both pairs of opposite sides are parallel, ABCD is a parallelogram.

Discuss

Would it be enough to show that two sides are parallel? Explain.

4.4   Exercises

1. For each slope below, choose a slope of a parallel line segment from the box at the right.

a) $\frac{6}{4}$ b) $\frac{2}{-1}$ c) $\frac{0}{5}$

d) $\frac{1}{4}$ e) $\frac{-2}{8}$ f) $\frac{3}{-4}$

$\frac{3}{12}$	-2	$-\frac{1}{2}$
$-\frac{3}{4}$	$-\frac{3}{2}$	0
$\frac{3}{2}$	$-\frac{1}{4}$	$\frac{6}{8}$

2. Which pairs of numbers are not slopes of parallel line segments? How do you know?

a) $\frac{2}{3}$, $\frac{4}{6}$ b) $\frac{3}{4}$, $-\frac{6}{8}$ c) $\frac{5}{10}$, $\frac{2}{1}$ d) $\frac{5}{6}$, $\frac{10}{12}$

e) $\frac{-1}{5}$, $\frac{-3}{15}$ f) $-\frac{8}{4}$, 2 g) $\frac{-2}{3}$, $\frac{4}{6}$ h) -3, $-\frac{9}{3}$

3. Which pairs of line segments are parallel? Explain how you know.

a) 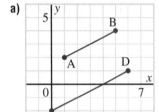   b) 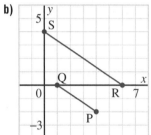   c)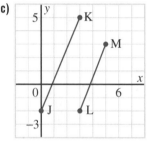

4. Knowledge/Understanding For each pair of points:

a) A(−2, −1), B(1, 5) and C(2, −1), D(4, 3)

b) E(−3, 2), F(5, 5) and O(0, 0), H(5, 2)

c) R(−1, 4), S(7, −2) and T(3, 4), U(9, 0)

   i) Graph the line segment with each set of endpoints.

   ii) Find its slope.

   iii) Are the line segments parallel? Explain how you know.

5. Graph each quadrilateral. Is it a parallelogram? Explain.

a) A(5, 3), B(−3, −3), C(−2, −8), D(6, −2)

b) P(−6, 1), Q(−2, −6), R(10, 2), S(7, 9)

c) J(−4, 5), K(−2, −1), L(6, −4), M(4, 2)

6. Application

a) Graph the points A(1, −2), B(3, 1), C(4, −1), and D(6, 2). Join the points to form a quadrilateral.

b) Find the slope of each side.

c) Identify the type of quadrilateral. Explain how you know.

7. a) What is the slope of the *x*-axis?

  b) Draw a line segment parallel to the *x*-axis. Find its slope. What do you notice?

8. a) What is the slope of the *y*-axis?

  b) Draw a line segment parallel to the *y*-axis. Find its slope. What do you notice?

9. a) The coordinates of the endpoints of a line segment are given. For each line segment, write the coordinates of the endpoints of a parallel line segment.

  i) A(7, 6), B(−6, 3)   **ii)** C(−3, 7), D(1, −5)

  iii) E(2, 3), F(−2, −7)   **iv)** G(−4, 2), H(6, −4)

  b) Compare your answers for part a with those of a classmate. Explain any differences.

✓ 10. Thinking/Inquiry/Problem Solving

  a) Plot points A(−2, 0), B(6, 4), and C(−3, 4).

  b) Find the coordinates of a point D on the *y*-axis so that line segment CD is parallel to AB.

✓ 11. a) On a staircase, how are the slopes of the treads related? How are the slopes of the risers related?

  b) Why is this important for walking on stairs?

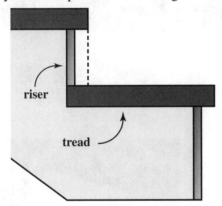

12. Communication How can you tell whether two line segments on a grid are parallel? Use examples to illustrate your explanation.

© 13. a) Graph four points that form a parallelogram.

  b) Find the slope of each side.

  c) Explain how you know the figure is a parallelogram.

Lines that meet at right angles (90°) are *perpendicular lines*.

What perpendicular line segments can you see in this picture?

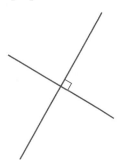

These lines are
perpendicular.

Perpendicular Line Segments

You will need grid paper and the cardboard
square used on page 152.

Adjacent sides of a square are perpendicular.

1. Draw a coordinate grid.

2. Place the square on the grid so that one side
   goes through 2 points where grid lines meet.
   Draw line segments along two perpendicular
   sides of the square.

3. Label the line segments AB and GH.

4. Find the slopes of AB and GH.

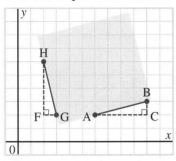

5. Move the square. Repeat exercises 2 to 4 to draw a different pair of perpendicular line segments.

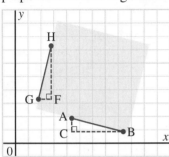 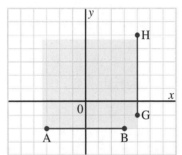

6. Repeat exercise 5 two more times. Include vertical and horizontal line segments.

7. For each pair of perpendicular line segments, what do you notice about the slopes of AB and GH?

8. Write a statement about the slopes of perpendicular line segments.

The *Investigation* shows that the slopes of perpendicular line segments are *negative reciprocals*.

> The product of negative reciprocals is −1.

Line segments AB and GH are perpendicular.

Slope of AB = $\dfrac{\text{rise}}{\text{run}}$ Slope of GH = $\dfrac{\text{rise}}{\text{run}}$

= $\dfrac{-3}{2}$ = $\dfrac{2}{3}$

= $-\dfrac{3}{2}$

The slopes $-\dfrac{3}{2}$ and $\dfrac{2}{3}$ are negative reciprocals.

$\left(-\dfrac{3}{2}\right)\left(\dfrac{2}{3}\right) = -1$

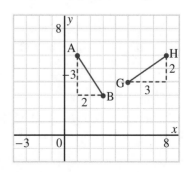

Perpendicular Line Segments

If the slopes of two line segments are negative reciprocals, the segments are perpendicular.

If two segments are perpendicular and neither is vertical, their slopes are negative reciprocals.

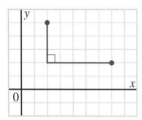

A vertical and a horizontal line segment are perpendicular. However, the slope of the vertical segment is undefined.
So, we cannot say that the slopes of these segments are negative reciprocals.

Example 1

Here are the endpoints of a line segment.
Which pair of line segments are perpendicular? How do you know?

a) R(−2, 5), S(2, 3) and S(2, 3), T(0, 0)

b) D(−2, −3), E(2, −3) and G(4, −3), F(4, 1)

Solution

a) Graph RS and ST.

$$\text{Slope of RS} = \frac{\text{rise}}{\text{run}} \qquad\qquad \text{Slope of ST} = \frac{\text{rise}}{\text{run}}$$

$$\qquad\qquad = \frac{-2}{4} \qquad\qquad\qquad\qquad\quad = \frac{-3}{-2}$$

$$\qquad\qquad = -\frac{1}{2} \qquad\qquad\qquad\qquad\quad = \frac{3}{2}$$

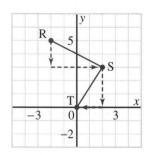

The slopes of RS and ST are not negative reciprocals.
So, line segments RS and ST are not perpendicular.

b) Graph DE and GF.

DE is horizontal and GF is vertical. So, segments DE and GF are perpendicular.

Discuss

Do segments need a common endpoint to be perpendicular?
Do they need to intersect to be perpendicular? Explain.

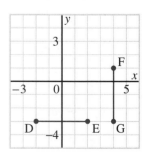

Example 2

A triangle has vertices A(–2, 3), B(8, –2), and C(4, 6).

Is it a right triangle? Explain.

Solution

Graph the triangle.

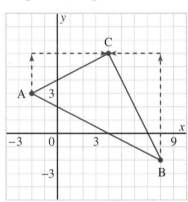

From the graph, ∠C appears to be a right angle. Calculate the slopes of AC and BC.

$$\text{Slope of AC} = \frac{\text{rise}}{\text{run}} \qquad \text{Slope of BC} = \frac{\text{rise}}{\text{run}}$$

$$= \frac{3}{6} \qquad\qquad\qquad = \frac{8}{-4}$$

$$= \frac{1}{2} \qquad\qquad\qquad = -2$$

Since $\frac{1}{2}$ and -2 are negative reciprocals, AC is perpendicular to BC.

So, △ABC is a right triangle.

Discuss

How does drawing the triangle help you determine if it is a right triangle?

4.5   Exercises

1. Which pairs of numbers are slopes of perpendicular line segments? How did you decide?

a) $\frac{3}{4}$, $-\frac{4}{3}$ b) $\frac{2}{3}$, $\frac{3}{2}$ c) $\frac{4}{5}$, $-\frac{4}{5}$ d) -4, $\frac{1}{4}$ e) 3, $\frac{1}{3}$

2. Which pairs of line segments are perpendicular? Explain how you know.

a)
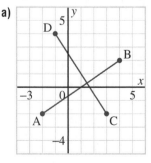

b)
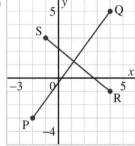

c)
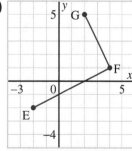

3. For each line segment with the given slope, write the slope of a perpendicular line segment.

a) $\dfrac{2}{3}$ b) $\dfrac{5}{8}$ c) $-\dfrac{3}{4}$ d) $-\dfrac{1}{2}$ e) $-\dfrac{1}{3}$

B **4. Knowledge/Understanding** For each pair of points:

a) O(0, 0), B(6, 4) and C(5, −1), D(1, 5)

b) H(−3, 1), I(6, 4) and J(2, 0), K(0, 6)

c) L(5, −3), M(1, 4) and N(1, −1), P(6, 2)

    i) Graph the line segment with each set of endpoints.

    ii) Find its slope.

    iii) Are the line segments perpendicular? Explain how you know.

5. Graph each triangle. Is it a right triangle? Explain.

a) D(−2, 2), E(−6, 2), F(−6, −1)   b) A(3, 0), B(−4, 4), C(−1, −2)

c) P(−3, 1), Q(3, −3), R(7, 3)   d) K(3, 2), L(−5, −1), M(−2, −8)

6. Application

a) Graph A(1, −2), B(3, 1), and C(6, −1). Join the points to form a triangle.

b) Find the slope of each side.

c) Identify the type of triangle. Explain your answer.

7. Graph each quadrilateral. Is it a rectangle? Explain.

a) A(5, 4), B(−4, −2), C(−2, −5), D(7, 1)

b) J(−3, 2), K(−2, −3), L(6, −2), M(5, 3)

c) P(5, 1), Q(−4, 4), R(−6, −2), S(3, −5)

> A rectangle has 4 right angles, so the adjacent sides of a rectangle are perpendicular.

8. Graph each line segment with the given endpoints. Find the coordinates of a point C so that AC is perpendicular to AB.

a) A(3, 2), B(6, 8)   b) A(0, 5), B(5, 3)   c) A(1, 3), B(1, −2)

9. Explain how to decide whether two line segments on a grid are perpendicular. Use examples to illustrate your explanation.

10. Communication Write or draw a plan to help you remember how to use slopes to decide whether line segments are parallel or perpendicular.

11. Thinking/Inquiry/Problem Solving The line segment that joins R(8, 6) and S(4, 8) is the shortest side of right △RST. Point T is on the *x*-axis. Find the possible coordinates of T. Explain your method.

1. Plot only the points with a negative *y*-coordinate.

   a) J(−1, −4)   **b)** K(4, 1)   **c)** L(5, −1)   **d)** M(−3, 0)

2. Find the slope of each line segment.

  a) 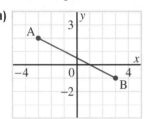 **b)** 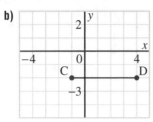 **c)**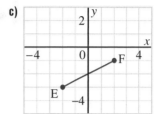

3. a) Sketch a line segment that has a positive slope.

  b) Sketch a line segment that has a negative slope.

  c) How are the line segments in parts a and b different?

4. Graph each pair of line segments. Use slopes to determine whether the segments are parallel, perpendicular, or neither.

  a) R(−3, 3), S(1, 1) and T(0, 0), U(6, −3)

  b) H(−4, −3), I(1, −1) and J(−3, 1), K(3, 4)

  c) E(−6, −2), F(1, −2) and G(−5, −4), H(−5, 4)

5. Graph quadrilateral KLMN with vertices K(1, 2), L(5, 1), M(3, −2), and N(−1, −1). Is quadrilateral KLMN a parallelogram? Use slopes to justify your answer.

Preparation for Ontario Testing

6. Examine the graph of the cost of a banquet at Vittoria's Banquet Hall.

  Which statement is true?

  a) As the number of people attending increases, the cost decreases.

  b) As the number of people attending increases, the cost stays constant.

  c) The graph "Cost at Vittoria's Banquet Hall" is linear.

  d) The graph "Cost at Vittoria's Banquet Hall" is non-linear.

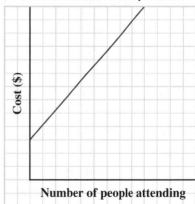

Cost at Vittoria's Banquet Hall

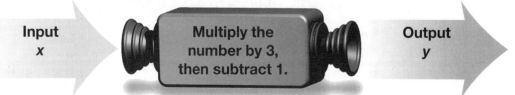

Recall, from Chapter 1, that the points on the graph of a linear relation lie on a straight line. A linear relation can be described by an *equation*. Consider this linear relation:

Input *x* → **Multiply the number by 3, then subtract 1.** → **Output** *y*

The equation $y = 3x - 1$ relates the values of *y* to the values of *x*. This relation can be expressed as a table of values and a graph.

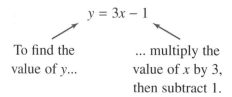

$y = 3x - 1$

To find the value of *y*... ... multiply the value of *x* by 3, then subtract 1.

If you have a graphing calculator, complete *Investigation 1*. If you do not have a graphing calculator, complete *Investigation 2*.

The Relation $y = 3x - 1$

Setting up an equation

- Press [Y=]. Use the scroll buttons and [CLEAR] to clear all equations.

- If Plot1, Plot2, and Plot3 at the top of the screen are highlighted, use the scroll buttons and [ENTER] to remove all highlighting.

- Make sure the cursor is beside Y₁. To enter the equation $y = 3x - 1$, press: 3 [X,T,θ,n] [-] 1

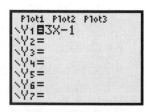

Setting up a table of values

- Press [2nd] [WINDOW] for TBLSET.
  Make sure TblStart = 0 so that the values of *x* begin at 0.
  Make sure △Tbl = 1 so that the values of *x* increase by 1.
  Make sure Auto is highlighted in the last two lines.

1. a) Press [2nd] [GRAPH] for TABLE.

b) Copy the table from the calculator to your notebook.

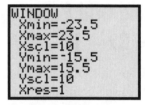

x	y
0	−1
1	2
2	5
3	8
4	11
5	14
6	17

Setting up a graph

• Press [WINDOW]. Enter these values.

2. a) Press [GRAPH].

b) Press [TRACE]. Press [▶] or [◀] to move the cursor along the line until $x = 3$. Compare the value of y on the calculator to the value in the table.

c) Repeat part b for different values of x.

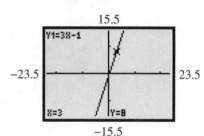

3. a) Add a third column to your table in exercise 1b. Label it *Difference*.
To complete the Difference column, take each y-coordinate and subtract the previous y-coordinate.

x	y	Difference
0	−1	
1	2	$2 - (-1) = 3$

b) What do you notice about the numbers in the Difference column?

4. a) Use the x- and y-columns of the table of values to graph the relation on grid paper.

b) Explain why it makes sense to connect the points with a straight line.

5. a) Label points A(0, −1) and B(1, 2). Find the slope of AB.

b) Label point C(2, 5). Find the slope of BC.

c) Continue labelling the points from the table of values (D, E, F, G). Find the slope of each line segment (CD, DE, EF, FG).

d) Compare the slopes in parts a to c with the numbers in the Difference column. What do you notice?

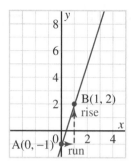

Using Grid Paper to Investigate $y = 3x - 1$

1. Copy this table. Use the rule below to complete the table.

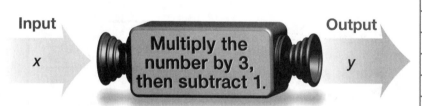

Input x	Output y
0	
1	
2	
3	
4	
5	
6	

You have made a table of values for the relation defined by $y = 3x - 1$. The x- and y-values in each row form an ordered pair.

2. a) Add a third column to your table in exercise 1. Label it *Difference*.

To complete the Difference column, take each y-coordinate and subtract the previous y-coordinate.

b) What do you notice about the numbers in the Difference column?

x	y	Difference
0	−1	2 − (−1) = 3
1	2	
2		
3		
4		
5		
6		

3. a) Use the x- and y-columns of the table of values to graph the relation on grid paper.

b) Explain why it makes sense to connect the points with a straight line.

4. a) Label points A(0, −1) and B(1, 2).
Find the slope of AB.

b) Label point C(2, 5). Find the slope of BC.

c) Continue labelling the points from the table of values (D, E, F, G). Find the slope of each line segment (CD, DE, EF, FG).

d) Compare the slopes in parts a to c with the numbers in the Difference column. What do you notice?

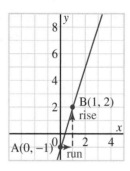

Each *Investigation* shows that:

- A linear relation can be represented by an equation, a table of values, or a graph.
- The graph of a linear relation is a straight line. On a coordinate grid:
  - When the *x*-coordinates increase by the same amount, the differences in *y*-coordinates are equal.
  - When the *x*-coordinates increase by 1, the differences in the *y*-coordinates are equal to the slope of any segment of the line.

Example 1

Graph the relation $y = 8 - 2x$.

Solution

$y = 8 - 2x$

Choose several values of *x*, for example, $x = -2, 0, 2, 4, 6$, and substitute each value in the equation.

When $x = -2$, $y = 8 - 2(-2)$ Press: 8 [−] 2 [(] [(−)] 2 [)] [ENTER =]
$ = 12$

$\boxed{8-2(-2) \hfill 12}$

When $x = 0$, $y = 8 - 2(0)$ Recall that $2(0) = 0$.
$ = 8$

When $x = 2$, $y = 8 - 2(2)$ Press: 8 [−] 2 [(] 2 [)] [ENTER =]
$ = 4$

$\boxed{8-2(2) \hfill 4}$

When $x = 4$, $y = 8 - 2(4)$
$ = 0$

When $x = 6$, $y = 8 - 2(6)$
$ = -4$

Make a table of values. Plot the points on a grid. Join the points with a straight line. Label the line with its equation.

x	y
-2	12
0	8
2	4
4	0
6	-4

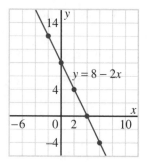

Discuss

Does the table of values show all possible values of x? Explain.

Example 2

Monique has a job at a garden centre. She is paid $10 per hour. Monique's pay, p dollars, and the time she works, h hours, are related by the equation $p = 10h$.

a) Copy and complete the table of values.

b) Graph the relation with h horizontally and p vertically.

c) Is the relation linear? How do you know?

d) What is the slope of any segment of the graph? How is this shown in the table?

e) How much does Monique earn for working 3.5 h?

f) Monique earned $45. How many hours did she work?

h (h)	p ($)	Difference
0	0	
1		
2		
3		
4		
5		
6		

Solution

a) Substitute each value of h in $p = 10h$ to find the corresponding value for p.

When $h = 0$, $p = 10(0)$
$$= 0$$

When $h = 1$, $p = 10(1)$
$$= 10$$

Continue in this way to complete the table.

Subtract consecutive values of p to complete the Difference column.

h (h)	p ($)	Difference
0	0	
1	10	$10 - 0 = 10$
2	20	$20 - 10 = 10$
3	30	$30 - 20 = 10$
4	40	$40 - 30 = 10$
5	50	$50 - 40 = 10$
6	60	$60 - 50 = 10$

b)

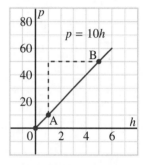

c) The relation is linear because all points on the graph lie on a straight line. The values of h increase by the same amount and the differences are equal. In this example, the differences are 10.

d) Choose points A(1, 10) and B(5, 50).

$$\text{Slope} = \frac{\text{rise}}{\text{run}}$$
$$= \frac{40}{4}$$
$$= 10$$

The slope of AB is 10. This is also the slope of any line segment on the graph. This can also be read from the table. Since the values of h increase by 1, the slope, 10, is the difference in the h-coordinates.

e) Draw a vertical line segment from 3.5 on the horizontal axis. It meets the graph at point (3.5, 35). Monique earns $35 in 3.5 h.

f) Draw a horizontal line segment from 45 on the vertical axis. It meets the graph at (4.5, 45). Monique worked for 4.5 h to earn $45.

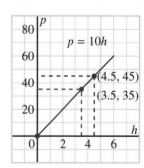

Discuss

Why do the points lie along a straight line?

Why does it make sense to join the points?

A   **1.** Does each graph represent a linear relation? Explain how you know.

a)

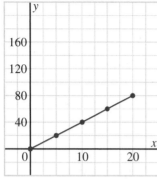

b)

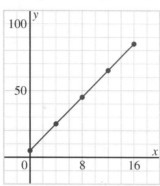

2. a) Does each table of values represent a linear relation? Explain how you know.

i)

x	y	Difference
0	0	
		8
1	8	
		8
2	16	
		8
3	24	
		8
4	32	

ii)

x	y	Difference
0	−3	
		−2
1	−5	
		−2
2	−7	
		−2
3	−9	
		−2
4	−11	

iii)

x	y	Difference
−2	6	
		0
−1	6	
		0
0	6	
		0
1	6	
		0
2	6	

b) For each table of values in part a that represents a linear relation, state the slope of the graph.

B   **3. a)** Copy and complete each table of values.

i) $y = 2x + 3$

x	y
0	
1	
2	
3	

ii) $y = 5 - 3x$

x	y
0	
2	
4	
6	

iii) $y = -12 + 4x$

x	y
0	
1	
2	
3	

b) Graph each equation.

c) Find the slope for any segment on each graph.

4. a) Copy and complete each table of values.

i) $y = 4x - 1$

x	y
-2	
-1	
0	
1	
2	

ii) $y = -3x + 2$

x	y
-4	
-2	
0	
2	
4	

b) Graph each equation.

c) Find the slope of any segment on each graph.

✓ **5. Knowledge/Understanding** For each equation below:

a) $y = 2x - 4$ **b)** $y = -5x + 10$

i) Copy and complete the table of values.

x	y	Difference
-2		
-1		
0		
1		
2		
3		
4		

ii) Graph the equation.

iii) Calculate the slope of any segment on the graph.

iv) Compare the slope in part iii and the numbers in the Difference column. Is the relation linear? Explain.

6. Enter these window settings. Graph each equation. Decide whether each relation is linear. Explain how you know.

a) $y = 5x + 3$ **b)** $y = x + 2$

c) $y = 4x$ **d)** $y = -2x - 4$

e) $y = -x + 6$ **f)** $y = 7x - 3$

To enter $y = -2x - 4$, press:

[Y=] [(-)] 2 [X,T,θ,n] [−] 4

```
WINDOW
 Xmin=-9.4
 Xmax=9.4
 Xscl=1
 Ymin=-10
 Ymax=10
 Yscl=1
 Xres=1
```

7. The equation $C = 40t + 20$ represents the cost to repair an appliance. C is the cost in dollars, and t is the time in hours for the repair.

a) Copy and complete this table.

b) Graph the relation on a grid like this:

t (h)	C ($)
0	
2	
3	
5	

c) Is the relation linear? How do you know?

d) Suppose it takes 4 h to repair an appliance. What would the repair cost?

e) Suppose a repair costs $100. How long would the repair take?

8. This diagram illustrates the relation $y = 2x + 3$.

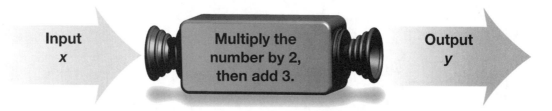

a) Copy and complete this table for 5 values of x from 0 to 10.

b) Graph the relation.

c) Is the relation linear? How does the table show this? How does the graph show this?

x	y	Difference

9. Application The cost, C cents, to print and bind n copies of a manual is modelled by the equation $C = 70 + 20n$.

a) Copy and complete this table.

n (copies)	0	20	40	60	80	100
C (¢)						

b) Use the table to draw a graph. Plot n horizontally and C vertically.

c) Use the graph to estimate the cost of 75 copies.

d) Use the graph to estimate how many copies can be printed for $10.

e) Is the relation linear? How do you know?

10. The cost, C dollars, for a school basketball team to play in a tournament is modelled by the equation $C = 300 + 20n$, where n is the number of players.

a) Copy and complete this table.

n (players)	0	2	4	6	8	10	12
C ($)							

b) Graph the relation. Plot n horizontally and C vertically.

c) What is the cost for 11 players to attend the tournament?

d) How many players can attend the tournament for $525?

11. Thinking/Inquiry/Problem Solving Suppose the extra cost for each basketball player in exercise 10 increased from $20 to $32. The equation becomes $C = 300 + 32n$.

a) Predict how the graph would change.

b) Predict how the cost for 11 players would change.

c) Explain how you made your predictions for parts a and b.

✓ **12. Communication** List three methods you can use to present a relation. Choose a relation from this section. Express the relation using each method.

C **13.** The temperature of an old oven is measured in degrees Fahrenheit. This formula converts Fahrenheit temperatures to Celsius temperatures.

$$C = \frac{5}{9}(F - 32)$$

a) Copy and complete this table. Graph the relation.

F (°F)	100	150	200	250	300	350	400
C (°C)							

b) Use the graph to estimate the temperature in degrees Celsius for each Fahrenheit temperature.
    i) 375°F   **ii)** 325°F   **iii)** 275°F

c) Use the graph to estimate the Fahrenheit temperature for each Celsius temperature.
    i) 90°C   **ii)** 120°C   **iii)** 200°C

d) Extend the graph to estimate the temperature in degrees Celsius for each Fahrenheit temperature.
    i) 20°F   **ii)** 0°F   **iii)** 425°F   **iv)** −20°F

e) What is the only temperature that is the same on both scales? How do you know?

Recall, from Chapter 1, that the points on the graph of a non-linear relation do not lie on a straight line.

If you have a graphing calculator, complete *Investigation 1*.
If you do not have a graphing calculator, complete *Investigation 2*.

The Relation $y = x^2 - 3x$

Setup

- Press $\boxed{Y=}$. Use the scroll buttons and $\boxed{\text{CLEAR}}$ to clear all equations.

- If any of Plot1, Plot2, and Plot3 at the top of the screen are highlighted, use the scroll buttons and $\boxed{\text{ENTER}}$ to remove the highlighting.

- Make sure the cursor is beside $Y_1 =$. To enter the equation $y = x^2 - 3x$, press: $\boxed{\text{X,T,θ,n}}$ $\boxed{x^2}$ $\boxed{-}$ 3 $\boxed{\text{X,T,θ,n}}$

- Press $\boxed{\text{2nd}}$ $\boxed{\text{WINDOW}}$ for TBLSET. Set the table to start at –2 with ΔTbl = 1.

- Press $\boxed{\text{WINDOW}}$. Enter these settings.

```
Plot1  Plot2  Plot3
\Y1◼X²-3X
\Y2=
\Y3=
\Y4=
\Y5=
\Y6=
\Y7=
```

```
TABLE SETUP
 TblStart=-2
 ∆Tbl=1■
Indpnt: AUTO  Ask
Depend: AUTO  Ask
```

```
WINDOW
 Xmin=-4.7
 Xmax=4.7
 Xscl=1
 Ymin=-3.1
 Ymax=3.1
 Yscl=1
 Xres=1
```

1. Press $\boxed{\text{2nd}}$ $\boxed{\text{GRAPH}}$ for TABLE.

2. Copy this table. Record the values of *y* from the graphing calculator.

x	y	Difference
–2	10	
–1		
0		
1		
2		
3		
4		
5		

3. a) Complete the Difference column by taking each *y*-coordinate and subtracting the previous *y*-coordinate.

b) What do you notice about the numbers in the Difference column?

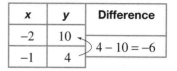

x	*y*	Difference
−2	10	
−1	4	4 − 10 = −6

4. a) Press GRAPH.

b) Press TRACE. Use the scroll buttons to move the cursor until $x = 0$. Compare the value of *y* on the calculator to that in the table.

c) Repeat part b for other values of *x* from the table.

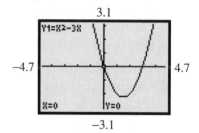

5. a) On grid paper, plot the points from your table of values. Draw a smooth curve through the points. Your graph should look like the graph at the right.

b) Label points A(−2, 10) and B(−1, 4). Find the slope of AB.

c) Label point O(0, 0). Find the slope of BO.

d) Continue labelling the points from your table of values (C, D, E, F, G). Find the slope of each line segment (OC, CD, DE, EF, FG).

e) Compare the slopes in parts b to d with the numbers in the Difference column. What do you notice?

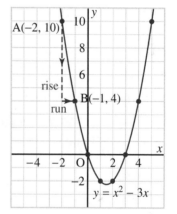

INVESTIGATION 2

Using Grid Paper to Investigate $y = x^2 - 3x$

1. Copy this table. Use the relation $y = x^2 - 3x$ to complete the *y*-column.

2. a) Complete the Difference column by taking each *y*-coordinate and subtracting the previous *y*-coordinate.

b) What do you notice about the numbers in the Difference column?

x	*y*	Difference
−2	10	
−1	4	4 − 10 = −6
0		
1		
2		
3		
4		
5		

3. a) On grid paper, plot the points from the first two columns of the table of values. Draw a smooth curve through the points.

b) Label points A(−2, 10) and B(−1, 4). Find the slope of AB.

c) Label point O(0, 0). Find the slope of BO.

d) Continue labelling the points from the table of values (C, D, E, F, G). Find the slope of each line segment (OC, CD, DE, EF, FG).

e) Compare the slopes in parts b to d with the numbers in the Difference column. What do you notice?

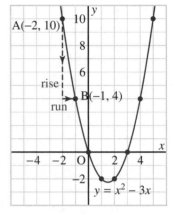

Each *Investigation* shows that:

- A non-linear relation can be represented by an equation, a table of values, or a graph.
- The graph of a non-linear relation is not a straight line.
- When the *x*-coordinates of a non-linear relation increase by the same amount, the differences in the *y*-coordinates are not equal.

Example

Use a table of values with a Difference column to determine whether each relation is linear or non-linear.

a) $y = 3x + 4$ **b)** $y = x^2 - 1$

Solution

a) $y = 3x + 4$

Draw a table. Choose values of x from −2 to 2.
Complete the y-column by substituting each value of x in $y = 3x + 4$.
For $x = -2$, $y = 3(-2) + 4$
$$= -6 + 4$$
$$= -2$$
Each x-value is substituted in a similar way.

Subtract the y-coordinates to complete the Difference column. Since the differences are equal, the relation is linear.

x	y	Difference
−2	−2	
		$1 - (-2) = 3$
−1	1	
		$4 - 1 = 3$
0	4	
		$7 - 4 = 3$
1	7	
		$10 - 7 = 3$
2	10	

b) $y = x^2 - 1$

Draw a table. Choose values of x from -2 to 2.
Complete the y-column by substituting each value
of x in $y = x^2 - 1$.

For $x = -2$, $y = (-2)^2 - 1$
$\qquad\qquad = 4 - 1$
$\qquad\qquad = 3$

Subtract the y-coordinates to complete the
Difference column.

x	y	Difference
-2	3	
		$0 - 3 = -3$
-1	0	
		$-1 - 0 = -1$
0	-1	
		$0 - (-1) = 1$
1	0	
		$3 - 0 = 3$
2	3	

Since the differences are not equal, the relation is non-linear.

Discuss

How are the tables of values for linear and non-linear relations different?
How are the graphs different? How are the equations different?

4.7 Exercises

1. Which graphs show non-linear relations? How do you know?

a)
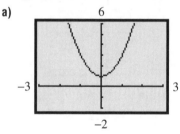

b)
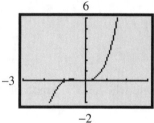

c)
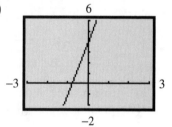

2. Which graphs show non-linear relations? How do you know?

a)
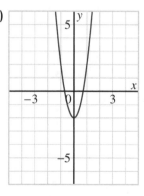

b)
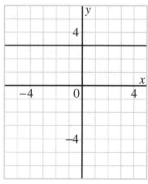

c)
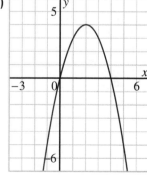

3. Determine whether each table of values represents a linear relation. Explain.

a)

x	y	Difference
−3	9	
		−5
−2	4	
		−3
−1	1	
		−1
0	0	
		1
1	1	
		3
2	4	
		5
3	9	
		7
4	16	

b)

x	y	Difference
−3	−5	
		2
−2	−3	
		2
−1	−1	
		2
0	1	
		2
1	3	
		2
2	5	
		2
3	7	
		2
4	9	

c)

x	y	Difference
−3	15	
		−7
−2	8	
		−5
−1	3	
		−3
0	0	
		−1
1	−1	
		1
2	0	
		3
3	3	
		5
4	8	

 4. Knowledge/Understanding

a) Copy and complete each table. Decide whether the relation is linear or non-linear.

i)

x	y	Difference
−2	5	
−1	2	
0	−1	
1	−4	
2	−7	
3	−10	
4	−13	

ii)

x	y	Difference
−2	5	
−1	9	
0	12	
1	14	
2	15	
3	15	
4	14	

iii)

x	y	Difference
−2	5	
−1	5	
0	5	
1	5	
2	5	
3	5	
4	5	

b) For each table in part a, decide whether the graph of the relation is a straight line. Explain how you know.

5. Copy and complete each table. Is each relation linear or non-linear? Explain.

a) $y = x^2 + 1$

x	y	Difference
−2		
−1		
0		
1		
2		

b) $y = 2 - x$

x	y	Difference
0		
2		
4		
6		
8		

c) $y = \dfrac{12}{x}$

x	y	Difference
1		
2		
3		
4		

d) $y = 3 + 4x$

x	y	Difference
−1		
0		
1		
2		
3		

6. Use a table of values with a Difference column to determine whether each relation is linear or non-linear.

a) $y = 1 - x$ **b)** $y = 2 + x^2$

c) $y = 2 + x$ **d)** $y = 2 - x^2$

7. Use the results of exercises 5 and 6.

a) List the equations of linear relations.

b) List the equations of non-linear relations.

c) How can you tell by looking at the equation of a relation whether it is linear or non-linear?

8. Enter these window settings. Graph each equation. Decide whether each relation is linear or non-linear. Explain how you know.

```
WINDOW
 Xmin=-9.4
 Xmax=9.4
 Xscl=1
 Ymin=-8
 Ymax=8
 Yscl=1
 Xres=1
```

a) $y = 5 - 2x^2$ **b)** $y = x + 6$

c) $y = -4x^2$ **d)** $y = \dfrac{2x}{5}$

e) $y = \dfrac{3}{x}$ **f)** $y = 5x - 4$

g) $y = x^2 + 5x$ **h)** $y = -3x^2 - 2$

i) $y = x + x^2$ **j)** $y = -\dfrac{1}{x}$

To enter $y = \dfrac{2x}{5}$, press: [Y=] 2 [X,T,θ,n] [÷] 5

To enter $y = -\dfrac{1}{x}$, press: [Y=] [(-)] 1 [÷] [X,T,θ,n]

9. a) For each relation, make a table of values for x-values from −2 to 3. Graph each relation.

   i) $y = -3x$ **ii)** $y = -1$ **iii)** $y = x^2 - x$

b) Is each relation linear or non-linear? How does the table of values show this? How does the graph show this?

 10. Communication Suppose you are given an equation for a relation. How can you decide whether the relation is linear without graphing it?

11. a) Identify the equations of straight lines.

i) $y = \dfrac{2}{x}$ **ii)** $y = 3x + 1$ **iii)** $y = -4x$ **iv)** $y = 2x^2 + 1$

v) $y = 2 - 3x$ **vi)** $y = -\dfrac{6}{x}$ **vii)** $y = \dfrac{1}{2}x + 4$ **viii)** $y = -x^2$

b) Explain how you identified the equations of straight lines.

12. Match each equation with a graph from the screens below.

i) $y = 5 - x$ **ii)** $y = \dfrac{x^2}{5}$ **iii)** $y = 5$

a)

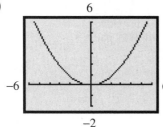

b)

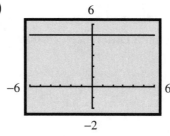

c)

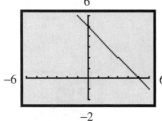

13. A baseball falls from rest. The approximate distance it falls, d metres, and the time, t seconds, are related by the equation $d = 5t^2$.

t (s)	d (m)	Difference
0		
1		
2		
3		
4		

a) Copy and complete this table.

b) Is the relation linear or non-linear? How do you know?

c) Graph the relation. Plot t horizontally and d vertically.

d) How does the graph show whether the relation is linear or non-linear?

14. **Application** Sunscreen protects the skin by reducing the amount of ultraviolet light that hits the skin. Sunscreen is labelled SPF 2, SPF 4, SPF 8, ..., SPF 35. SPF is the sunscreen protection factor, s. The percent of ultraviolet light that hits the skin is p. The relation between s and p is $p = \dfrac{100}{s}$.

a) Copy and complete this table.

s (SPF)	p (%)	Difference
2		
8		
15		
25		
35		

b) Is the relation linear or non-linear? Explain how you know.

c) Graph the relation. Plot s horizontally and p vertically.

d) How does the graph show whether the relation is linear or non-linear?

15. **Thinking/Inquiry/Problem Solving**
Usually, light does not penetrate deeper than 100 m below the surface of the ocean. This table shows the percent of surface light present at various depths.

a) Is the relation between light penetration and depth linear or non-linear? Explain how you know.

b) Estimate the depth at which 30% of the light is present.

Depth (m)	Percent of light present
0	100
20	63
40	40
60	25
80	16
100	10

Staircases come in many shapes and sizes. There are circular staircases, wide and narrow staircases, long and short staircases.

Recall from page 151 that all staircases have three main parts.

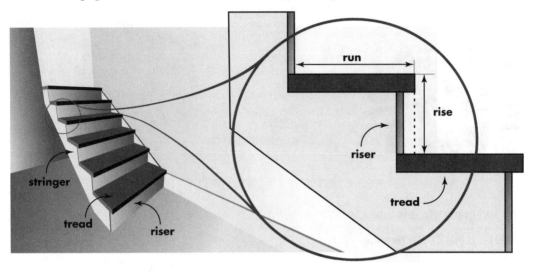

The run or *tread* is the horizontal part of a stair.

The rise or *riser* is the vertical part of a stair.

The *stringers* are the sloping boards running diagonally between floors, on both ends of the treads.

The stringers support and stabilize the staircase. The slope of each stringer determines the steepness of the staircase.

1. Look at these 3 staircases.

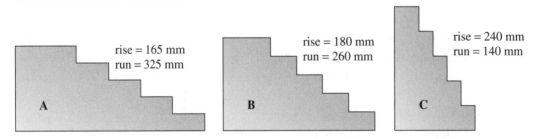

A   rise = 165 mm   run = 325 mm

B   rise = 180 mm   run = 260 mm

C   rise = 240 mm   run = 140 mm

   a) How is the number of risers related to the number of treads?

   b) Which staircase would most likely be used as the main staircase in a home? Explain your choice.

c) Which staircase is best suited for going up to an attic? Explain.

d) Most staircase accidents occur when the person is going down. Which staircase do you think would be safest? Explain.

2. In the 17th century, architect Francois Blondel used a person's normal walking stride to suggest measurements for the "ideal" staircase. He said the measurement of the run plus twice the rise should equal 620 mm. Carpenters still use the rule today.

The equation that represents the rule is $x + 2y = 620$.

a) Assume that the rule was based on safety. Do you think the rule is equally safe for all people? Explain.

b) Use the equation. Calculate the rise for a staircase with a run of 520 mm. Where might you find a staircase with these measurements?

3. The Canadian Mortgage and Housing Corporation (CMHC) recommends staircase measurements. The maximum rise should be 200 mm and the minimum run should be 250 mm.

a) Use Blondel's rule. Calculate the run that corresponds to the maximum rise recommended by the CMHC. What is the slope of the stringer?

b) Calculate the rise that corresponds to the minimum run. What is the slope of the stringer?

c) The vertical distance between two floors is 2.95 m. Use the CMHC guidelines and Blondel's rule. Calculate the minimum number of treads for a staircase between these floors.

4. A staircase may be constructed off site, then delivered and installed. Suppose a carpenter miscalculated and made a staircase with stringers 55 mm too long. The staircase was installed. Explain the problems that might arise with this staircase.

CHAPTER 4

MATHEMATICS TOOLKIT

Slope

- Slope $= \dfrac{\text{rise}}{\text{run}}$

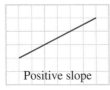
Positive slope

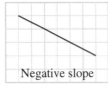
Negative slope

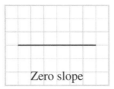
Zero slope

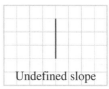
Undefined slope

Parallel Line Segments

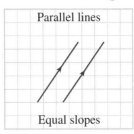
Parallel lines
Equal slopes

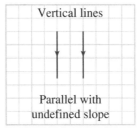
Vertical lines
Parallel with undefined slope

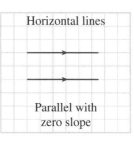
Horizontal lines
Parallel with zero slope

Perpendicular Line Segments

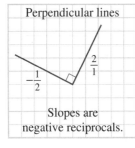
Perpendicular lines
Slopes are negative reciprocals.

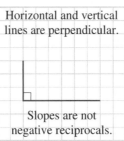
Horizontal and vertical lines are perpendicular.
Slopes are not negative reciprocals.

Linear Relations

- A linear relation can be represented by an equation, a table of values, or a straight-line graph.

$$y = 2x + 1$$

x	y	Difference
−2	−3	
		+2
−1	−1	
		+2
0	1	
		+2
1	3	
		+2
2	5	

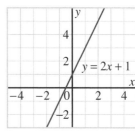

- When the x-coordinates increase by the same amount, the differences in the y-coordinates are equal.

- When the x-coordinates increase by 1, the differences in the y-coordinates are equal to the slope of any segment of the line.

Non-Linear Relations

- A non-linear relation can be represented by an equation, a table of values, or a graph that is not a straight line.

$$y = x^2 - 1$$

x	y	Difference
−2	3	
		3
−1	0	
		1
0	−1	
		−1
1	0	
		−3
2	3	

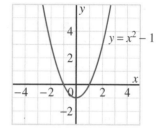

- When the x-coordinates increase by the same amount, the differences in the y-coordinates are not equal.

4.1

1. This diagram is a side view of a roller coaster. Find the slope of each section.

a) AB   b) BC

2. Find the slope of each line segment.

a)    b)    c)   d)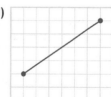

4.2 **3.** Name the coordinates of each point on the coordinate plane at the right.

4. Plot and label these points on a coordinate plane.

a) A(−2, 5)   b) B(0, 0)   c) C(6, −1)

d) D(0, −4)   e) E(−1, −3)   f) F(−3, −5)

4.3 **5.** Plot points A(3, −2), B(0, 5), C(3, 5), and D(−1, −1). Find the slope of each segment.

a) AB   b) AC   c) BC   d) CD

4.4 **6.** Start at (1, 1). Draw a line segment with each given slope. Describe each segment, including its direction.

a) −2   b) 0   c) $\frac{1}{4}$ d) $-\frac{2}{3}$ e) −4

7. Graph each pair of line segments with the given endpoints. Are the line segments parallel?

a) R(−2, 3), S(3, −2) and T(−4, 0), U(−1, −3)

b) L(−5, 7), M(4, 7) and N(0, −2), P(1, −2)

c) H(5, 4), I(0, 0) and J(2, −3), K(−4, −7)

d) W(−4, −3), S(−2, 0) and T(−3, −7), Z(2, −1)

8. A quadrilateral has vertices A(−1, 4), B(−3, −2), C(3, −1), and D(4, 5). Is it a parallelogram? How do you know?

4.5 **9.** Graph each pair of line segments with the given endpoints. Are the line segments perpendicular?

a) A(−5, 6), B(1, 3,) and C(−4, 3), D(−3, 5)

b) E(0, −7), F(4, −1) and G(2, −4), H(7, −6)

c) P(−6, 4), Q(−3, 0) and R(−2, 0), S(1, −4)

d) K(2, −1), L(4, 3) and M(−1, 3), N(3, 1)

10. A triangle has vertices P(−4, −2), Q(6, 4), and R(−7, 3). Show that △QPR is a right triangle.

11. A quadrilateral has vertices A(−2, 2), B(−1, 3), C(5, −2), and D(4, 3).

a) Is ABCD a parallelogram? Explain.   b) Is ABCD a rectangle? Explain.

4.6 **12. a)** Copy and complete the table of values for $y = -3x + 2$.

b) Graph the equation.

c) Calculate the slope of any segment on the graph.

d) What do you notice about the slope in part c and the numbers in the Difference column?

e) Is the relation linear? Explain how you know.

x	y	Difference
−2		
−1		
0		
1		
2		

13. a) Copy each table. Complete the Difference column. Decide whether the relation is linear. Explain how you know.

i)

x	y	Difference
−2	−2	
−1	1	
0	4	
1	7	
2	10	
3	13	
4	16	

ii)

x	y	Difference
−2	9	
−1	7	
0	5	
1	3	
2	1	
3	−1	
4	−3	

b) For each table of values in part a that represents a linear relation, state the slope of the graph.

14. The equation $C = 10h + 5$ represents the cost to rent a video game. C is the cost in dollars, and h is the time in hours playing the video game.

a) Copy and complete this table.

b) Graph the relation.

c) Is the relation linear? How do you know?

d) How much does it cost to play the video game for 3 h?

e) How many hours can you play the video game for $45?

h (h)	C ($)
0	
1	
2	
4	

4.7 **15. a)** For each relation, make a table of values for x-values from −2 to 2. Graph each relation on a separate coordinate plane.

i) $y = 2x - 5$ ii) $y = x^2 + 4$ iii) $y = -2x^2 - 2x$

b) Is each relation linear or non-linear? How does the table of values show this? How does the graph show this?

16. Enter these window settings. Graph each equation. Decide whether each relation is linear or non-linear. Explain how you know.

a) $y = x^2 + 3$ **b)** $y = -x + 2$ **c)** $y = 6 - 2x$ **d)** $y = 2x^2 - x$

e) $y = x + 5$ **f)** $y = -3x^2$ **g)** $y = 5 - x^2$ **h)** $y = \dfrac{12}{x}$

```
WINDOW
 Xmin=-9.4
 Xmax=9.4
 Xscl=1
 Ymin=-10
 Ymax=10
 Yscl=1
 Xres=1
```

17. Decide whether each relation is linear or non-linear. Justify each decision.

a) $y = 5x - 1$ **b)** $y = -2x^2 - 6x$ **c)** $y = -2x^2$ **d)** $y = \dfrac{4}{x}$

4.8 **18.** What is the slope of this staircase?

1. Find the slope of each line segment.

a)

b)

c)

2. Graph the line segment with each pair of endpoints. Find its slope.

a) A(−1, 5), B(−4, −1)   b) C(3, 2), D(8, −2)   c) E(−2, −5), F(0, −5)

3. **Application** A ramp is built to a door as shown on right.

a) What is the slope of the ramp?

b) Suppose the length of the ramp is increased. What happens to its slope? Explain how you know.

c) Suppose the door is lower than 0.3 m from the ground. What would happen to the slope of the ramp? Explain how you know.

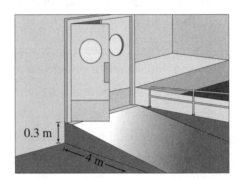

0.3 m

4 m

4. **Knowledge/Understanding** Graph each pair of line segments. Decide whether they are parallel, perpendicular, or neither. Justify your answers.

a) W(−3, 3), S(5, 1) and T(−1, −2), Z(1, 2)

b) A(−4, −3), B(0, 1) and C(−5, 0), D(−1, −4)

c) Q(−4, −2), R(2, −4) and S(1, 2), T(4, 1)

5. Enter these window settings. Graph each equation. Decide whether each relation is linear or non-linear. Explain how you know.

a) $y = x^2 - 5$

b) $y = 5x + 4$

c) $y = 4x^2 + 7x$

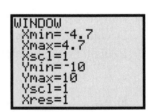

```
WINDOW
 Xmin=-4.7
 Xmax=4.7
 Xscl=1
 Ymin=-10
 Ymax=10
 Yscl=1
 Xres=1
```

6. **Communication** Explain how you know whether each relation is linear or non-linear by using an equation, a table of values, and a graph.

a) $y = 3x + 4$ b) $y = 2x^2 - 6$ c) $y = -x^2 - 2x$

7. **Thinking/Inquiry/Problem Solving** One side of a parallelogram has slope $\frac{3}{4}$.

a) Draw the parallelogram.

b) How many different parallelograms are possible? Explain.

1. A month ago, Juan built a skateboard ramp with run 5 m, rise 4 m, and slope $\frac{4}{5}$. Juan wants to change the length of the run to 15 m. How much will he need to increase the rise of the ramp to preserve the $\frac{4}{5}$ slope?

Rise = 4 m

Run = 5 m

2. This diagram is part of a side view of a roller coaster. Segments AB and CD represent 2 uphill segments of the ride. Which segment is steeper? Justify your answer.

5 The Line

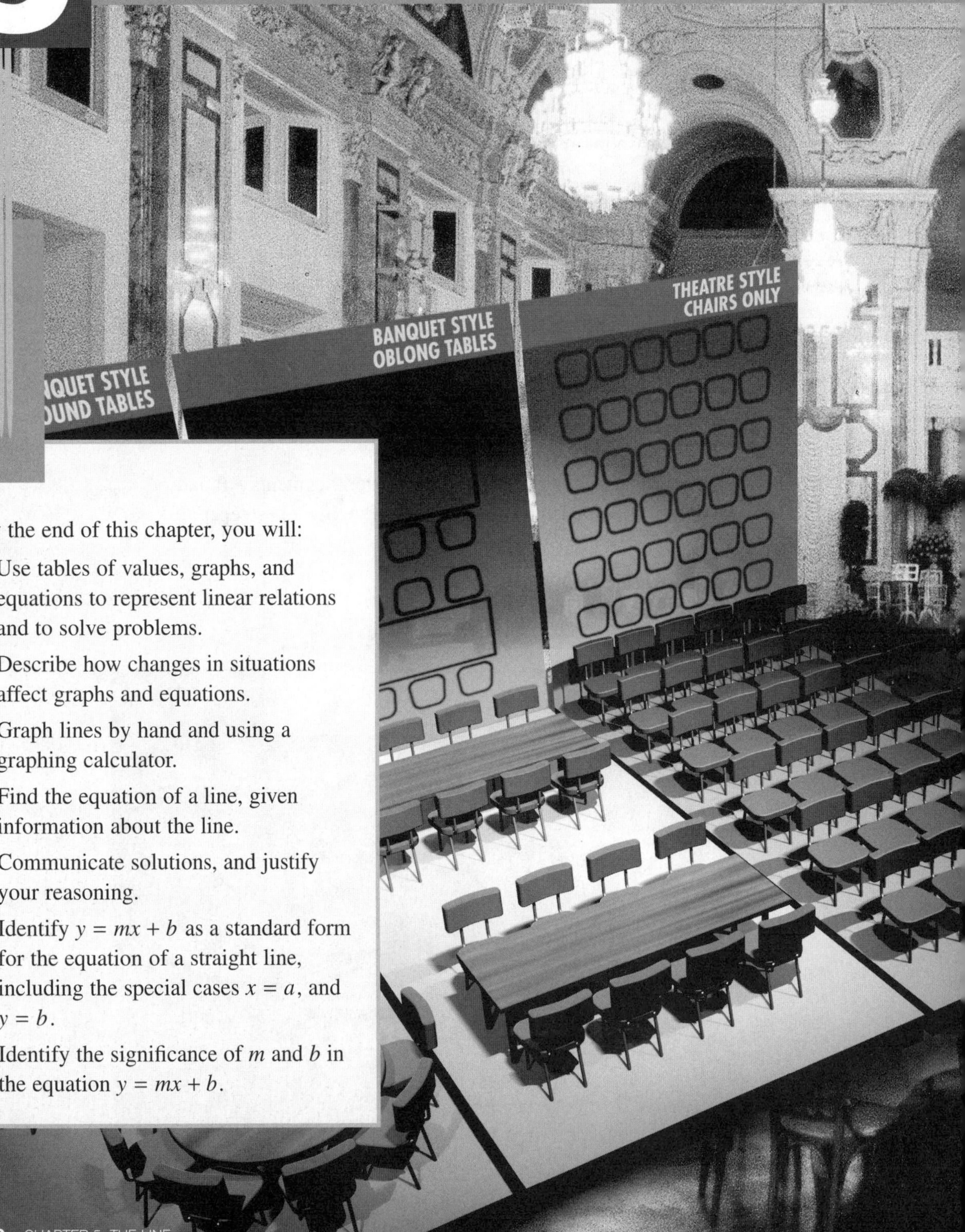

By the end of this chapter, you will:

- Use tables of values, graphs, and equations to represent linear relations and to solve problems.

- Describe how changes in situations affect graphs and equations.

- Graph lines by hand and using a graphing calculator.

- Find the equation of a line, given information about the line.

- Communicate solutions, and justify your reasoning.

- Identify $y = mx + b$ as a standard form for the equation of a straight line, including the special cases $x = a$, and $y = b$.

- Identify the significance of m and b in the equation $y = mx + b$.

BANQUET STYLE
ROUND TABLES

BANQUET STYLE
OBLONG TABLES

THEATRE STYLE
CHAIRS ONLY

Setting Up for a Banquet

People sometimes rent large room in hotels to hold a banquet or some other function. The number of guests depends on the area of the room and the way the tables and chairs are arranged. On page 190, there are 3 possible seating arrangements for one room.

In Section 5.8, you will use mathematical modelling to estimate the number of people that can be seated in each arrangement. You will apply the models to your classroom, your cafeteria, and some hotel rooms.

Necessary Skills

Slope of a Line Segment

The slope of a line segment is $\frac{\text{rise}}{\text{run}}$.

For AB, the rise is 5 and the run is 2.

So, the slope of AB is $\frac{5}{2}$.

For CD, the rise is −3 and the run is 1.

So, the slope of CD is $\frac{-3}{1}$, or −3.

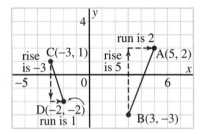

Exercises

1. Find the slope of each line segment.

a) 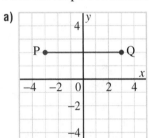 **b)** 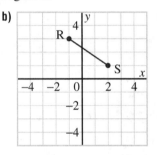 **c)**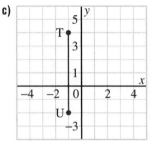

2. Graph each line segment. Find its slope.

a) A(−2, 4), B(3, 2)   **b)** C(3, 1), D(0, −3)

c) E(−2, 1), F(−6, 1)   **d)** G(1, 2), H(1, 9)

e) I(−4, 10), J(−3, 4)   **f)** K(−5, 3), L(0, 0)

g) M(0, 5), N(0, −5)   **h)** P(−6, −2), Q(4, 3)

3. a) What is the slope of any horizontal line segment?

b) What is the slope of any vertical line segment?

Linear Relations

For a linear relation:

- The points on the graph lie on a straight line.
- When the x-coordinates increase by 1, the differences in the y-coordinates equal the slope of any segment of the graph.

For the graph of $y = 3x + 2$, the slope of any segment is 3.

x	y	Difference
−1	−1	
		3
0	2	
		3
1	5	
		3
2	8	

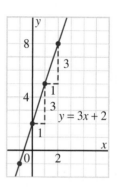

Exercises

1. For each relation:

a) Copy and complete the table of values.

b) Graph the equation.

c) What is the slope of any segment of the graph?

d) What do you notice about the slope and the numbers in the Difference column?

i) $y = -3 + 4x$

x	y	Difference
1		
2		
3		
4		
5		

ii) $y = 2x - 5$

x	y	Difference
1		
2		
3		
4		
5		

2. For each equation in exercise 1:

a) Is the relation linear?

b) Explain how the table of values shows whether the relation is linear.

c) Explain how the slope shows whether the relation is linear.

In Chapter 4, we calculated the slope of a line segment. In this section, we will calculate the slope of a line.

Suppose several line segments with the same slope are connected.

For example, start at A(1, 3). Move 2 up and 3 right to B. Then move 2 up and 3 right to C. Continue in this way to D and E.

Observe that A, B, C, D, and E lie on a straight line.

Choose any 2 segments of this line, for example, AB and BD, or AD and CE. Find their slopes.

$$\text{Slope of AB} = \frac{\text{rise}}{\text{run}}$$
$$= \frac{2}{3}$$

$$\text{Slope of BD} = \frac{\text{rise}}{\text{run}}$$
$$= \frac{4}{6}$$
$$= \frac{2}{3}$$

$$\text{Slope of AD} = \frac{\text{rise}}{\text{run}}$$
$$= \frac{6}{9}$$
$$= \frac{2}{3}$$

$$\text{Slope of CE} = \frac{\text{rise}}{\text{run}}$$
$$= \frac{4}{6}$$
$$= \frac{2}{3}$$

The slope of the line through AE is $\frac{2}{3}$.

TAKE NOTE

Slope of a Line

The slopes of all segments of a line are equal.

The slope of a line is the slope of any segment of the line.

We can use these results to draw a line when we know its slope and the coordinates of a point on the line.

Example 1

On a grid, draw a line through A(2, 5) with slope 2.

Solution

Mark the point A(2, 5).

Write slope 2 as $\frac{2}{1}$.

The rise is 2 and the run is 1.

Move 2 up and 1 right. Mark a point.

Move 2 up and 1 right again. Mark another point.

Draw a line through the points.

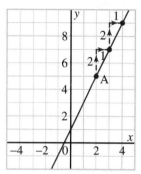

Discuss

Could you draw the line with slope 2 by marking points on the opposite side of A? Explain.

Example 2

On a grid, draw a line through K(4, −2) with slope $-\frac{1}{3}$.

Solution

Mark the point K(4, −2).

Write slope $-\frac{1}{3}$ as $\frac{-1}{3}$.

The rise is −1 and the run is 3.

Move 1 down and 3 right. Mark a point.

Move 1 down and 3 right again. Mark a point.

Draw a line through the points.

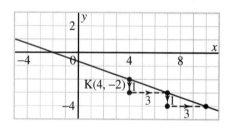

Discuss

Could you have drawn the line by using the slope as $\frac{1}{-3}$? Explain.

A **1.** State the slope of each line.

a)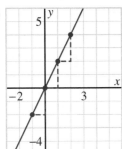

b)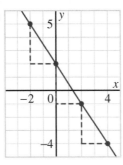

c)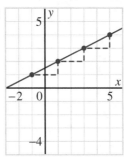

2. State the slope of each line.

a)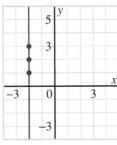

b)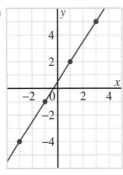

c)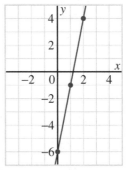

d)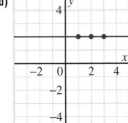

e)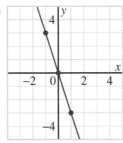

f)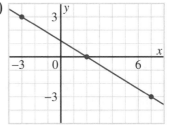

B **3.** Draw a line through each point with each given slope.

a) A(−2, 1), slope 3

b) B(4, 0), slope $\frac{3}{2}$

c) C(0, 0), slope $-\frac{1}{4}$

d) D(−1, −3), slope −4

4. Knowledge/Understanding Draw a line through B(3, 2) with each slope.

a) 2   **b)** $-\frac{1}{2}$ **c)** −3   **d)** 0

5. Draw a line through E(0, 4) with each slope. Find the coordinates of 2 more points on each line.

a) 3   **b)** $\frac{1}{2}$ **c)** −2   **d)** $-\frac{1}{4}$

6. Draw a line with each slope. Find the coordinates of 2 points on the line.

a) 3   **b)** $\frac{4}{3}$ **c)** −2   **d)** $-\frac{2}{5}$

7. Communication Choose a slope from exercise 6. Compare your coordinates of the 2 points with a classmate's. Do your points lie on your classmate's line? Do your classmate's points lie on your line? Explain why the points lie on the same or different lines.

8. a) Draw a line through C(−2, 3) with slope 0.

b) Find the coordinates of 3 other points on this line. What do you notice about the coordinates of these points?

9. a) Draw a line through D(4, −3) with an undefined slope.

b) Find the coordinates of 3 other points on this line. What do you notice about the coordinates of these points?

 10. Draw the line through each pair of points. Find the coordinates of 2 more points on each line.

a) E(2, 3) and F(1, 7)   **b)** G(−4, 7) and H(1, 0)

c) J(−6, −2) and K(5, 8)   **d)** L(−3, −7) and M(−4, −6)

11. Graph each set of points.

    i) A(0, 1), B(3, 3), C(9, 7)

    ii) A(−6, 1), B(−2, −1), C(4, −4)

    iii) A(8, 5), B(−2, 1), C(3, 3)

a) Find the slopes of AB, BC, and AC. What do you notice? Explain whether this makes sense.

b) Suppose D is another point on the line. What is the slope of AD? How do you know?

12. Application Points that lie on the same line are *collinear* points. In the diagram, points A, B, and C appear to be collinear.

a) Find the slopes of AB, BC, and AC.

b) Are the 3 points collinear?

c) Find another way to determine whether the points are collinear.

13. Thinking/Inquiry/Problem Solving A line has slope −1. It passes through the points C(q, 3) and D(4, −2). What is the value of q? Explain how you got your answer.

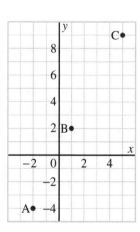

If you have a graphing calculator, complete *Investigation 1*.
If you do not have a graphing calculator, complete *Investigation 2*.

The Equation $y = mx$

Set-up

- Press WINDOW. Enter these settings.
- Press Y=. Use the scroll buttons and CLEAR to clear all equations.
- If Plot1, Plot2, and Plot3 are highlighted, use the scroll buttons and ENTER to remove the highlighting.

```
WINDOW
 Xmin=-9
 Xmax=9
 Xscl=1
 Ymin=-6
 Ymax=6
 Yscl=1
 Xres=1
```

Graph $y = x$, $y = 2x$, and $y = 4x$ on the same screen.

1. To enter the equation $y = x$, make sure the cursor is beside $Y_1 =$. Press X,T,θ,n.

To enter $y = 2x$, make sure the cursor is beside $Y_2 =$. Press 2 X,T,θ,n.

To enter $y = 4x$, make sure the cursor is beside $Y_3 =$. Press 4 X,T,θ,n.

Press GRAPH.

```
Plot1 Plot2 Plot3
\Y1■X
\Y2■2X
\Y3■4X■
\Y4=
\Y5=
\Y6=
\Y7=
```

2. How are the graphs in exercise 1 alike? How are they different?

Graph $y = -x$, $y = -2x$, and $y = -4x$ on the same screen.

3. To enter $y = -x$, make sure the cursor is beside $Y_4 =$.
Press (-) X,T,θ,n.

To enter $y = -2x$, make sure the cursor is beside $Y_5 =$.
Press (-) 2 X,T,θ,n.

To enter $y = -4x$, make sure the cursor is beside $Y_6 =$.
Press (-) 4 X,T,θ,n.

To differentiate the graphs of Y_4, Y_5, and Y_6, move the cursor to the left of $Y_4 =$, $Y_5 =$, and $Y_6 =$. Press ENTER to select the thick line. Press GRAPH.

```
Plot1 Plot2 Plot3
\Y1■X
\Y2■2X
\Y3■4X
\Y4■-X
\Y5■-2X
\Y6■-4X
\Y7=■
```

4. How are the thick-lined graphs alike? How are they different?

5. How are the thick-lined graphs similar to the thin-lined graphs? How are they different?

6. Press [2nd] [WINDOW] for TBLSET. Make sure TblStart = 0 and ΔTbl = 1.

```
TABLE SETUP
 TblStart=0
 ΔTbl=1
Indpnt: Auto Ask
Depend: Auto Ask
```

7. Press [2nd] [GRAPH] for TABLE.

   a) To find the slope of $y = x$, calculate the differences in the Y_1 values.

   b) To find the slope of $y = 2x$, calculate the differences in the Y_2 values.

   c) Compare the slope of each line with its equation. What do you notice?

8. Each equation is in $y = mx$ form. What do you think m represents?

Using Grid Paper
to Investigate $y = mx$

1. Copy and complete this table of values for each equation.

   a) $y = x$ **b)** $y = 2x$

   c) $y = -x$ **d)** $y = -2x$

x	y
−2	
0	
2	

2. a) Use the coordinates from each table. Graph each equation in exercise 1 on the same grid. Label each line.

   b) How are the graphs alike?

   c) How are the graphs different?

3. Find the slope of each line in exercise 1.

4. Compare the slope of each line with its equation. What do you notice?

5. Each equation in exercise 1 is in $y = mx$ form. What do you think m represents?

Each *Investigation* shows that for the line $y = mx$:

- m is the slope of the line.
- The line passes through the origin O(0,0).
- When m is positive, the line rises to the right. When m is negative, the line falls to the right.
- For positive slopes, the greater the slope, the steeper the line.
- The value of y *varies directly* with the value of x. For example, if x is doubled, y is doubled. If x is tripled, y is also tripled.

TAKE NOTE

The Line $y = mx$

- The graph of the equation $y = mx$ is a straight line with slope m.
- The value of m indicates the direction and steepness of the line.
- The line $y = mx$ passes through the origin O(0, 0).
- The equation $y = mx$ represents direct variation since y varies directly with x.

We can use these results to graph a line when its equation has the form $y = mx$.

Example 1

Graph each line.

a) $y = 3x$ 　　　　　　　　　**b)** $y = -\dfrac{2}{5}x$

Solution

Each equation has the form $y = mx$, so each line passes through the origin.

a) $y = 3x$

The slope is $\dfrac{3}{1}$.

The rise is 3 and the run is 1.
Mark a point at the origin.
Move 3 up and 1 right. Mark a point.
From that point, move 3 up and 1 right again.
Mark another point.
Draw a line through the points.

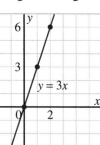

b) $y = -\frac{2}{5}x$

The slope is $-\frac{2}{5}$, or $\frac{-2}{5}$.

The rise is −2 and the run is 5.

Mark a point at the origin.

Move 2 down and 5 right. Mark a point.

From that point, move 2 down and 5 right again.

Mark another point.

Draw a line through the points.

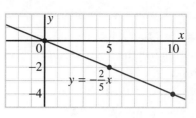

If we are given a line that passes through the origin, we can find its equation.

Example 2

Find the equation of each line.

a)

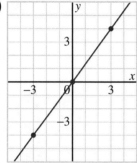

b)

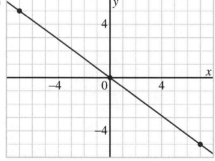

Solution

a) The line passes through the origin.
So, the equation has the form $y = mx$.
Find the slope, m, of the line.
Label any point A on the line.

The slope of segment OA is: $\dfrac{\text{rise}}{\text{run}} = \dfrac{4}{3}$

The slope of the line is equal to the slope of OA, $\dfrac{4}{3}$.

So, the equation of the line is $y = \dfrac{4}{3}x$.

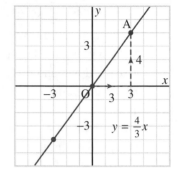

b) The line passes through the origin.
So, the equation has the form $y = mx$.
Find the slope, m, of the line.
Label point B.

The slope of segment OB is: $\dfrac{\text{rise}}{\text{run}} = \dfrac{-5}{7}$

The slope of the line is equal to the slope of OB, $-\dfrac{5}{7}$.

So, the equation of the line is $y = -\dfrac{5}{7}x$.

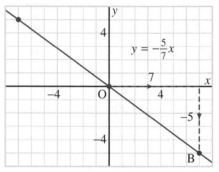

A special case of $y = mx$ occurs when $m = 0$.
The x-axis is a horizontal line. Its slope is 0.
When $m = 0$, $y = mx$ becomes $y = 0x$, or $y = 0$.

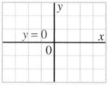

The y-axis is a vertical line. Its slope is undefined.
Each point on the y-axis has x-coordinate 0.
Its equation is $x = 0$.

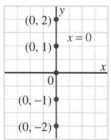

TAKE NOTE

Equations of the Axes

The x-axis has equation $y = 0$.

The y-axis has equation $x = 0$.

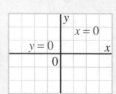

5.2   **Exercises**

A   **1.** Each equation has the form $y = mx$. State each value of m.

    a) $y = 2x$ **b)** $y = -\dfrac{1}{5}x$ **c)** $y = -x$ **d)** $y = -\dfrac{4}{3}x$

2. State the slope of each line.

    a) $y = -2x$ **b)** $y = \dfrac{1}{4}x$ **c)** $y = 10x$

    d) $y = -\dfrac{4}{7}x$ **e)** $y = 0$ **f)** $x = 0$

3. Write the equation of a line through the origin with each slope.

    a) $m = 1$ **b)** $m = -1$ **c)** $m = -\dfrac{1}{4}$

    d) $m = \dfrac{1}{3}$ **e)** $m = 0$ **f)** $m = 10$

B   **4.** Find the slope of each line, then write its equation.

a) 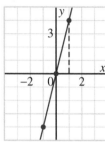   **b)** 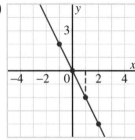   **c)**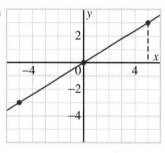

5. Find the equation of each line.

a) 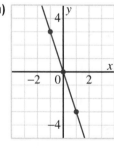   **b)** 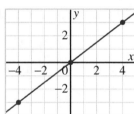   **c)**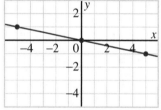

6. Knowledge/Understanding Graph each line.

    a) $y = 4x$ **b)** $y = \dfrac{7}{2}x$ **c)** $y = -\dfrac{1}{6}x$

    d) $y = -x$ **e)** $y = 0$ **f)** $x = 0$

7. a) Write the next 2 equations for each list. Graph the lines from each list on the same grid.

i) $y = 2x$

$y = 3x$

$y = 4x$

ii) $y = \frac{1}{2}x$

$y = \frac{1}{4}x$

$y = \frac{1}{6}x$

iii) $y = -x$

$y = -2x$

$y = -3x$

b) For each list, what do you notice about the lines represented by the equations?

8. Graph each line, then write its equation.

a) Every point on the line has x-coordinate 0.

b) Every point on the line has y-coordinate 0.

 9. Communicaiton Explain why a vertical line through the origin does not have the form $y = mx$.

10. Application The price of a ticket to a museum is $6. The total cost is represented by the equation $y = 6x$, where y dollars represents the total cost and x represents the number of tickets.

a) Graph $y = 6x$.

b) State the slope of the graph.

c) What does the slope tell you about the tickets?

11. Thinking/Inquiry/Problem Solving Are the lines represented by the equations $y = 0$ and $x = 0$ perpendicular? Explain how you know.

 12. • Enter these window settings.

• Use a graphing calculator to graph each line.

• Press [TRACE] and use the scroll buttons to move the cursor along the line.

• State the coordinates of two points on each line, other than the origin.

```
WINDOW
Xmin=-4.7
Xmax=4.7
Xscl=1
Ymin=-8
Ymax=8
Yscl=1
Xres=1
```

a) $y = 6x$ **b)** $y = -\frac{4}{5}x$ **c)** $y = \frac{6}{5}x$ **d)** $y = -7x$

If you have a graphing calculator, complete *Investigation 1*.
If you do not have a graphing calculator, complete *Investigation 2*.

INVESTIGATION 1

The Equation $y = mx + b$

Set-up

- Press [WINDOW]. Enter these settings.
- Press [Y=]. Use the scroll buttons and [CLEAR] to clear all equations.
- If Plot1, Plot2, and Plot3 are highlighted, use the scroll buttons and [ENTER] to remove the highlighting.

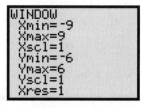

1. Make sure the cursor is beside $Y_1 =$.
   To enter the equation $y = x + 1$, press [X,T,θ,n] [+] 1.

   Graph each equation on the same screen.

   $y = 2x + 1$
   $y = -x + 1$
   $y = 3x + 1$

2. a) How are the graphs in exercise 1 alike?

   b) How are they different?

3. Each equation in exercise 1 has the form $y = mx + b$.

   a) What does m represent?

   b) What do you think b represents?

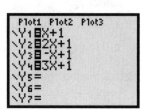

4. Press [Y=]. Clear all equations. Graph $y = x$.

5. Graph each equation on the same screen.

   $y = x + 1$ $\qquad$ $y = x + 3$ $\qquad$ $y = x - 2$

6. How are the graphs in exercises 4 and 5 similar? How are they different?

7. Each equation in exercise 5 has the form $y = mx + b$. Compare the equation and the graph of each line. What does b represent?

Using Grid Paper to Investigate $y = mx + b$

1. Copy and complete this table of values for each equation.

   a) $y = x + 1$ b) $y = 2x + 1$

   c) $y = -x + 1$ d) $y = 3x + 1$

x	y
−2	
0	
2	

2. Graph the equations in exercise 1 on the same grid. Label each line.

   a) How are the graphs alike?

   b) How are they different?

3. Each equation in exercise 1 has the form $y = mx + b$.

   a) What does m represent?

   b) What do you think b represents?

4. Copy and complete this table of values for each equation.

   a) $y = x + 1$ b) $y = x + 3$ c) $y = x - 2$

x	y
−2	
0	
2	

5. Graph each equation in exercise 4 on the same grid. Label each line.

   a) How are the graphs alike?

   b) How are they different?

6. Each equation in exercise 4 has the form $y = mx + b$. Compare the equation and the graph of each line. What does b represent?

Each *Investigation* shows that for the line $y = mx + b$:

- m is the slope of the line.

- b is the y-intercept; that is, the y-coordinate of the point where the line crosses the y-axis.

- The value of y *varies partially* with the value of x.

- The graph does not go through the origin.

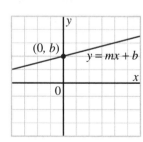

Consider the equation $y = 2x + 3$. The slope of the graph is 2. The y-intercept is 3; so, the graph crosses the y-axis at $(0, 3)$.

$$y = 2x + 3$$

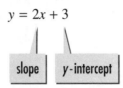

slope y-intercept

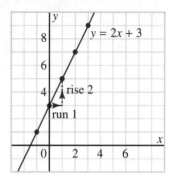

The equation $y = mx + b$ is called the *slope y-intercept form* of the equation of a line.

The Line $y = mx + b$

- The graph of $y = mx + b$ is a straight line with slope m and y-intercept b.
- The equation $y = mx + b$ represents *partial variation*.

We can graph an equation in this form without making a table of values.

Example 1

Graph each line.

a) $y = \frac{2}{3}x - 5$ **b)** $y = -2x + 4$

Solution

a) $y = \frac{2}{3}x - 5$

The slope is $\frac{2}{3}$. The rise is 2 and the run is 3.
The y-intercept is -5 with coordinates $(0, -5)$.
Begin at $(0, -5)$. Move 2 up and 3 right.
Mark a point. Find points on the line by continuing
2 up and 3 right or moving 2 down and 3 left.
Join the points.

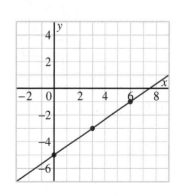

b) $y = -2x + 4$

The slope is -2, or $\frac{-2}{1}$. The rise is -2 and the run is 1.
The y-intercept is 4.
Begin at (0, 4). Move 2 down and 1 right.
Mark a point. Find other points on the line by
continuing 2 down and 1 right, or moving
2 up and 1 left. Join the points.

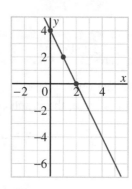

Discuss

In what direction do you move for a positive rise? a negative rise?
In what direction do you move for a positive run? a negative run?

We can also find the equation of a line in the slope y-intercept form when its
graph is given.

Example 2

Find the equation of each line.

a)

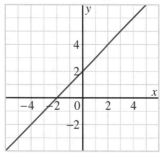

b)

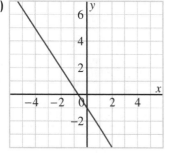

Solution

Read the y-intercept and slope from the graph.
Each equation has the form $y = mx + b$.

a) The y-intercept is 2. Mark a point at $(0, 2)$.
Locate another point with integer coordinates.
The slope is 1.
The equation is $y = 1x + 2$, or $y = x + 2$.

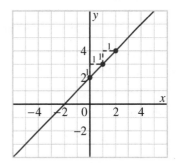

b) The y-intercept is −1. Mark a point at $(0, -1)$.
Locate another point with integer coordinates.
The slope is $-\dfrac{3}{2}$.
The equation is $y = -\dfrac{3}{2}x - 1$.

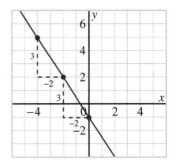

A special case occurs for $y = mx + b$ when $m = 0$.
When $m = 0$, $y = mx + b$ becomes $y = 0x + b$, or $y = b$.
The line $y = b$ is a horizontal line with y-intercept b.
For example, $y = 3$ is a horizontal line with y-intercept 3.
And, $y = -2$ is a horizontal line with y-intercept −2.

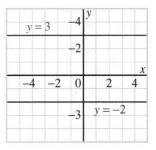

Another special case occurs for vertical lines.
A vertical line has a slope that is undefined.
So, its equation does not have the form $y = mx + b$.

For example, consider the vertical line with x-intercept 2.
Each point on the line has x-coordinate 2.
So, the equation of the line $x = 2$.

Similarly, a vertical line with x-intercept −3 has
equation $x = -3$.

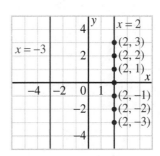

Equations of Horizontal and Vertical Lines

A horizontal line has equation $y = b$,
where b is the y-intercept.

A vertical line has equation $x = a$,
where a is the x-intercept.

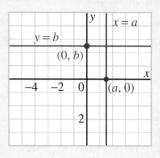

5.4　　Exercises

1. Each equation has the form $y = mx + b$. State each value of m and b.

　　a) $y = 3x + 5$　　　**b)** $y = -2x + 3$　　　**c)** $y = \frac{2}{5}x - 4$　　　**d)** $y = -\frac{1}{2}x + 6$

2. State the slope and y-intercept for each line.

　　a) $y = -4x - 7$　　　**b)** $y = \frac{3}{8}x - 5$　　　**c)** $y = \frac{4}{3}x - 2$　　　**d)** $y = \frac{9}{5}x + 1$

3. Write the equation of the line with each slope and y-intercept.

　　a) $m = 2$, $b = 3$　　　　　**b)** $m = -1$, $b = 4$　　　　　**c)** $m = \frac{2}{3}$, $b = -1$

　　d) $m = -\frac{4}{5}$, $b = 8$　　　**e)** $m = -3$, $b = \frac{5}{2}$　　　**f)** $m = 0$, $b = 3$

4. State the y-intercept of each line.

　　a)
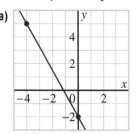
　　b)
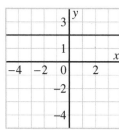
　　c)
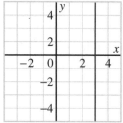

5. a) For each line, find the slope and y-intercept.

　　i)
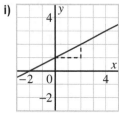
　　ii)
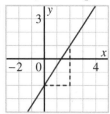

　　iii)
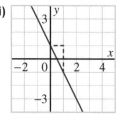

　　b) State the equation of each line in part a.

6. Find the equation of each line.

a)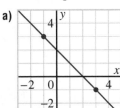
b)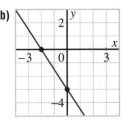
c)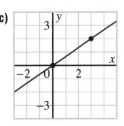

7. Graph each line.

a) $y = \frac{2}{3}x + 3$
b) $y = \frac{3}{4}x - 2$
c) $y = -\frac{1}{2}x + 1$

8. Graph each line.

a) $y = -\frac{3}{2}x - 1$
b) $y = x - 3$
c) $y = -3x + 2$

9. Graph each line.

a) $y = 1$
b) $x = 4$
c) $y = -6$
d) $x = -3$

10. Knowledge/Understanding

a) Graph the line $y = -\frac{1}{2}x + 3$.

b) What are the coordinates of the point where the line intersects the x-axis?

11. a) Graph the lines $y = 2x + 4$ and $y = -x + 7$.

b) What are the coordinates of the point where the lines intersect?

12. Application The equations of the 3 sides of a triangle are $y = 2x - 4$, $y = -\frac{1}{2}x + 6$, and $y = -3x + 1$.

a) Graph the lines on the same grid.

b) Find the coordinates of the vertices of the triangle.

13. Graph each line, then write its equation.

a) Every point on the line has the x-coordinate 9.

b) Every point on the line has the y-coordinate -8.

14. Communication Maria graphed the equation $y = 3x - 2$ on a grid. When she checked with a classmate, she realized her graph was different. Is Maria's graph correct? If so, explain how you know. If not, explain what Maria did incorrectly.

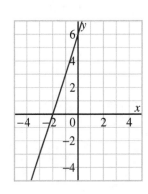

15. a) Identify the pattern in the values of m and b in each list.

  i) $y = 2x + 4$

  $y = x + 3$

  $y = 0x + 2$

  $y = -x + 1$

  $y = -2x + 0$

  ii) $y = 2x - 6$

  $y = x - 3$

  $y = 0.5x - 1.5$

  $y = -0.5x + 1.5$

  $y = -x + 3$

  $y = -2x + 6$

b) Graph the lines in each list on the same grid. Describe what you see.

16. a) Describe the patterns in the values of m and b in these equations.

  $y = x + 1$

  $y = 2x + 0.5$

  $y = 0.5x + 2$

  $y = -x - 1$

  $y = -2x - 0.5$

  $y = -0.5x - 2$

b) Plot the 6 graphs on the same grid. Describe what you see.

17. Use a graphing calculator. Set the window as shown. Graph each line on the same screen. Sketch the graphs.

a) $y = -2x + 7$

b) $y = \frac{2}{5}x - 1$

c) $y = -\frac{4}{3}x - 5$

d) $y = -3x + 4$

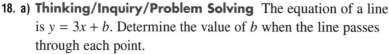

```
WINDOW
Xmin=-9.4
Xmax=9.4
Xscl=1
Ymin=-10
Ymax=10
Yscl=1
Xres=1
```

18. a) Thinking/Inquiry/Problem Solving The equation of a line is $y = 3x + b$. Determine the value of b when the line passes through each point.

  i) R(2, 1) **ii)** K(−1, 4) **iii)** A(3, −2)

b) Choose one point from part a. Explain how you determined the value of b.

19. Make a prediction about either the y- or x-intercept for the graphs of the equations in each list. Give reasons for your predictions. Use a calculator to check your predictions.

a) $y = x + 3$

  $y = 2x + 3$

  $y = 3x + 3$

  $y = 4x + 3$

b) $y = x$

  $y = 2x$

  $y = 3x$

  $y = 4x$

c) $y = x + 3$

  $y = 2x + 6$

  $y = 3x + 9$

  $y = 4x + 12$

1. On a grid, draw a line through each point with each given slope.

    a) O(0, 0), slope $\frac{1}{4}$ **b)** F(−4, −1), slope −3

2. Graph the line through each point with the given slope. Write the coordinates of 2 more points on each line.

    a) C(−2, 3), slope $-\frac{4}{3}$ **b)** D(0, 1), slope 2

3. Draw a line through J(−1, 3) with each slope. Find the coordinates of 2 more points on each line.

    a) $\frac{3}{2}$ **b)** −2   **c)** 1   **d)** $\frac{1}{5}$ **e)** $-\frac{2}{3}$

4. Write the equation of a line passing through the origin with each slope.

    a) $m = 3$ **b)** $m = -1$ **c)** $m = -\frac{1}{2}$ **d)** $m = 0$

5. Graph each line.

    a) $y = x$ **b)** $y = -\frac{4}{3}x$ **c)** $y = -5x$ **d)** $y = -\frac{1}{5}x$

6. Write the equation of a line with each slope and y-intercept.

    a) $m = -3, b = -1$ **b)** $m = \frac{1}{2}, b = 2$ **c)** $m = -\frac{3}{5}, b = -4$

7. Find the equation of each line.

    a) 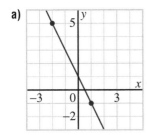   **b)** 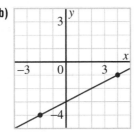   **c)**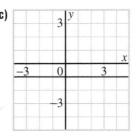

8. Graph each line.

    a) $y = -\frac{3}{4}x - 2$ **b)** $y = 3x + 3$ **c)** $y = -x - 1$ **d)** $y = \frac{1}{3}x - 5$

Preparation for Ontario Testing

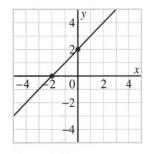

9. Which equation best represents this graph?

    a) $y = 2$

    b) $x = 2$

    c) $x = -2$

    d) $y = x + 2$

We can use the equation $y = mx + b$ to write the equation of a line if we know its slope, m, and its y-intercept, b.

The coordinates of all the points on a line satisfy its equation. That means we can substitute the x-coordinate and y-coordinate of a point into the equation. Once evaluated, the result for the left side equals the result for the right side.

For example, the point C(8, 5) lies on the line $y = \frac{1}{2}x + 1$.

Substitute $x = 8$ and $y = 5$ into the equation $y = \frac{1}{2}x + 1$.

Left side = y Right side = $\frac{1}{2}x + 1$
      = 5   = $\frac{1}{2}(8) + 1$
                                = $4 + 1$
                                = 5

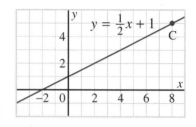

Since left side = right side, the coordinates (8, 5) satisfy the equation of the line.

We can graph a line and find its equation by using other information about the line.

Given the slope and a point on the line

For a given slope, there is only one line that passes through a given point.

Example 1

---

a) Graph the line with slope $-\frac{1}{2}$ that passes through the point A(4, 1).

b) Find the equation of the line.

c) Check that the coordinates of A satisfy the equation of the line.

Solution

a) The slope is $-\frac{1}{2}$, or $\frac{-1}{2}$.

   So, the rise is -1 and the run is 2.
   Plot point A(4, 1).
   From A, move 1 down and 2 right. Mark point B.
   Move 1 down and 2 right again. Mark point C.
   Draw a line through the points.

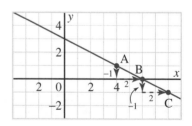

b) Let the equation of the line be $y = mx + b$.

   To write the equation of the line, we need m, the slope, and b, the y-intercept.

   Since the slope is $-\frac{1}{2}$, $m = -\frac{1}{2}$.

From the graph, the y-intercept is 3, so $b = 3$.

The equation of the line is $y = -\dfrac{1}{2}x + 3$.

c) Substitute $x = 4$ and $y = 1$ into the equation $y = -\dfrac{1}{2}x + 3$.

Left side $= y$　　　　　Right side $= -\dfrac{1}{2}x + 3$

$\qquad\quad = 1$　　　　　　　　　　　$= -\dfrac{1}{2}(4) + 3$

$\qquad\qquad\qquad\qquad\qquad\qquad\ = -2 + 3$

$\qquad\qquad\qquad\qquad\qquad\qquad\ = 1$

Since left side = right side, the coordinates of A satisfy the equation of the line.

Given two points on the line

There is only one line that passes through 2 given points.

Example 2

Find the equation of the line that passes through the points A$(-2, -1)$ and C$(2, 5)$.

Solution

Plot A and C. Join them with a line.
Let the equation of the line be $y = mx + b$.
Find the slope and y-intercept from the graph.
From the graph,

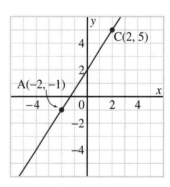

the slope is $\dfrac{\text{rise}}{\text{run}} = \dfrac{6}{4}$

$\qquad\qquad\quad = \dfrac{3}{2}$

So, $m = \dfrac{3}{2}$

The y-intercept is 2, so $b = 2$.
Substitute for m and b in $y = mx + b$.

The equation of the line is $y = \dfrac{3}{2}x + 2$.

A 1. The slope, m, and y-intercept, b, of a line are given. Write the equation of each line.

a) $m = 4$ **b)** $m = -2$ **c)** $m = -\dfrac{2}{3}$ **d)** $m = \dfrac{7}{4}$

    $b = 3$ $b = \dfrac{1}{2}$ $b = \dfrac{3}{4}$ $b = -\dfrac{1}{4}$

2. The coordinates of the y-intercept and the slope of a line are given. Write the equation of each line.

a) y-int $(0, -3)$, slope 5   **b)** y-int $(0, 4)$, slope -2 **c)** y-int $(0, -6)$, slope $\dfrac{2}{3}$

3. Point A is marked on each line.

a) Write the coordinates of A.

b) Find the slope of the line from the graph.

c) Find the y-intercept from the graph.

d) Write the equation of the line.

i) 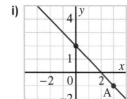   **ii)** 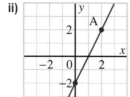   **iii)**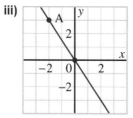

4. Points A and B are marked on each line.

a) Write the coordinates of A and B.

b) Find the slope of AB.

c) Find the y-intercept from the graph.

d) Write the equation of the line.

i) 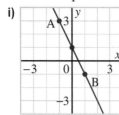   **ii)** 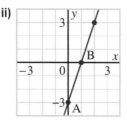   **iii)**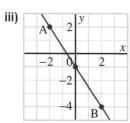

5. Find the equation of each line.

a) 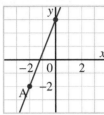   **b)** 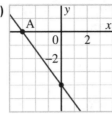   **c)**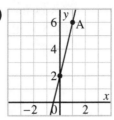

6. Find each equation.

a) 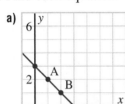   **b)** 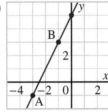   **c)**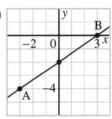

7. The coordinates of a point and the slope of a line are given.
   i) Graph each line.
   ii) Write each equation.
   a) A(2, 5), slope 3   **b)** R(–4, 2), slope $-\dfrac{1}{2}$ **c)** K(4, –6), slope –3

8. Which points lie on the line $y = 3x + 6$?
   a) A(3, 15)   **b)** B(–4, 0)   **c)** C(0, 6)
   d) E(–2, 0)   **e)** F(–2, 3)   **f)** G(–1, 3)

9. Which lines pass through the point (–4, 2)?
   a) $y = -x$ **b)** $y = x + 6$ **c)** $y = 3x + 14$ **d)** $y = -2x + 2$

10. The coordinates of a point and the slope of a line are given.
   i) Graph each line.
   ii) Write the equation of each line.
   iii) Check that the coordinates of the point satisfy the equation.
   a) G(1, 4), slope –2   **b)** H(–5, –6), slope 1   **c)** J(–2, 5), slope $\dfrac{1}{2}$

11. The coordinates of 2 points are given.
   i) Draw a line through the points.
   ii) Write the equation of the line.
   a) B(3, 0), C(–1, –8)   **b)** D(–2, 4), E(1, –5)   **c)** F(–3, –2), G(–1, 6)

12. Knowledge/Understanding The coordinates of 2 points are given.
   i) Draw a line through the points.
   ii) Write the equation of the line.
   a) H(2, 5), J(–2, –1)   **b)** K(0, –4), L(10, 0)   **c)** P(–2, 5), Q(2, –7)

✓ **13. Application** The equation $y = mx + b$ represents a line with slope m and y-intercept b. So, the line passes through $(0, b)$.

a) Graph the line through $(0, 5)$ with each slope.

i) 3	ii) 2	iii) 1	iv) 0
v) -1	vi) -2	vii) -3	

b) Find the y-intercept of each line in part a.

c) Write the equation of each line in part a. When you notice a pattern, use it to write the remaining equations.

d) Describe the pattern in the equations.

14. Communication To find the equation of a line, you need 2 facts about it. List as many pairs of facts as you can that determine a line. Use examples and exercises in this chapter for ideas.

15. To visit the Ontario Science Centre and see one movie, the cost is $220 for 20 visitors and $330 for 30 visitors. These costs are represented by the points $(20, 220)$ and $(30, 330)$.

a) Draw the line through points $(20, 220)$ and $(30, 330)$.

b) Use the graph to estimate the cost for each group of visitors.

i) 25	ii) 17	iii) 48

c) Let C dollars represent the cost and n represent the number of visitors. Write the equation for the cost of a group visit to the Science Centre.

d) Use the equation to calculate the cost for each group in part b.

e) Compare estimates from part b with calculations from part d. What are advantages of using the graph? What are advantages of using the equation? What are advantages of comparing results from both?

16. Thinking/Inquiry/Problem Solving

a) i) Graph the line through K$(-4, 4)$ with slope $-\frac{2}{3}$.

ii) To find the approximate y-intercept, read the integer closest to the y-intercept on the graph. Write the equation of the line with the slope and approximate y-intercept.

iii) Graph the line for your equation on the same grid. Does this line pass through K$(-4, 4)$ with slope $-\frac{2}{3}$? Is it close?

iv) Check whether the coordinates of K satisfy your equation. Does your equation represent a line through K with slope $-\frac{2}{3}$? Does it represent a line that passes close to K with slope $-\frac{2}{3}$?

v) Explain why your equation is an estimate of the equation of the line through K$(-4, 4)$ with slope $-\frac{2}{3}$.

b) Use a similar method as in part a to estimate the equation of a line through M$(-3, 0)$ and N$(5, 6)$.

Many relations in business and science are linear relations. The slope and intercepts of the graphs of these relations represent different things. Variables other than x and y may be used.

When graphing variables other than x and y, plot the *dependent variable* vertically. Plot the *independent variable* horizontally.

TAKE NOTE

Dependent and Independent Variables

Dependent Variable: the output of a relation; often denoted y

Independent Variable: the input of a relation; often denoted x

Example 1

Sam sells computers and earns 5% commission on her sales.
Her commission, C dollars, varies directly with her sales, s dollars.
The equation is $C = 0.05s$.

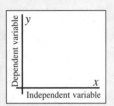

a) Make a table of values for the relation.

b) Graph the relation.

c) Use the graph.
   i) What is Sam's commission on sales of $8000?
   ii) Sam earns $200 commission. What are her sales?

d) Suppose Sam's commission increases to 10%.
   How would the graph change?

e) Suppose Sam's commission decreases to 3%.
   How would the graph change?

Solution

a) Substitute some values for s into the equation $C = 0.05s$.
   Calculate the corresponding values of C.

   When $s = 0$, $C = 0.05(0)$
   $\qquad\qquad\quad = 0$

   When $s = 3000$, $C = 0.05(3000)$
   $\qquad\qquad\qquad\quad = 150$

   When $s = 6000$, $C = 0.05(6000)$
   $\qquad\qquad\qquad\quad = 300$

s ($)	C ($)
0	0
3000	150
6000	300

b) Plot the data from the table. Since the variable C is used instead of y, plot C vertically. Extend the graph to include $s = 8000$ because that value is needed in part c.

c) i) From 8000 on the s-axis, draw a vertical line to the graph. Then draw a horizontal line to the C-axis. This line meets the C-axis at 400. Sam earns $400 commission on sales of $8000.

   ii) From 200 on the C-axis, draw a horizontal line to the graph. Then draw a vertical line to the s-axis. This line meets the s-axis at 4000. Sam has sales of $4000 to earn a commission of $200.

d) If Sam's commission increases to 10%, she will earn more commission. The graph would still pass through the origin, but all other points would be higher. The slope of the graph would be steeper.

e) If Sam's commission decreases to 3%, she will earn less commission. The graph would still pass through the origin, but all other points would be lower. The slope of the graph would be less steep.

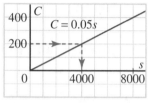

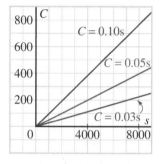

Discuss

Does the graph illustrate direct variation or partial variation? Explain. What are the slope and C-intercept for the line?

Example 2

When you exercise, your pulse should not exceed a maximum rate. The relation between the maximum rate and your age is represented by the equation $p = 220 - a$, where p is the number of beats per minute and a is your age in years.

a) Make a table of values for the equation $p = 220 - a$, for ages between 18 and 50.

b) Graph p against a.

c) Find the slope of the line. What does the slope represent?

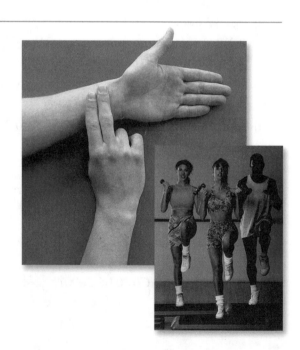

Solution

a) Substitute some values of a in the equation $p = 220 - a$.
Find the corresponding values of p.

When $a = 18$, $p = 220 - 18$
$\qquad = 202$

When $a = 25$, $p = 220 - 25$
$\qquad = 195$

When $a = 40$, $p = 220 - 40$
$\qquad = 180$

When $a = 50$, $p = 220 - 50$
$\qquad = 170$

Age, a (years)	Maximum pulse, p (beats/min)
18	202
25	195
40	180
50	170

b) Plot the data. Since the variable p is used instead of y, plot p vertically.

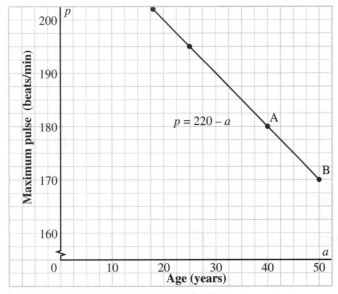

c) The graph is a straight line. Choose any 2 points on the line,
such as A(40, 180) and B(50, 170).

Slope of AB $= \dfrac{\text{rise}}{\text{run}}$

$\qquad = \dfrac{-10}{10}$

$\qquad = -1$

The slope of the line is -1.

The slope is negative. So, as age increases, the maximum pulse decreases.
Since the slope is -1, for each year increase in age, the maximum pulse
decreases by 1 beat/minute.

Discuss

What would a positive slope show? Explain.

A 1. State the slope of each line.

　　a) $m = 60n$　　　　　b) $T = 1.15c$　　　　　c) $E = 16h$

✓ 2. State the slope and vertical intercept for each line.

　　a) $E = 19s + 15$　　　b) $C = 145 + 9t$　　　c) $m = 159 + 25n$

✓ 3. State whether each equation illustrates direct variation or partial variation. How do you know?

　　a) $C = 100 + 20n$　　b) $C = 60n$　　　　　c) $C = 8n + 240$

　　d) $C = 315n$　　　　　e) $C = 1000n$　　　　f) $C = 125n + 5$

✓ 4. State whether each graph illustrates direct variation or partial variation. How do you know?

a) 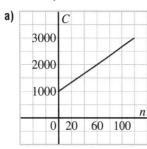　　b) 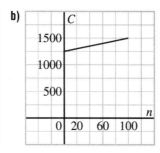　　c)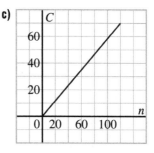

B 5. **Knowledge/Understanding** A child receives a weekly allowance
✓　　from age 6 to 16. The allowance is $1 per week the first year. It increases by
　　$1 each year. The weekly allowance, a dollars, is related to the age, n years,
　　by the equation $a = n - 5$.

　　a) Copy and complete this table.

n (years)	6	8	10	12	14	16
a ($)						

　　b) Graph the data. Plot n horizontally and a vertically.

　　c) Does it make sense to join the points? Explain why.

　　d) What is the slope? What does it represent?

　　e) Extend the graph to find the weekly allowance the child would receive
　　　　at age 18.

6. This table shows the cost of processing a roll of film. The cost, C dollars, is related to the number of photos, n, by the equation $C = \frac{1}{4}n + 2$.

Numbers of photos, n	Cost, C ($)
12	5.00
24	8.00
36	11.00

a) Graph C against n.

b) Does it make sense to join the points? Explain why.

c) What is the slope? What does it represent?

d) Use the graph to find the cost to process 48 photos.

7. Turkeys are cooked at an oven temperature of 165°C. For turkeys between 3 kg and 8 kg, the cooking time is 30 min per kilogram. The time, t hours, is related to the mass, k kilograms, by this equation: $t = \frac{1}{2}k$.

a) Copy and complete this table.

k (kg)	3	4	5	6	7	8
t (h)						

b) Graph t against k.

c) Does it make sense to join the points? Explain why.

d) What is the slope? What does it represent?

e) Turkeys larger than 8 kg need less cooking time per kilogram. How would the graph change for these turkeys?

f) Turkeys with stuffing need more cooking time per kilogram. How would the graph change for stuffed turkeys?

8. **Thinking/Inquiry/Problem Solving** The yearbook club is choosing a company to print the school yearbook. Blue Heron Yearbooks charges $8000 for set-up and $4 per copy. The equation that represents this relation is $C = 8000 + 4n$, where C is the cost in dollars and n is the number of books printed. Miles Ahead Yearbooks charges $8400 for set-up and $3 per copy. The equation that represents this relation is $C = 8400 + 3n$. Which company charges less? Explain.

9. **Application** A car travels at an average speed of 80 km/h from Hearst to Nipigon. The towns are 400 km apart. The distance, d kilometres, from Nipigon after t hours of driving is given by the equation $d = 400 - 80t$.

a) Copy and complete this table.

t (h)	0	1	2	3	4	5
d (km)						

b) Graph d against t.

c) Does it make sense to join the points? Explain why.

d) What is the slope? What does it represent?

e) Suppose the average speed increased. How would the graph change?

f) Suppose the average speed decreased. How would the graph change?

g) What is the d-intercept? What does it represent?

h) Suppose a longer route was taken. How would the graph change?

i) Suppose a shorter route was taken. How would the graph change?

10. **Communication** Find an exercise in this section that illustrates direct variation and another that illustrates partial variation. Explain how the equations, tables, and graphs show whether each relation illustrates direct or partial variation.

11. The trip from Toronto to the cross-country running provincial finals in Ottawa costs $1940 for the bus and $80 per runner for meals and accommodation. The cost, C dollars, is modelled by the equation $C = 1940 + 80n$, where n represents the number of runners.

a) Copy and complete this table.

n	0	10	20	30	40	50
C ($)						

b) Graph the relation.

c) Does it make sense to join the points? Explain why.

d) What is the C-intercept? What does it represent?

e) What is the slope? What does it represent?

f) Use the graph to estimate the cost for each number of runners.
   i) 25   ii) 12   iii) 48

g) Suppose the runners stay with local families so the cost per runner is reduced to $32. How would the graph and equation change?

h) Suppose the cost of the bus is covered by fundraising. So, the only expense is $80 per runner. How would the graph and equation change?

We can use the description of a linear relation to write an equation to represent it.

Example 1

A banquet hall charges $40 per person for a reception. Let C dollars represent the total cost and n represent the number of people attending.

a) Write an equation to relate C and n.

b) Graph the relation.

c) Find the slope and the C-intercept.

d) What does the slope tell us?

Solution

a) In words, the equation is:
Total cost = $40 × number of people
Using algebra, the equation is:
$C = 40n$

b) *Using a graphing calculator*
Use the indicated window settings, which assume a maximum of 100 people will attend. To find the cost for 100 people, substitute $n = 100$ in the equation.
When $n = 100$, $C = 40(100)$
$$= 4000$$

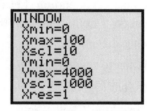

Press [Y=]. Use the scroll button and [CLEAR] to delete any previous equations.
Press: 40 [X,T,θ,n] [GRAPH]

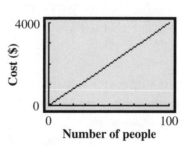

Using grid paper
Choose 2 values of n. Find each corresponding cost.
When $n = 0$, $C = 40(0)$
$$= 0$$
When $n = 100$, $C = 40(100)$
$$= 4000$$

Draw axes on grid paper. Label the horizontal axis n and the vertical axis C. Plot the points (0, 0) and (100, 4000). Join the points with a straight line. Label the graph with its equation.

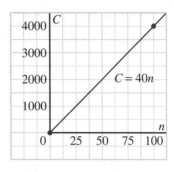

c) For the equation $C = 40n$, the slope is 40 and the C-intercept is 0.

d) The slope tells us that the cost increases by $40 per person.

Discuss

How would the graph change if the cost per person decreased?

In *Example 1*, C varies directly with n. Recall that the graph of a direct variation relation is a straight line through the origin. The equation has the form $y = mx$; in this case, $C = 40n$.

Example 2

To hold a banquet, it costs $1000 to rent the hall, plus $25 for each person attending. Let C dollars represent the total cost. Let n represent the number of people attending.

a) Write an equation to relate C and n.

b) Graph the relation.

c) Find the slope and the C-intercept.

d) What do the rise, run, and slope represent?

e) What does the C-intercept tell us?

Solution

a) C represents the total cost in dollars and n represents the number of people attending. In words, the equation is:
Total cost = $25 × number of people + $1000
Using algebra, the equation is:
$C = 25n + 1000$.

b) *Using a graphing calculator*
Use the window settings from *Example 1*.
Press [Y=]. Use the scroll buttons and [CLEAR] to delete any previous equations.
Press: 25 [X,T,θ,n] [+] 1000 [GRAPH]

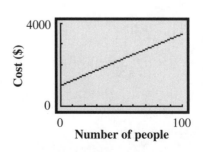

Using grid paper

Choose 2 values of n and find the corresponding costs.

When $n = 0$, $C = 25(0) + 1000$
$$= 1000$$

When $n = 100$, $C = 25(100) + 1000$
$$= 3500$$

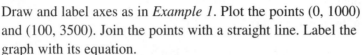

Draw and label axes as in *Example 1*. Plot the points (0, 1000) and (100, 3500). Join the points with a straight line. Label the graph with its equation.

c) Use the equation $C = 25n + 1000$.

Compare the equation with $y = mx + b$.

The slope, m, is 25 and the C-intercept, b, is 1000.

d) The rise is the change in total cost in dollars.
The run is the change in the number of people attending the banquet.
The slope represents the cost increase of $25 per person.

e) The C-intercept is the fixed cost; that is, the rent for the hall.
The fixed cost is $1000.

Discuss

How would the graph change if the $1000 rent increased? decreased?
How would the graph change if the $25 per person increased? decreased?

In *Example 2*, C varies partially with n. Recall that the graph of a partial variation relation is a straight line that does not pass through the origin. The equation has the form $y = mx + b$; in this case, $C = 25n + 1000$.

5.7   Exercises

1. What does each variable in the equations below represent?

   a) Paul earns 4% commission on his sales. The equation is $C = 0.04s$.

   b) The federal government charges 7% GST on goods and services.
   The equation is $T = 0.07c$.

   c) A bus is travelling at a constant rate of 55 km/h. The equation is $d = 55t$.

   d) The length of time to set up is 100 min. The time to paint each poster is
   20 min. The equation is $t = 100 + 20n$.

✓ **2.** Let T dollars represent the total cost and d days represent the rental time. Write an equation to relate the variables.

    a) A rental agency charges $31/day for a small car.

    b) A room in a hotel costs $134/day.

    c) A room in a different hotel costs $239/day.

    d) Renting a popcorn machine costs $90/day.

    e) Renting a tent that is 6 m by 6 m costs $160 plus $305/day.

3. A car is driven on the highway at an average speed of 65 km/h. Let d kilometres represent the distance travelled in h hours. Write an equation to relate the variables.

✓ **4.** Let C dollars represent the total cost and h hours represent the length of rental time. Write an equation for each situation.

    a) At the least expensive times, the cost of renting Lakeside Arena is $86/h.

    b) At the most expensive times, the cost of renting Lakeside Arena is $164/h.

    c) Another arena charges a rental fee of $110 plus $95/h.

✓ **5.** State whether each relation illustrates a direct variation or a partial variation. How do you know?

a) 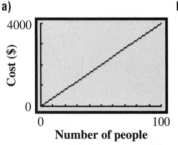   **b)** 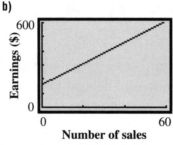   **c)**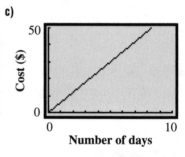

6. Knowledge/Understanding The table shows the production of cans at a soft drink company. The number of cans produced, C, is related to d, the number of days of production.

    a) Write an equation to relate C and d.

    b) Graph this relation.

    c) How many cans will be produced on day 10?

Day, d	Number of cans produced, C
1	4000
2	4200
3	4400
4	4600
5	4800

✓ **7. Communication** Compare the costs to have a banquet in *Examples 1* and *2*. Which hall would you choose? Explain your choice.

8. The mass of each candy in a box is 5 g. The mass of the empty box is 20 g. Let t grams represent the total mass of the box and candies. Let n represent the number of candies.

a) Write an equation to relate t and n.

b) Graph the relation.

c) Find the slope and the t-intercept.

d) What does the t-intercept represent?

e) What does the slope represent? What are the units for the slope?

f) How would the graph change in each situation?
   i) The mass of each candy is 7 g.   **ii)** The mass of the box is 30 g.

g) Write the equation for each situation in part f.

9. A tanker truck contains crude oil. The mass of an empty truck is 14 000 kg. The mass of one barrel of oil is 180 kg. Let T kilograms represents the total mass of the truck and the oil. Let b represent the number of barrels of oil.

a) Write an equation to relate T and b.

b) Graph the relation.

c) Find the slope and the T-intercept.

d) What does the T-intercept represent?

e) What does the slope represent? What are the units for the slope?

f) How would the graph and the equation change for a heavier truck?

✓ **10. Application** The average temperature of Earth's surface is 20°C. For every kilometre below the surface, the temperature increases by 10°C. Let T°C represent the temperature at a depth of d kilometres.

a) Write an equation to relate T and d.

b) Graph the relation.

c) Find the slope and the T-intercept.

d) What does the T-intercept represent?

e) What does the slope represent? What are the units for the slope?

f) How would the graph change in each situation?
   i) The surface temperature is 5°C.   **ii)** The surface temperature is 40°C.

g) Write the equation for each situation in part f.

11. Thinking/Inquiry/Problem Solving The cost of organizing a concert in the park is $12 000. Each ticket costs $25. Let t represent the number of tickets sold, and P dollars represent the promoter's profit.

a) How many tickets must be sold to break even?

b) How is this shown on a graph of P against t?

12. The boiling point of water, $T°C$, depends upon h, the height in kilometres above sea level. The boiling point at sea level is 100°C. For every kilometre above sea level, the boiling point decreases by approximately 3.4°C.

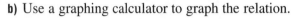

a) Write an equation to relate T and h.

b) Use a graphing calculator to graph the relation.

c) Find the slope and the T-intercept.

d) What does the T-intercept represent?

e) What does the slope represent? What are the units for the slope?

f) The world's highest mountain is Mt. Everest at 8848 m. Use TRACE to find the temperature at which water boils at the top of Mt. Everest.

13. The amount of batter mix for pancakes varies directly with the number of people who eat breakfast. It takes 4 cups of batter mix to serve 6 people.

a) Create a table of values.

b) Graph the relation.

c) How many cups of batter mix are needed for 30 people?

d) How many people can be served with 12 cups of batter mix?

e) Suppose you use a mix that requires 5 cups of batter mix for 8 people. How would the graph change?

14. Riverdale Collegiate is planning an athletic banquet. The community centre charges a fixed cost of $200 plus $5 per guest. Let T dollars represent the total cost. Let g represent the number of guests.

a) Write an equation to relate T and g.

b) Graph the relation.

c) Find the slope and the T-intercept.

d) What does the slope represent?

e) What does the T-intercept represent?

f) Use the graph to estimate each cost.
   i) 45 guests attend   ii) 52 guests attend   iii) 81 guests attend

g) Use the equation to calculate each cost. Check by comparing your results with estimates from part f.
   i) 47 guests attend   ii) 50 guests attend   iii) 79 guests attend

h) Suppose the cost was $2 more per guest. How would the graph and the equation change?

i) Is this relation best represented by an equation, a table of values, a graph, or a description in words? Justify your opinion.

5.8   Setting Up for a Banquet

On page 190, you saw different arrangements for tables and chairs for a banquet or some other function. One company uses rules to estimate the number of chairs and tables needed. To use these rules, the area of the room must be in square feet. (One square metre is approximately 10 square feet.)

Gathering Data

1. Estimate or measure the area, in square metres, of these rooms in your school.

   a) your classroom   **b)** the cafeteria

2. The approximate dimensions of some rooms in the Royal York Hotel in Toronto are given. Assume each room is rectangular. Calculate the area of each room.

   a) Canadian Room   length: 187 ft   width: 71 ft

   b) Imperial Room   length: 96 ft   width: 63 ft

   c) Manitoba Room   length: 55 ft   width: 22 ft

3. Multiply the areas of the rooms in exercise 1 by 10.76 to convert the areas to square feet. Copy this table. Complete the *Area* column. You will complete the other columns in the exercises that follow.

Room	Area (sq. ft.)	Number of people		
		Theatre style	Oblong table	Round table
Classroom				
Cafeteria				
Canadian Room				
Imperial Room				
Manitoba Room				

The Theatre Style Model

The rule for theatre style:

For the number of people, divide the room area (in square feet) by 6.

4. a) Let x represent the room area in square feet.
   Let y represent the number of people who can be seated.
   Use the rule to write an equation for y in terms of x for this model.

   b) Graph the equation.

5. a) Determine how many people can be seated in each room in exercise 3. Enter the results in the 3rd column of the table.

   b) Are the results for the rooms in your school reasonable? Explain.

The Oblong Table Model

The rule for oblong tables:

For the number of people, divide the room area (in square feet) by 8.

6. a) Write an equation for y in terms of x for this model.

   b) Graph the equation.

7. a) Determine how many people can be seated at oblong tables in each room in exercise 3. Enter the results in the 4th column of the table.

   b) Are the results for the rooms in your school reasonable? Explain.

The Round Table Model

The rule for round tables:

For the number of people, divide the room area (in square feet) by 10.

8. a) Write an equation for y in terms of x for this model.

   b) Graph the equation.

9. a) Determine how many people can be seated at round tables in each room in exercise 3. Enter the results in the 5th column of the table.

   b) Are the results for the rooms in your school reasonable? Explain.

10. Communication Explain how rules can be used to find the number of people who can be seated at a banquet.

MATHEMATICS TOOLKIT

Slope of a Line

- The slopes of all segments of a line are equal.
- The slope of a line is the slope of any segment on the line.

The Line $y = mx$

- Graph is a straight line with slope m.
- Passes through the origin $O(0, 0)$.
- Represents *direct variation* since y varies directly with x.

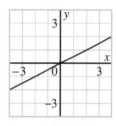

The Line $y = mx + b$

- Graph is a straight line with slope m and y-intercept b.
- Does not pass through the origin.
- Represents *partial variation* since y varies partially with x.
- Called slope y-intercept form.

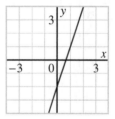

Horizontal and Vertical Lines

Horizontal line

- Has the equation $y = b$, where b is the y-intercept.

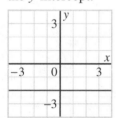

Vertical line

- Has the equation $x = a$, where a is the x-intercept.

Equation of a Line

To find the equation of a line, one of the following is needed:

- slope and y-intercept
- slope and the coordinates of a point on the line
- the coordinates of two points on the line

5.1 **1.** Graph the line through each point with each given slope.

    a) C(–4, 2), slope –1   **b)** D(5, –3), slope $\frac{5}{2}$ **c)** E(–6, –1), slope undefined

2. Draw a line with slope $-\frac{3}{4}$ through each point. Find the coordinates of 2 more points on each line.

    a) Q(1, –2)   **b)** R(3, 0)   **c)** S(0, 0)   **d)** T(–3, –1)

3. Graph the line through each point with each given slope. Find the coordinates of 2 more points on each line.

    a) M(2, 5), slope $\frac{1}{4}$ **b)** N(–2, –4), slope $-\frac{2}{3}$ **c)** P(–1, 3), slope 0

5.2 **4.** Write the equation of each line.

a) 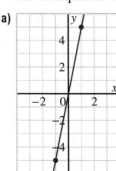   **b)** 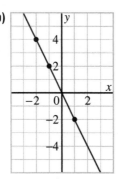   **c)**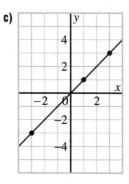

5. Graph each line.

    a) $y = -\frac{3}{2}x$ **b)** $y = 4x$ **c)** $y = -x$ **d)** $y = \frac{1}{3}x$

5.4 **6.** Write the equation of the line with each slope and y-intercept.

    a) $m = -\frac{1}{4}, b = 3$ **b)** $m = 1, b = -2$ **c)** $m = \frac{2}{5}, b = -4$

7. Match each line, right, with an equation.

    a) $y = -2$ **b)** $y = \frac{1}{2}x + 2$

    c) $y = -x + 2$ **d)** $y = \frac{1}{2}x - 2$

    e) $y = 2x + 2$ **f)** $y = -2x + 2$

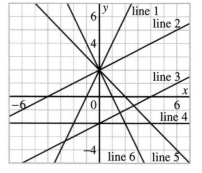

8. Graph each line then write its equation.

    a) Every point on the line has the x-coordinate –3.

    b) Every point on the line has the y-coordinate 2.

9. Graph each line.

    a) $y = -2x - 5$ **b)** $y = \frac{2}{3}x + 2$ **c)** $y = -\frac{1}{6}x - 1$

5.5 **10.** Write each equation.

a)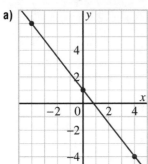

b)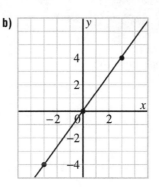

c)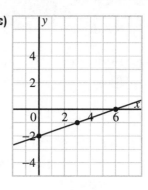

11. The coordinates of a point on a line and the slope of the line are given.

   i) Graph each line.   **ii)** Write each equation.

   a) J(1, 3), slope −3   **b)** K(−5, −2), slope $\frac{2}{5}$ **c)** L(4, 0), slope −2

12. Find the equation of the line that passes through each pair of points.

   a) A(3, 5) and B(−5, −3)   **b)** C(2, −7) and D(−1, −1)

   c) G(4, 2) and H(−2, −1)   **d)** L(6, 0) and M(0, 5)

5.6 **13.** A car travels at an average speed of 65 km/h. The distance travelled, d kilometres, after t hours is given by the equation $d = 65t$.

   a) Copy and complete this table.

t (h)	0	1	2	3	4	5
d (km)						

   b) Graph d against t.

   c) What is the d-intercept? What does it represent?

   d) What is the slope? What does it represent?

   e) Suppose the average speed increased. How would the graph change?

5.7 **14.** Olaf is paid $75/day plus $15 commission for each product he sells. Let T dollars represent Olaf's total pay and p represent the number of products he sells.

   a) Write an equation to relate T and p.

   b) Graph the relation. Should the points be joined? Explain why.

   c) Find the T-intercept. What does it represent?

   d) Is the relationship between T and p direct variation or partial variation? Explain how the equation and the graph show this.

   e) How much would Olaf earn on a day he sells 6 products?

   f) Suppose Olaf was paid $95/day plus $10 commission for each product he sells. Write an equation to relate T and p.

1. **Knowledge/Understanding** Graph each line.

   a) $y = \frac{1}{4}x$

   b) $y = -3x$

   c) $y = -\frac{5}{3}x$

   d) $y = 4x - 1$

   e) $y = 4$

   f) $y = -\frac{2}{3}x + 3$

2. Graph the line for each pair of points.

   a) S(4, 1), T(0, −3)   b) V(−2, 5), Z(−2, −6)   c) L(−5, −1), M(7, −1)
       i) State the slope.
       ii) Find the coordinates of 2 more points on each line.
       iii) Write the equation of each line.

3. **Application** For a business trip, Gina took a flight 450 km north, then rented a car and drove further north at a speed of 70 km/h. Let d kilometres represent the total distance travelled and h, the hours of driving.

   a) Write an equation to relate d and h.

   b) Graph the relation. Estimate the total distance Gina travelled after driving 3 h.

   c) What is the d-intercept? What does it represent?

   d) Suppose Gina drove at a faster speed. How would the graph and the equation change?

   e) Suppose the flight distance had been shorter. How would the graph and the equation change?

4. The coordinates of a point on a line and the slope of the line are given. Graph each line, then write its equation.

   a) D(5, −3), slope $-\frac{1}{5}$ b) E(−4, 1), slope −1   c) F(0, −6), slope $\frac{4}{3}$

5. **Communication**

   a) Describe the steps for substituting the coordinates of a point into an equation of a line to find out whether the point is on the line.

   b) Illustrate the steps from part a with a line from exercise 4.

6. **Thinking/Inquiry/Problem Solving** A line passes through D(−5, 4). The run is 3. The rise is either 2 or −2. When the line crosses the x-axis, the x-coordinate is positive. Write the equation of the line.

1. The graph below shows the number of hectares of trees remaining in a northern forest each year after the logging season.

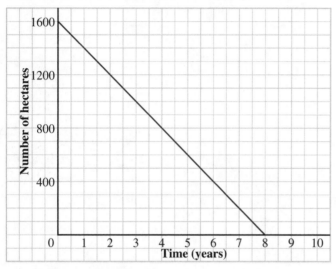

For the situation above, give the meaning of each number below.

- −2000, the slope of the line
- 1600, the vertical intercept
- 8, the horizontal intercept

2. The graph below shows Yoshikatsu's walk in front of a motion detector.

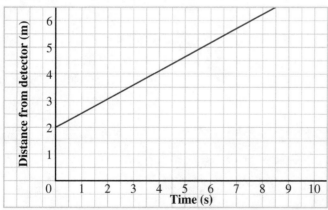

Yoshikatsu decided to repeat his walk. This time he started 1 m in front of the detector and walked at the same speed.

Copy the graph above. Draw a line for the second walk. Determine the equation of the line for the second walk.

CHAPTER
6 Polynomials

By the end of this chapter, you will:

- Substitute into and evaluate algebraic expressions with exponents.
- Use exponent rules for multiplying and dividing monomials, and the exponent rule for the power of a power.
- Add and subtract polynomials.
- Multiply a polynomial by a monomial.
- Expand and simplify polynomials.

Could a Giant Survive?

The Guinness Book of Records reports some real-life examples of exceptionally tall people. The tallest person ever, Robert Wadlow, was 272 cm tall. Wadlow died at age 22. The tallest woman, Zeng Jinlian, was 248 cm tall. She died at age 18.

In Section 6.7, you will develop a mathematical model to help you understand what happens to the body if all the body's dimensions become much larger than normal.

Necessary Skills

Exponent Laws for Multiplying and Dividing Powers

Recall the exponent law for multiplying powers: $a^n \times a^m = a^{n+m}$

Recall the exponent law for dividing powers: $\dfrac{a^n}{a^m} = a^{n-m}$

Example

Express as a single power, then evaluate.

a) $3^2 \times 3^3$

b) $\dfrac{5^3}{5^2}$

Solution

a) $3^2 \times 3^3 = 3^{2+3}$ Use a calculator.   **b)** $\dfrac{5^3}{5^2} = 5^{3-2}$

$\qquad\qquad\quad = 3^5$ $\qquad\qquad\qquad\qquad\qquad\qquad = 5^1$

$\qquad\qquad\quad = 243$ $\qquad\qquad\qquad\qquad\qquad\qquad = 5$

Exercises

1. Express as a single power, then evaluate.

a) $2^3 \times 2^2$

b) $4^1 \times 4^3$

c) $3^2 \times 3^5$

d) $10^2 \times 10^5$

e) $6^4 \div 6^2$

f) $10^7 \div 10^3$

g) $7^6 \div 7$

h) $4^9 \div 4^6$

2. Express as a single power, then evaluate.

a) $\dfrac{3^8}{3^6}$

b) $\dfrac{10^8}{10^5}$

c) $\dfrac{4^5}{4^2}$

d) $\dfrac{5^4}{5^2}$

e) $\dfrac{6^4}{6^3}$

f) $\dfrac{2^9}{2}$

g) $\dfrac{10^6}{10^2}$

h) $\dfrac{1^7}{1^3}$

Exponent Law for a Power of a Product

Sometimes we apply the exponent law for a power of a power to an algebraic term.

We raise an algebraic term to an exponent; for example, $(2x)^3$.

$(2x)^3$ means $(2x)(2x)(2x) = (2)(2)(2)(x)(x)(x)$
$$= (2^3)(x^3)$$
$$= 8x^3$$

The term, $2x$, is a product of 2 and x.

To raise a product to an exponent, raise each factor to that exponent.

TAKE NOTE

Exponent Law for a Power of a Product

$(ab)^n = a^n b^n$, where n is an integer

Example

Simplify.

a) $(4a)^3$ 						**b)** $(-3a)^3$

Solution

Use the power of a product law.

a) $(4a)^3 = 4^3 a^3$ 				**b)** $(-3a)^3 = (-3)^3 a^3$
$$ = 64a^3$$ 				$$ = -27a^3$$

Exercises

1. Simplify.

  a) $(2a)^2$ **b)** $(2a)^3$ **c)** $(2a)^4$ **d)** $(2a)^5$

2. Simplify.

  a) $(-3x)^2$ **b)** $(-5a)^3$ **c)** $(-2x)^4$ **d)** $(-2a)^5$

3. Simplify.

  a) $(4b)^4$ **b)** $(-6z)^2$ **c)** $(-3c)^5$ **d)** $(5m)^4$

  e) $(-2t)^6$ **f)** $(-7x)^3$ **g)** $(-4z)^7$ **h)** $(3q)^8$

The Distributive Law

Recall the distributive law: $a(b + c) = ab + ac$

Example

Expand.

a) $2(x + 4)$　　　　　　　　　**b)** $-3(2a - 5)$

Solution

a) $2(x + 4) = 2(x) + 2(4)$
$\quad\quad\quad\quad = 2x + 8$

b) $-3(2a - 5) = -3(2a) - 3(-5)$
$\quad\quad\quad\quad\quad = -6a + 15$

Exercises

1. Expand.

　　a) $3(2 + a)$　　**b)** $3(2 - a)$　　**c)** $4(2x + 1)$　　**d)** $4(2x - 1)$

2. This diagram represents a parking lot. Use the distributive law. Write two expressions for the total area of the parking lot.

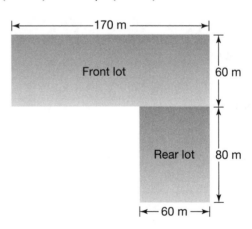

3. Expand.

　　a) $6(4x + 9)$　　　　　**b)** $-3(5c + 3)$　　　　　**c)** $11(3 - 8z)$

　　d) $-10(-2 + 7y)$　　　**e)** $5(6z + 2)$　　　　　**f)** $-(3y - 6)$

6.1 What Is a Polynomial?

Jennifer has U.S. bills from a vacation in the United States and some Canadian bills.

To calculate the amount, Jennifer adds the U.S. money: $20 + $10 + $10 + $5 + $1 = $46 U.S.
and the Canadian money: $10 + $5 + $5 = $20 Can

All the terms that represent Canadian money are like terms. They can be combined into a single value. Similarly, all the terms that represent U.S. money are like terms. However, a term that represents Canadian money and a term that represents U.S. money are unlike terms. They cannot be combined into a single value.

We can only say that Jennifer has $46 U.S. and $20 Can.

In Chapter 3, you worked with algebra tiles and like and unlike terms.

Recall:

This is a 1-tile.

It measures 1 unit on each side.
Its area is 1 square unit.

This is a variable tile, or x-tile.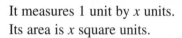

It measures 1 unit by x units.
Its area is x square units.

This new algebra tile is a square measuring x units on each side.
Its area is $x \times x$, or x^2 square units.
It is an x^2-tile.

All three tiles represent unlike terms.

Forming Rectangles with Algebra Tiles

1. Arrange 4 green 1-tiles to form a rectangle.

    a) What is the length of the rectangle?

    b) What is the width of the rectangle?

    c) What is the area of the rectangle?

    d) What is the perimeter of the rectangle?

2. Arrange the tiles from exercise 1 to form a different rectangle. Repeat exercise 1a to d for the new rectangle.

3. Compare your answers to exercises 1 and 2. What do you notice about the perimeter and area?

4. a) Arrange 4 green x-tiles to form a rectangle. Repeat exercise 1 for this rectangle.

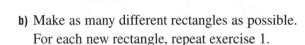

    b) Make as many different rectangles as possible. For each new rectangle, repeat exercise 1.

5. Use the tiles from exercises 1 and 4 together. Make as many different rectangles as possible. Repeat exercise 1 for each rectangle.

6. When you arrange algebra tiles to form different rectangles:

    a) What do you notice about the areas?

    b) What do you notice about the perimeters?

From the *Investigation*, for a fixed number of tiles, when the rectangle changed:

- The area remained constant.
- The perimeter changed.

Since x is a variable, we cannot combine the areas of a 1-tile, an x-tile, and an x^2-tile to form a single term. The tiles represent unlike terms.

To represent these tiles:

We think: 3 x^2-tiles + 2 x-tiles + 5 1-tiles

We write: $3x^2 + 2x + 5$

There are special names for terms and combinations of terms.
Terms are separated by plus or minus signs. The sign belongs to the term.

A term is a constant or a coefficient and one or more variables.
A coefficient is the number that precedes a variable.
The term $3x^2$ has coefficient 3 and variable x.

A *polynomial* is one term or the sum of two or more terms.
These are polynomials: $-3x$, $3a^2 - 5a - 14$, $11 - d^2$

A *monomial* is a polynomial with one term.
These are monomials: $3x^2$, $4x$, $-6m^3$

A *binomial* is a polynomial with two terms.
These are binomials: $3x + 7$, $4 - a^4$

A *trinomial* is a polynomial with three terms.
These are trinomials: $3x^2 + 7x - 6$, $a^2 - 2a + 1$

The trinomial $3x^2 - 2x + 5$ contains coefficients 3 and -2; 5 is a constant term.
The variable is x.

We can use algebra tiles to represent the polynomial $3x^2 + 2x + 5$. The terms in this polynomial have positive coefficients. We can also represent a polynomial such as $3x^2 - 2x + 5$, which has a term with a negative coefficient. We do this by flipping the two x-tiles.

We see: $3x^2 - 2x + 5$
We think: 3 x^2-tiles, 2 flipped x-tiles, and 5 1-tiles

We display:

Recall that we can evaluate an expression by substituting a number for a variable.

Example 1

a) Evaluate $2x - 3$ for $x = 4$.

b) Evaluate $-4a^2 + 3a + 3$ for $a = -2$.

Solution

a) Substitute $x = 4$ in $2x - 3$.

$$2x - 3 = 2(4) - 3$$
$$= 8 - 3$$
$$= 5$$

b) Substitute $a = -2$ in $-4a^2 + 3a + 3$.

$-4a^2 + 3a + 3 = -4(-2)^2 + 3(-2) + 3$ Recall that $(-2)^2 = 4$.
$$= -4(4) - 6 + 3$$
$$= -16 - 3$$
$$= -19$$

As you discovered in the *Investigation*, we can combine algebra tiles to form a rectangle. We can write the area and the perimeter of the rectangle as a polynomial.

Example 2

Write polynomials that represent the perimeter and area of each rectangle.

a)

b)

Solution

a) The rectangle has 5 x-tiles.
Its length is 5.
Its width is x.
The perimeter is $x + 5 + x + 5 = 2x + 10$.
The area is $5 \times x = 5x$.

b) The rectangle has 3 x^2-tiles.
Its length is $3x$.
Its width is x.
The perimeter is $x + 3x + x + 3x = 8x$.
The area is $3x \times x = 3x^2$.

A 1. How much money is represented?

10 Can	10 U.S.	1 U.S.
10 Can	5 Can	2 Can
10 U.S.	5 U.S.	1 U.S.
10 Can	5 U.S.	5 U.S.

2. Let x represent Canadian money.
   Let y represent U.S. money.
   Write an expression to represent the total money in exercise 1.

3. Is each expression a monomial, binomial, or trinomial? Give reasons.
   a) $3x + 4$ b) $-x^2$ c) $-2 - y^2$ d) 10
   e) $5 - 2x + 3x^2$ f) $4x$ g) $5x^2 + 4 + x$ h) $-3 - y$

4. For each, write a polynomial that represents the total area.

   a)

   b)

   c) 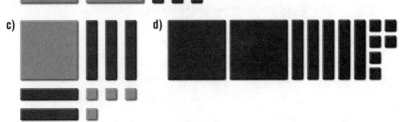   d)

5. Use algebra tiles to represent each polynomial.
   a) $x^2 + 3x + 2$ b) $2x^2 + x + 7$ c) $-2x^2 - 3$ d) $2x^2 - 5x - 4$
   e) $-x^2 - 3x + 2$ f) $x^2 - 4x$ g) $6 - x$ h) 5

6. State the coefficient in each term.

a) $14x$　　b) $7y^2$　　c) a　　d) $-b^2$　　e) $3r^2$

 7. State the constant term in each polynomial.

a) $5x^2 - 2x + 6$　b) $-x^2 - 5$　c) $7 - 3x - 2x^2$　d) $7x^2 - 5x$

8. State the coefficient for each variable term.

a) $6p + 2p^2 + 3$　b) $6 - 2c + 9c^2$　c) $1.8C + 32$

d) $2r$　e) $7y^2 - 3y - 9$　f) $4s^3 - s^2 - 5s + 2$

9. State the like terms in each group.

a) $5a, 3b, 5c, a^2, -a, 3d, 3e$　　b) $4x, 3y^2, 4z, 2y, y^2, 4w$

c) $9g, 6h, 9g^2, \frac{1}{9}g, \frac{1}{6}h^2, g^2$　　d) $16, d^2, d, f, -8, 0.5d, 7d^3$

 10. Evaluate $3n + 4$ for each value of n.

a) 1　　b) 3　　c) 4　　d) -1

11. Evaluate $3x - 5$ for each value of x.

a) 0　　b) 1　　c) -1　　d) 7

12. Evaluate $2a^2 - 6a + 1$ for each value of a.

a) 0　　b) -1　　c) 2　　d) -3

13. Knowledge/Understanding Write a polynomial to represent the perimeter of each rectangle.

a)　　　　　　b)　　　　　　c)

14. Write a polynomial to represent the area of each rectangle in exercise 13.

15. Represent each rectangle using algebra tiles.

a)　　　　　　b)

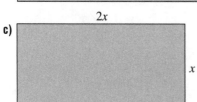 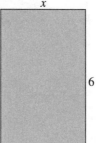

c)

16. For each rectangle in exercise 15, write a polynomial to represent its perimeter and a polynomial to represent its area.

17. Communication

a) Is a binomial a polynomial? Explain.

b) Is a monomial a binomial? Explain.

18. Write a polynomial to represent the perimeter of each rectangle.

a)
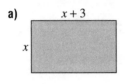
$x + 3$

x

b)
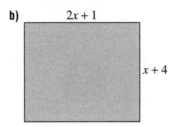
$2x + 1$

$x + 4$

c)
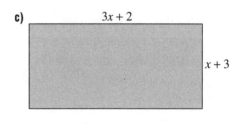
$3x + 2$

$x + 3$

19. For exercise 18, determine the perimeter of each rectangle when $x = 4$ cm and when $x = 2$ m.

20. a) Write a polynomial to represent the area of a square with side length x.

b) Write a polynomial to represent the area of:
  i) the large square
  ii) the small square
  iii) the shaded region

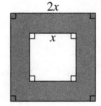
$2x$

x

c) Determine the area of each figure in part b when $x = 3$ cm.

21. Application The formula, $d = 0.20v + 0.015v^2$, gives the approximate stopping distance, d metres, for a car travelling at v kilometres per hour. Estimate the stopping distance for a speed of 50 km/h and a speed of 100 km/h.

22. Thinking/Inquiry/Problem Solving Use the variable x. Make up a trinomial, a binomial, and a monomial that result in -3 when $x = 2$.

6.2   Adding Polynomials

To add two polynomials, we combine like terms. We can use algebra tiles to add polynomials. We combined like terms in Section 3.2. Now we include x^2-tiles.

Suppose we add $2x^2 + 3x + 1$ and $-x^2 + 2x - 4$.
We write: $(2x^2 + 3x + 1) + (-x^2 + 2x - 4)$

We think:

Combine like terms. Use the Zero Principle. Each pair of opposite tiles has the sum 0.
1 x^2-tile, 5 x-tiles, and 3 flipped 1-tiles remain.

From the tiles,
$(2x^2 + 3x + 1) + (-x^2 + 2x - 4) = x^2 + 5x - 3$

To add polynomials algebraically, we group like terms, then simplify. When grouping like terms, the sign in front of the term belongs to the term. The sign should move with the term.

We display:

Example 1

Simplify $(-2x^2 + 6x - 7) + (3x^2 - x - 2)$.

Solution

$$(-2x^2 + 6x - 7) + (3x^2 - x - 2) = -2x^2 + 6x - 7 + 3x^2 - x - 2$$ — Remove brackets
$$= -2x^2 + 3x^2 + 6x - x - 7 - 2$$ — Group like terms
$$= x^2 + 5x - 9$$ — Add like terms

Discuss
Explain how to use algebra tiles to add $(-2x^2 + 6x - 7) + (3x^2 - x - 2)$.

Some polynomials cannot be represented with algebra tiles. We use algebra to combine these polynomials.

Example 2

Simplify $(2x^4 - 3x^2 + x - 1) + (-x^4 - 3x + 3)$.

Solution

$$(2x^4 - 3x^2 + x - 1) + (-x^4 - 3x + 3) = 2x^4 - 3x^2 + x - 1 - x^4 - 3x + 3$$
$$= 2x^4 - x^4 - 3x^2 + x - 3x - 1 + 3$$
$$= x^4 - 3x^2 - 2x + 2$$

Remove brackets

Group like terms

Add like terms

Discuss

Why can we not represent these polynomials with algebra tiles?

When we evaluate the sum of two polynomials, we simplify first.

Example 3

a) Simplify $(-2x^3 + 3x + 1) + (x^3 - 4x - 2)$.

b) Evaluate the polynomial in part a for $x = -2$.

Solution

a) $(-2x^3 + 3x + 1) + (x^3 - 4x - 2) = -2x^3 + 3x + 1 + x^3 - 4x - 2$
$$= -2x^3 + x^3 + 3x - 4x + 1 - 2$$
$$= -x^3 - x - 1$$

b) $-x^3 - x - 1$

Substitute $x = -2$.

$$-x^3 - x - 1 = -(-2)^3 - (-2) - 1 \qquad \text{Note: } (-2)^3 = (-2) \times (-2) \times (-2)$$
$$= -(-8) + 2 - 1 \qquad\qquad\qquad\qquad = 4 \times (-2)$$
$$= 8 + 2 - 1 \qquad\qquad\qquad\qquad\quad = -8$$
$$= 9$$

Discuss

Suppose we evaluated $(-2x^3 + 3x + 1) + (x^3 - 4x - 2)$ for $x = -2$ without simplifying first. What would be the result? Why does this make sense? How can you check?

A 1. Use algebra tiles to add.

a) $(x^2 + 2x - 1) + (2x^2 + 3x + 3)$ b) $(3x^2 - x + 5) + (x^2 - 2x - 4)$

c) $(-2x^2 - 3x - 4) + (-2x^2 - 5x - 1)$ d) $(x^2 - 2x - 4) + (-x^2 + 2x + 4)$

2. a) Use the variable x. What polynomials do these tiles represent?

b) Use algebra tiles to find the sum of the polynomials in part a.

3. Use the variable x. Add.

a)
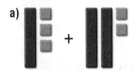

b)

c)

d)
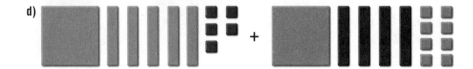

 4. Add.

a) $(a + 1) + (a + 1)$ b) $(a + 1) + (2a + 2)$

c) $(a + 1) + (3a + 3)$ d) $(a + 1) + (4a + 4)$

e) $(a + 1) + (5a + 5)$ f) $(a + 1) + (6a + 6)$

 5. Add.

a) $(2k + 3) + (k - 1)$ b) $(2k + 3) + (2k - 2)$

c) $(2k + 3) + (3k - 3)$ d) $(2k + 3) + (4k - 4)$

B **6.** Add.

a) $(h^2 + 1) + (4h^2 + 5)$ b) $(h^2 - 1) + (4h^2 - 5)$

c) $(h^2 + h) + (4h^2 + 3h)$ d) $(h^2 - h) + (4h^2 - 3h)$

e) $(h^2 + h + 1) + (4h^2 + 3h + 5)$ f) $(h^2 - h - 1) + (4h^2 - 3h - 5)$

7. Add.

a) $(6x + 2) + (3x + 4)$ b) $(5a - 3) + (2a + 7)$

c) $(8 - 4m) + (-3 - 2m)$ d) $(-x + 4) + (7x - 2)$

8. Knowledge/Understanding Add.

a) $(4n^2 - 3n - 1) + (2n^2 - 5n - 3)$ b) $(3x^2 + 6x - 8) + (-5x^2 - x + 4)$

c) $(2 - 3c + c^2) + (5 - 4c - 4c^2)$ d) $(8 - 2n - n^2) + (-3 - n + 4n^2)$

e) $(b^3 + 3b - 5) + (2b^3 - 4b - 6)$ f) $(m^4 - 5m^2 + 6m - 2) + (-6m^4 + 3m^2 + 7)$

9. Add.

a) $(3x^2 + 2x + 4) + (x^2 + 3)$ b) $(3x^2 - 2x - 4) + (x^2 - 3)$

c) $(5m + 2m^2) + (m^2 + 6)$ d) $(5m - 2m^2) + (m^2 - 6)$

10. Add.

a) $(5c^4 + 2c^3 - 7) + (3c^4 - c^3 + 1)$

b) $(-4q^5 + 3q^2 - 5q - 7) + (-q^4 - 6q^3 + 2q)$

c) $(2t^3 - 6 + 2t^2) + (4t^3 + t - 1)$

d) $(3 + t + 4t^4) + (-7 - t - 5t^3 + t^4)$

11. a) Add $(2x^5 + 3x^4 + 4x^3 + 5x^2) + (-2x^3 + 3x^2 - 7)$.

b) **Communication** Explain why you cannot use algebra tiles to simplify the polynomial sum in part a.

12. Simplify. Then determine the value of the polynomial when $x = 1$.
$(1 - 2x^2 - x) + (2x - 3x^2 - 7)$

13. Simplify. Then determine the value of the polynomial when $x = -2$.
$(3 - 2x^2 - x) + (2x - 3x^2 - 7)$

14. Simplify. Then evaluate for $y = -3$.

a) $(y^2 + y + 2) + (3y^2 - y + 1)$

b) $(-2y^4 - y^3 + y - 1) + (3y^4 - y^3 - y^2 - 5)$

c) $(5y^3 + 2y^2 - 4y) + (-y^4 - y^3 + 4)$

15. **Application** Each rectangle is divided into squares and rectangles. Write one polynomial for the area of each section and one polynomial for the area of the entire rectangle.

a)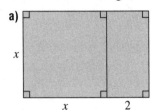

b)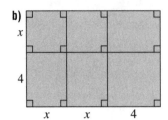

c)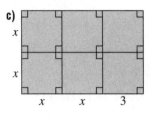

16. Simplify.

a) $(3x^2 - 7x + 4) + (5x - 7x^2 + 6)$ b) $(6 - 3x + x^2) + (9 - x)$

c) $(1 - 7x^2 + 2x) + (x^3 - 3x^2 + 7)$ d) $(5x - x^2) + (3x + x^2 - 7)$

17. What hint would you give about using algebra tiles to represent the addition of polynomials?

18. **Thinking/Inquiry/Problem Solving**
Choose any month on a calendar.
Then choose a 3 by 3 square of 9 dates.
Let x represent the date at the centre
of the square.

a) Write a polynomial for:
   i) the date one week before x
   ii) the date one week after x
   iii) the sum of the dates in each column
   iv) the sum of all 9 dates

b) Suppose you know the sum of all 9 dates.
   How could you determine the value of x?

19. a) Write a polynomial expression for the perimeter of the triangle shown.

b) Find the perimeter when $x = 2$.

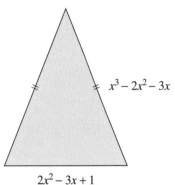
one week before
x
one week after

$x^3 - 2x^2 - 3x$

$2x^2 - 3x + 1$

6.3 Subtracting Polynomials

Polynomials can be subtracted. We can use algebra tiles to subtract polynomials.

Polynomials that have a sum of 0 are called *opposites*.
Flipping the tiles representing $-2x^2 + x - 9$ gives its opposite, $2x^2 - x + 9$.
We can use this to subtract one polynomial from another.

Suppose we subtract $-2x^2 + x - 9$ from $3x^2 + 5x - 6$.
We write: $(3x^2 + 5x - 6) - (-2x^2 + x - 9)$

We think:

Flip the tiles representing $(-2x^2 + x - 9)$.
Combine like terms.
Use the Zero Principle.
5 x^2-tiles, 4 x-tiles, and 3 1-tiles remain.
From the tiles,
$(3x^2 + 5x - 6) - (-2x^2 + x - 9) = 5x^2 + 4x + 3$

We display:

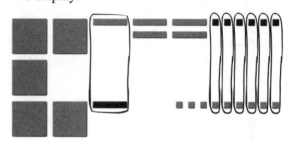

When we subtract a polynomial from itself,
we get zero.
For example, $(x^2 - 2x - 4) - (x^2 - 2x - 4) = 0$

We get the same result if we add the polynomial and its opposite.
For example, $(x^2 - 2x - 4) + (-x^2 + 2x + 4) = 0$

So, to subtract a polynomial, we add its opposite.

Example 1

Simplify $(3x^2 + 5x - 6) - (-2x^2 + x - 9)$.

Solution

$$
\begin{aligned}
(3x^2 + 5x - 6) - (-2x^2 + x - 9) &= (3x^2 + 5x - 6) + (2x^2 - x + 9) \\
&= 3x^2 + 5x - 6 + 2x^2 - x + 9 \\
&= 3x^2 + 2x^2 + 5x - x - 6 + 9 \\
&= 5x^2 + 4x + 3
\end{aligned}
$$

Add the opposite of $-2x^2 + x - 9$

Remove brackets

Group like terms

Add like terms

We can subtract polynomials using algebra.

Example 2

Simplify $(3x^4 - 2x^2 + 3x - 9) - (x^2 - 4x + 2)$.

Solution

$$(3x^4 - 2x^2 + 3x - 9) - (x^2 - 4x + 2)$$
$$= (3x^4 - 2x^2 + 3x - 9) + (-x^2 + 4x - 2)$$
$$= 3x^4 - 2x^2 + 3x - 9 - x^2 + 4x - 2$$
$$= 3x^4 - 2x^2 - x^2 + 3x + 4x - 9 - 2$$
$$= 3x^4 - 3x^2 + 7x - 11$$

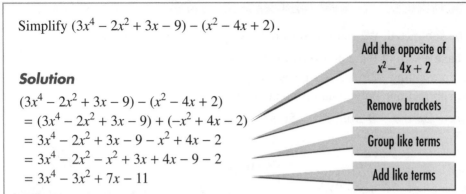

Add the opposite of $x^2 - 4x + 2$

Remove brackets

Group like terms

Add like terms

Discuss

Why can we not represent these polynomials with algebra tiles?

When we evaluate the difference of two polynomials, we simplify first.

Example 3

a) Simplify $(2x^3 - 3x^2 + x - 1) - (-x^2 + 2x - 1)$.

b) Evaluate the polynomial in part a for $x = 3$.

Solution

a) $(2x^3 - 3x^2 + x - 1) - (-x^2 + 2x - 1) = 2x^3 - 3x^2 + x - 1 + x^2 - 2x + 1$
$$= 2x^3 - 3x^2 + x^2 + x - 2x - 1 + 1$$
$$= 2x^3 - 2x^2 - x$$

b) $2x^3 - 2x^2 - x$

Substitute $x = 3$.
$$2x^3 - 2x^2 - x = 2(3)^3 - 2(3)^2 - 3 \quad \text{Note: } 3^3 = 27 \text{ and } 3^2 = 9$$
$$= 2(27) - 2(9) - 3$$
$$= 54 - 18 - 3$$
$$= 33$$

6.3   Exercises

  1. Show each polynomial using algebra tiles. Then flip the tiles and state its opposite.

a) $3x^2 + 7$ **b)** $2x^2 - 5x + 3$ **c)** $-4n^2 + 3n - 5$

2. a) Use the variable x. What polynomials do these tiles represent?

b) Use algebra tiles to find the difference of the polynomials in part a.

3. Use the variable m. Subtract.

a)

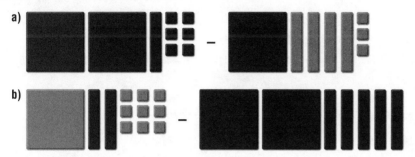

b)

4. Use algebra tiles to subtract.

a) $(-x^2 + 5x + 4) - (2x^2 + 3x + 3)$ **b)** $(3x^2 + 4) - (x^2 + 2)$

5. State the opposite of each polynomial.

a) $5x + 2$ **b)** $2 - 3a$ **c)** $7x^2 - 5x + 4$

d) $5 - 2m - 4m^2$ **e)** $6n^2 - 3n + 1$ **f)** $-2x^3 - 5$

6. Write each subtraction statement as an addition statement.

a) $(3x^2 + 5) - (2x^2 + 1)$

b) $(x^2 + 2x) - (-x - 1)$

c) $(x^2 + 3x - 2) - (-x^2 - x + 1)$

7. Communication Explain why the two polynomials in each pair are not opposites.

a) $5x^2 - 3x - 2$ **b)** $x^2 + 7x - 9$ **c)** $-4y + y^2 + 11$ **d)** $x^3 - 4x^2 + 9$

$\quad 5x^2 + 3x + 2$ $\quad -x^3 - 7x + 9$ $\quad 4y - y^2 + 11$ $\quad -x^3 + 4x^2 - x$

8. Subtract.

a) $(8s + 8) - (s + 1)$ **b)** $(8s^2 + 8s + 8) - (s^2 + s + 1)$

c) $(8s + 8) - (-s - 1)$ **d)** $(8s^2 + 8s + 8) - (-s^2 - s - 1)$

9. Simplify.

a) $(-2x + 3) - (3x + 2)$ **b)** $(4 - 5n) - (-6n + 2)$

c) $(8a^2 + 2a - 3) - (-6a^2 + 4a + 7)$ **d)** $(-6x^2 + 5x + 1) - (4x^2 + 5 - 2x)$

10. Knowledge/Understanding Simplify.

a) $(3 - 2n - n^2) - (7 - 6n + n^2)$ b) $(2 + 6x^2) - (7 - 3x^2)$

c) $(5 - 6t^2) - (3 - t^2)$ d) $(5x^2 - 3x) - (-3x + 5x^2)$

11. a) What is the sum of a polynomial and its opposite? Explain.

   b) Is there a polynomial that is equal to its opposite? Explain.

12. Simplify.

a) $(3x - 2) - (x - 1)$ b) $(2a + 3) - (6a - 1)$

c) $(5x^2 - 3x) - (x^2 + 2x)$ d) $(5t - 4) - (3t - 1)$

e) $(3 - 4x + x^2) - (2x - x^2)$ f) $(3n^2 - 6n + 5) - (3n^2 - 2n - 1)$

13. Simplify.

a) $(5x^2 + 7x + 9) - (3x^2 + 4x + 2)$ b) $(11m^2 - 5m + 8) - (7m^2 + m - 3)$

c) $(4a^2 - 3a^3 - 7) - (a^2 - 2a^3 - 13)$ d) $(-6x^2 + 17x - 4) - (3x^2 + 12x + 8)$

14. Simplify. Then find the value of the polynomial when $x = 3$.

$(3x^2 - 8x + 6) - (-2x^2 + 7x + 3)$

15. Simplify. Then find the value of the polynomial when $x = -2$.

$(x^2 - 4x + x^3) - (3x + 5 - x^3)$

16. a) Simplify.

     i) $(5 - 2m - m^2) - (7m + 4 - 5m^2)$ ii) $(2m^2 - 5m + 3) - (4 - 3m)$

   b) Determine the value of each polynomial in part a when $m = 0$ and when $m = -2$.

17. a) Simplify.

     i) $(y^2 - 2y) - (5 - 2y)$ ii) $(8y - 5) - (y - 4) + (3y + 1)$

   b) Determine the value of each polynomial in part a when $y = 4$ and when $y = 1$.

18. Application When the terms of a polynomial in x are arranged from the highest to the lowest powers of x, the polynomial is in *descending* powers of x.

   a) Simplify. Write the polynomial in descending powers of x.

$7 - (3x^2 + 2x) - (5x + x^2 - 6) - (3x + 3x^2 - 12)$

   b) Determine the value of the polynomial in part a when $x = 2$.

19. Thinking/Inquiry/Problem Solving

   a) Plan a method of adding to check subtraction with polynomials. Show your method with an example.

   b) Plan a method of subtracting to check addition with polynomials. Show your method with an example.

   c) Explain whether your methods in parts a and b are related.

6.4 Multiplying Monomials

In Sections 6.2 and 6.3, we added and subtracted polynomials.

We now multiply one-term polynomials, called monomials.

Recall the exponent laws for multiplying powers.
We apply this to multiply monomials.

$$(a^m)(a^n) = a^{m+n}$$

Consider this product:

$$
\begin{aligned}
(3a^2)(5a^3) &= (3 \times a \times a)(5 \times a \times a \times a) \qquad \text{Write each term as a product of factors.} \\
&= (3)(5)(a \times a \times a \times a \times a) \qquad \text{Rearrange the factors.} \\
&= 15a^5 \qquad \text{Write } a \times a \times a \times a \times a \text{ as } a^5.
\end{aligned}
$$

The above example illustrates this rule for multiplying monomials:

TAKE NOTE

Multiplying Monomials

To multiply two monomials, multiply their coefficients and multiply their variables.
If the variables are the same, add their exponents.

We use this rule to multiply $3a^2$ by $5a^3$.
Multiply the coefficients: $3 \times 5 = 15$
To multiply the variables, write the variable and add the exponents: $a^2 + a^3 = a^{2+3}$
$$= a^5$$

$$(3a^2)(5a^3) = 15a^5$$

Example

Simplify $(3x^2)(-2x^3)$.

Solution

$$
\begin{aligned}
(3x^2)(-2x^3) &= (3)(-2)(x^2)(x^3) \\
&= -6x^{2+3} \\
&= -6x^5
\end{aligned}
$$

A **1.** Simplify.

✓ **a)** $(2)(5)(x^4)(x^2)$ **b)** $(5)(2)(x^2)(x^4)$ **c)** $(-2)(5)(x^3)(x^3)$

d) $(2)(-5)(x)(x^5)$ **e)** $(-9)(4)(t^6)(t^2)$ **f)** $(-7)(-6)(z)(z^6)$

✓ **2.** Simplify.

a) $(3x^2)(4x^3)$ **b)** $(-x^2)(2x^6)$ **c)** $(a^2)(a^4)$ **d)** $(-5a)(6a^2)$

3. Simplify.

a) $(6x)(6x)(x^3)$ **b)** $(3z^2)(3z^2)(3z^2)(-z)(-z)$

c) $(-4a^3)(-4a^3)(-a^2)(-a^2)(-a^2)$ **d)** $(-2n)(-2n)(-2n)(-2n)(n^2)(n^2)$

B **4.** Simplify.

✓ **a)** $4(3b)$ **b)** $(-7)(2k)$ **c)** $5(4t)$ **d)** $(-2)(8p)$

e) $a(5a)$ **f)** $p(-3p)$ **g)** $n(4n)$ **h)** $x(-2x)$

5. Knowledge/Understanding Simplify.

a) $(3a)(2a)$ **b)** $(-2c)(5c)$ **c)** $(-2a)(-5a)$

d) $(7x)(3x)$ **e)** $(8y)(-7y)$ **f)** $(-x)(-5x)$

✓ **6.** Simplify.

a) $(12x)^2$ **b)** $(-3y)^3$ **c)** $-(5b)^2$

d) $-(9m^5)^2$ **e)** $(-5b^2)^3$ **f)** $-(3n^4)^2$

✓ **7.** Simplify.

a) $(x^3)(-x^2)$ **b)** $(2p^2)(3p^3)$ **c)** $(6y^3)(-2y)$ **d)** $(3b)(2b^2)$

8. Simplify.

a) $(3m^4)(7m^5)$ **b)** $(2x^2)(4x^3)$ **c)** $(8a^3)(7a^{11})$

d) $(-5b^3)(2b^4)$ **e)** $(6x^5)(-3x^3)$ **f)** $(-8p^4)(-6p^2)$

✓ **9. Application**

a) Write the area of the square as a product of monomials.

b) Write the area of the square as a monomial.

3x

3x

10. Communication When is the product of two monomials a monomial? Explain using an example.

11. Thinking/Inquiry/Problem Solving Name a pair of monomials that will satisfy each equation. Is there only one possible answer for each equation? Explain.

a) $\square \times \square = 3x^6$ **b)** $\square \times \square = -5b^3$ **c)** $\square \times \square = -6x$

6.5 Dividing Monomials

To divide two monomials, use the exponent law for dividing powers.

$$\frac{a^m}{a^n} = a^{m-n}$$

Consider this quotient:

$$\frac{18a^6}{3a^2} = \frac{2 \times 3 \times 3 \times a \times a \times a \times a \times a \times a}{3 \times a \times a}$$

Write each term as a product of factors.

$$= \frac{2 \times 3 \times 3^1 \times a \times a \times a \times a \times a^1 \times a^1}{3^1 \times a^1 \times a^1}$$

Reduce by dividing common factors.

$$= 6a^4$$

Write $a \times a \times a \times a$ as a^4.

The above example illustrates this rule for dividing monomials:

TAKE NOTE

Dividing Monomials

To divide two monomials, divide their coefficients and divide their variables.
If the variables are the same, subtract their exponents.

We use this rule to divide $18x^6$ by $3x^2$.
Divide the coefficients: $18 \div 3 = 6$
To divide the variables, write the variable
and subtract the exponents: $x^6 \div x^2 = x^{6-2}$
$$= x^4$$

$$\boxed{\frac{18x^6}{3x^2} = 6x^4}$$

Example

Simplify $8a^4 \div 2a^2$.

Solution

$$8a^4 \div 2a^2 = \frac{8a^4}{2a^2}$$
$$= \frac{8}{2} \times \frac{a^4}{a^2} \qquad \text{Note: } \frac{8}{2} = 4$$
$$= 4a^{4-2}$$
$$= 4a^2$$

1. Divide.

✓

    a) $\dfrac{6x}{3}$ **b)** $\dfrac{12x^2}{4}$ **c)** $\dfrac{20x^3}{5}$

    d) $\dfrac{32x^4}{8}$ **e)** $\dfrac{x^3}{x}$ **f)** $\dfrac{x^5}{x^2}$

2. Simplify.

    a) $\dfrac{2x^2}{x}$ **b)** $\dfrac{2x^3}{x^2}$ **c)** $\dfrac{4x^2}{2x}$ **d)** $\dfrac{4x^3}{2x^2}$

✓ **3.** Simplify.

    a) $\dfrac{-3x^2}{x}$ **b)** $\dfrac{-3x^3}{x^2}$ **c)** $\dfrac{-9x^2}{3x}$ **d)** $\dfrac{-9x^3}{3x^2}$

4. Simplify.

    a) $\dfrac{(3x)(3x)(3x)(3x)}{(-x)(-x)}$ **b)** $\dfrac{(-4d)(-4d)(-4d)(-4d)(-4d)}{(2d)(2d)(2d)(2d)}$

    c) $\dfrac{(-10a)(-10a)(-10a)}{(-5a)}$ **d)** $\dfrac{(6t)(6t)(6t)(6t)}{(3t)(3t)(3t)}$

 5. Simplify.

✓

    a) $\dfrac{5m^5}{2m^3}$ **b)** $\dfrac{-25x^5}{10x^2}$ **c)** $\dfrac{30x^6}{-6x^2}$

6. Knowledge/Understanding   Simplify.

    a) $\dfrac{12x^3}{3}$ **b)** $\dfrac{32y^4}{16}$

    c) $\dfrac{27m^3}{-9m}$ **d)** $(-45y^6) \div (-5y^4)$

    e) $3n^6 \div 5n^4$ **f)** $25x^4 \div (-5x^4)$

✓ **7.** Simplify.

    a) $15x^3 \div 3x$ **b)** $(-6y^2) \div 2y$

    c) $20a^3 \div (-4a^2)$ **d)** $\dfrac{6b^3}{2b^2}$

    e) $\dfrac{15m^5}{3m^2}$ **f)** $\dfrac{21x^2}{7x^2}$

✓ **8.** Simplify.

    a) $\dfrac{-28a^7}{4a^2}$ **b)** $\dfrac{20s^3}{-5s}$

    c) $\dfrac{-32c^8}{-8c^2}$ **d)** $45x^9 \div 9x^3$

    e) $18y^4 \div 3y^2$ **f)** $12b^3 \div 4b^2$

9. Simplify.

a) $42m^{12} \div 6m^4$

b) $36k^4 \div 9k^3$

c) $25w^3 \div 5w^3$

d) $\dfrac{49z^7}{7z^4}$

e) $\dfrac{56a^4}{8a^3}$

f) $\dfrac{60x^3}{15x^3}$

10. Simplify.

a) $\dfrac{(-10v)^6}{(5v^2)^2}$

b) $\dfrac{(4p)^6}{(2p)^2}$

✓ **11. Communication** Javier's solution to the exercise $\dfrac{6x^{10}}{3x^2}$ is $2x^5$. Is his solution correct? Explain why.

✓ **12.** Multiply or divide.

a) $(2m^3)(5m^2)$

b) $(-x^4)(3x)$

c) $\dfrac{2x^5}{3x^3}$

d) $\dfrac{-9m^8}{12m^5}$

e) $(3b^3)(2b^4)$

f) $\dfrac{15x^3}{-5x}$

13. Multiply or divide.

a) $(2d^3)(5d^4)$

b) $(-30m^2) \div (-6m)$

c) $(-x^2)(5x)$

d) $(-3a)(-10a^3)$

e) $\dfrac{12x^3}{2x}$

f) $\dfrac{-25a^7}{15a^2}$

14. When is the quotient of two monomials a monomial? Explain using an example.

15. Thinking/Inquiry/Problem Solving Name a pair of monomials that will satisfy each equation. Is there only one possible answer for each equation? Explain.

a) $\square \div \square = 2x^2$

b) $\square \div \square = 6x^3$

c) $\square \div \square = 4$

16. Application Evaluate each expression for $x = 2$.

a) $\dfrac{12x^5}{3x^2}$

b) $\dfrac{-9x^7}{2x^3}$

c) $\dfrac{-10x^4}{-5x}$

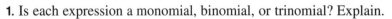
1. Is each expression a monomial, binomial, or trinomial? Explain.

   a) $x^2 - 5$ b) $y - 1 + 4y^2$ c) $6x^2$ d) $4 - c$

2. Write the polynomial these algebra tiles represent.

3. Simplify.

   a) $(6x + 3) + (3x - 1)$ b) $(x^2 - 2x + 4) + (2x^2 - 3x - 4)$

   c) $(5n - 3n^2 - 7) + (-3n + 2n^2 - 5)$ d) $(6 - 5a + a^2) + (2 - 7a^2)$

4. Simplify.

   a) $(-3x - 5) - (4x + 3)$ b) $(3x^2 + 5x - 6) - (x^2 - x + 4)$

   c) $(2g^2 + 1) - (5g^2 - 2)$ d) $(-5b^2 - 3b + 2) - (b^3 - 2b^2 + 7)$

5. Simplify. Find the value of each polynomial when $x = -4$.

   a) $(-3x^2 + 2x - 3) - (-4x^2 - x + 1)$ b) $(2x^4 - 4x + x^3) - (x^4 + 5 - x^3)$

6. Simplify.

   a) $(6f)(-2f)$ b) $(-5)(-3r)$ c) $(-4t)(9t)$

   d) $(-p^3)(-7p^5)$ e) $(2w^4)(8w^3)$ f) $(6)(-8x^2)$

7. Simplify.

   a) $(4x)^3$ b) $(-5y^3)^5$ c) $(-2t^5)^2$

   d) $(-6f^5)^4$ e) $(-w^3)^6$ f) $(3g^6)^4$

8. Simplify.

   a) $16x^2 \div 4x$ b) $28h^3 \div (-7h)$ c) $(-54y^5) \div (-9y^3)$

   d) $\dfrac{-15b^7}{5b^4}$ e) $\dfrac{-6s^6}{-s^2}$ f) $\dfrac{30c^8}{-6c^5}$

Preparation for Ontario Testing

9. Simplify $\dfrac{-15x^6}{3x^2}$.

   a) $-5x^4$ b) $-5x^3$ c) $5x^8$ d) $-5x^8$

Multiplying a Polynomial by a Monomial

In Section 3.1, you expanded a product such as $3(x + 4)$ using the distributive law. We can represent this product by combining these 3 sets of algebra tiles:

We can represent the product 3×5:

with a rectangle and...   with algebra tiles arranged in a rectangle

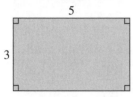

The area is $3 \times 5 = 15$.

Similarly, we can represent the product $2(x + 4)$ with algebra tiles in a rectangle.

The area is $2(x + 4) = 2x + 8$.

Instead of writing the length and width as algebraic terms, we use algebra tiles.

length

width

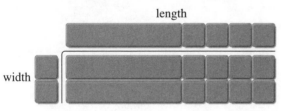

To represent the product $2x(x + 4)$ with algebra tiles, we make a rectangle $2x$ units wide and $(x + 4)$ units long. We use tiles to represent the length and the width.

We fill in the rectangle with 2 x^2-tiles and 8 x-tiles. The total area of the rectangles is $2x^2 + 8x$. We write: $2x(x + 4) = 2x^2 + 8x$

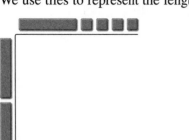

The Distributive Law in Arithmetic and in Algebra

To multiply in arithmetic, we use the distributive law.

$$3 \times 27 = 3(20 + 7)$$
$$= 3(20) + 3(7)$$
$$= 60 + 21$$
$$= 81$$

To multiply in algebra, we use the distributive law.

$$2x(x + 4) = 2x(x) + 2x(4)$$
$$= 2x^2 + 8x$$

When we use the distributive law to multiply a polynomial by a monomial, we are *expanding* the product of the monomial and polynomial.

Example 1

Expand $8x(x - 3)$.

Solution

$$8x(x - 3) = 8x(x) - 8x(3) \quad \text{Use the distributive law.}$$
$$= 8x^2 - 24x$$

Discuss

Can we use algebra tiles to expand this product? Explain.

We apply the same method when a polynomial has more than two terms.
When polynomials cannot be represented with algebra tiles, we use the distributive law.

Example 2

Expand $(-5a)(a^2 - 4a - 7)$.

Solution

$(-5a)(a^2 - 4a - 7) = (-5a)(a^2) - (-5a)(4a) - (-5a)(7)$ Use the distributive law.
$= -5a^3 + 20a^2 + 35a$

Discuss

Can we use algebra tiles to expand this product? Explain.

6.6   Exercises

A   **1.** What product does each diagram represent?

a)

b)

c)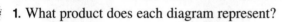

d)

e)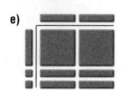

f)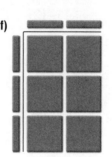

2. Use algebra tiles to expand each product.

     a) $x(x + 1)$ **b)** $x(3x + 2)$ **c)** $2(x^2 + x + 3)$ **d)** $2x(x + 2)$

✓ **3.** Expand.

     a) $2(x + 3)$ **b)** $(-2)(x + 3)$ **c)** $3(x - 2)$ **d)** $(-3)(x - 2)$

     e) $4(2x + 1)$ **f)** $(-4)(2x + 1)$ **g)** $5(4 - x^2)$ **h)** $(-5)(4 - x^2)$

4. Expand.

     a) $x(x + 3)$ **b)** $(-x)(x + 3)$ **c)** $x(x - 2)$ **d)** $(-x)(x - 2)$

     e) $x(2x + 1)$ **f)** $(-x)(2x + 1)$ **g)** $x(4 - x^2)$ **h)** $(-x)(4 - x^2)$

✓ **5.** Expand.

     a) $5(x - 3)$ **b)** $7(a + 1)$ **c)** $(-3)(2 + n)$

     d) $(-4)(-x - 2)$ **e)** $3(6x - 4)$ **f)** $5(x^2 - 6x + 3)$

6. Match each product with a set of algebra tiles.

a) $2x(x + 1)$ **b)** $2x(2x + 3)$ **c)** $2x(x + 5)$

d) $3x(x + 1)$ **e)** $x(x + 3)$ **f)** $x(2x + 2)$

i)

ii)

iii)

iv)

v)

vi)

B **7.** Expand.

a) $x(3x + 2)$ **b)** $a(5a - 1)$ **c)** $n(3 - 7n)$

d) $(-x)(x - 2)$ **e)** $y(5 - y)$ **f)** $(-x)(7 - 2x + x^2)$

8. Expand.

a) $x(x + 3)$ **b)** $(-5)(a - 3)$ **c)** $b(2b^2 - 3b + 1)$

d) $p(4 - 3p - p^2)$ **e)** $(-12)(-3t^2 + 2t)$ **f)** $(-k)(k^2 - 5k + 1)$

9. Expand.

a) $x(5x^2 - 6)$ **b)** $2(x + 3x^2)$ **c)** $(-3b)(b^3 - b^2)$

d) $2a(3a + 1)$ **e)** $(-4m)(m^2 - m)$ **f)** $x^2(1 - x^3)$

10. Knowledge/Understanding Expand.

a) $5x(2x + 3)$ **b)** $2a(3a - 4)$ **c)** $3c(5 - 2c)$

d) $(-4n)(2n - 1)$ **e)** $(-q)(2q^2 + 3q - 1)$ **f)** $6k(3 - k + 2k^2)$

11. Communication

a) Use the distributive law to multiply 7×236.

b) Use the distributive law to expand $7(2x^2 + 3x + 6)$. Evaluate this polynomial for $x = 10$.

c) Compare your answers in parts a and b. Explain any relationship you discover.

12. Application The dimensions of a cereal box, in centimetres, are $5x - 1$, $3x$, and x.

a) Write an expression for each measurement:
   i) the area of the base of the box
   ii) the height of the box
   iii) the volume, V, of the box
   iv) the area of the top of the box
   v) the area of the front of the box
   vi) the area of a side of the box
   vii) the surface area, A, of the box

b) Determine the volume and surface area of the box when $x = 7$ cm.

 13. Thinking/Inquiry/Problem Solving The height of any television screen is about $\frac{3}{4}$ of its width.

a) Write an expression for the height of a television screen x units wide.

b) Write an expression for the height of a television screen that is 4 units wider than the screen in part a.

c) Write an expression for the area of the screen in part b.

d) Suppose the difference in the areas of the screens in part a and part b is 120 square units. What is the area of each screen?

6.7　　Could a Giant Survive?

See page 239 for some examples of fantasy giants and exceptionally tall people. In the book, *Gulliver's Travels*, the giants in the land of Brobdingnag were 12 times as tall as a normal adult. Could these giants survive?

To model this situation, think about a sequence of cubes like this:

   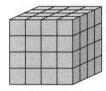

1. Make and complete a table for larger and larger cubes.

Edge length, x (cm)	Volume, V (cm^3)	Surface area, A (cm^2)	$\dfrac{\text{Volume, } V}{\text{Surface area, } A}$
1			
2			
3			
:			
10			

2. a) As the edge length increases, which grows more rapidly, surface area or volume?

   b) As the edge length increases, what happens to the value of $\dfrac{\text{Volume}}{\text{Surface area}}$?

3. a) Use the data in the completed table.
      i) Graph Volume, V, against Edge length, x.
      ii) Graph Surface Area, A, against Edge length, x.
      iii) Graph $\dfrac{\text{Volume}}{\text{Surface area}}$ against Edge length, x.

   b) Explain how the graphs in part a support your answers to exercise 2.

4. Suppose you multiply each dimension of a person by 12.

   a) Approximately how many times as great would the surface area and the volume be for the giant than for the person?

   b) How would the value of $\dfrac{\text{Volume}}{\text{Surface area}}$ for a giant compare with this value for a person?

5. In the movie *Honey, I Blew Up the Kid*, an inventor accidentally enlarges his child. The child eventually grows from 1 m to 32 m tall. Suppose you multiply each dimension of a person by 32. Repeat parts a and b of exercise 4.

6. Choose one of the biological systems described below. What health problems might the giants in the land of Brobdingnag have, or the giant child in the movie *Honey, I Blew Up the Kid*?

Respiratory system All the cells in your body require oxygen. The number of cells in your body depends on your volume, but the amount of oxygen absorbed by your lungs depends on the surface area of your lungs.

Skeletal system Your mass depends on your volume, but the strength of your bones depends on the area of their cross-section.

7. See page 239 for two real-life examples of the gigantic. Jinlian suffered from severe scoliosis, or curvature of the spine. Wadlow died of an infected blister on his ankle, caused by a poorly fitting brace.

a) Do you think that Jinlian's and Wadlow's ailments might have been related to their size? Explain.

b) How do you think their exceptional heights may have contributed to their early deaths?

8. Communication What is your answer to the question "Could a Giant Survive?" Explain how mathematical modelling supports your answer.

MATHEMATICS TOOLKIT

Exponent Law for a Power of a Product

- $(xy)^n = x^n y^n$, where n is an integer

Polynomials

- A term is a constant or a coefficient and one or more variables.
- A *polynomial* is one term or the sum of two or more terms.
- A *monomial* is a polynomial with one term.
- A *binomial* is a polynomial with two terms.
- A *trinomial* is a polynomial with three terms.

Adding Polynomials

- To add polynomials, group like terms. Simplify by adding the coefficients of like terms.

Zero Principle

- Polynomials with a sum of 0 are opposites.

Subtracting Polynomials

- To subtract a polynomial, add its opposite.

$$
\begin{aligned}
(4x + 2) - (2x - 5) &= 4x + 2 + (-2x + 5) \\
&= 4x + 2 - 2x + 5 \\
&= 2x + 7
\end{aligned}
$$

Multiplying Monomials

- To multiply two monomials, multiply their coefficients and multiply their variables. If the variables are the same, add their exponents.

$$5a \times 3a^2 = 15a^3$$

Dividing Monomials

- To divide two monomials, divide their coefficients and divide their variables. If the variables are the same, subtract their exponents.

$$\frac{6x^7}{3x^2} = 2x^5$$

The Distributive Law

- Use the distributive law to multiply a polynomial by a monomial.

6.1 **1.** Use algebra tiles to represent each polynomial.

    a) $2x^2 + 5x + 3$ **b)** $x^2 - 3x + 2$ **c)** $4x^2 - 2x - 3$ **d)** $-3x^2 - 4x$

2. Write a polynomial to represent the perimeter and a polynomial to represent the area of each rectangle.

  a) $x + 4$ **b)** $2x + 3$ **c)** $x + 5$

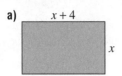
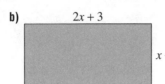
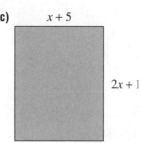

3. Which expressions are polynomials?

    a) $x^2 + 4$ **b)** $5x$ **c)** $1 - 4x$ **d)** $7 - 2x + 3x^2$

4. Classify each polynomial in exercise 3 as a monomial, binomial, or trinomial. Explain.

5. State the coefficient in each term.

    a) $5x$ **b)** $-2z^3$ **c)** y^2 **d)** $3c^4$

6. State the constant term in each polynomial.

    a) $4 - 2x$ **b)** $a^2 + 2a + 3$ **c)** $4y^2 - 1 + 3y$ **d)** $5x^2 + 2x - 1$

6.2 **7.** Simplify.

    a) $(4x - 1) + (x - 2)$

    b) $(3s + 4) + (2s - 3)$

    c) $(a^2 - 3) + (2a^2 + 3)$

    d) $(d^2 - 2d + 1) + (d^2 + d - 2)$

8. Simplify. Then evaluate for $x = -2$.

    a) $(x + 5) + (3x - 2)$

    b) $(2x^2 - x) + (-x^2 + 4x)$

    c) $(7 - 6x) + (2x + 1)$

    d) $(-x^2 - 3x - 4) + (3x^2 + 3x - 1)$

9. Simplify.

a) $(u^2 - 4u + 1) + (5u^2 - 3u)$

b) $(r^3 + r - 2) + (r^3 - 5r + 6)$

c) $(6 - 2j^4) + (2 - 3j^2 + 3j^4)$

d) $(-3k^4 - 2k^3 - 1) + (2k^3 + 6k^2 + k)$

e) $(4t^3 - 5t^2 + 4) + (-2t^3 + 7t - 3)$

f) $(p^4 + 5p - 6) + (-p^4 - 3p + 1)$

6.3 **10.** Simplify.

a) $(q - 3) - (2q + 3)$

b) $(2r - 1) - (4r - 5)$

c) $(x^2 - 4x + 1) - (5x^2 + 2x - 6)$

d) $(8 - 3h^2) - (2 + 4h - 5h^2)$

e) $(6t^4 + 3t^3 - 2t) - (t^3 + 3t - 4)$

f) $(4d^2 + 2 - 3d^4) - (2d^2 + 1 - 2d^4 - 5d^3)$

11. Simplify.

a) $(5y - 3y^2) - (y + 4y^2)$ b) $(-2x - 7) - (-14x - 6)$

c) $(9a^2 + 2a - 3) - (-6a^2 + 4a + 7)$ d) $(5z^2 - 3z - 2) - (2z^4 + 3z^2 - z - 1)$

e) $(4x^2 - 3x) - (x^2 + 2x)$ f) $(3c^2 + 5c + 7) - (2c^2 - 4c + 9)$

12. Simplify. Evaluate when $x = 2$ and when $x = -3$.

a) $(5 - 2x) - (3 - x)$ b) $(5x^2 - 5x + 7) - (2x^2 - 3x - 5)$

6.4 **13.** Simplify.

a) $(2y)(2y)(2y)(y^2)(y^2)$ b) $(-a^2)(-a^2)(-4a)(-4a)(-4a)$

c) $(-3m^3)(m^4)(m^4)(m^4)(m^4)$ d) $(c)(c)(c)(c)(2c^3)(2c^3)$

14. Simplify.

a) $(-3)(3r)$ b) $6(-y)$ c) $(-2)(-5k)$ d) $7(4q)$

e) $(-8x)(-2x)$ f) $(-5b)(7b)$ g) $(4a)(6a)$ h) $(c)(-9c)$

15. Simplify.

a) $(7m)^3$ b) $(-2d)^4$ c) $-(4q)^2$ d) $(-5p)^3$

e) $(-g^2)^5$ f) $(-4y^2)^3$ g) $(3w^5)^4$ h) $-(2t^3)^2$

16. Simplify.

a) $(-3n^2)(6n^2)$ b) $(-4c^3)(-4c^2)$ c) $(7x^2)(5x^3)$

d) $(-8n)(5n^3)$ e) $(2j^2)(-3j^4)$ f) $(-t^4)(-6t^5)$

17. Simplify.

a) $(-2a^2)^2(a^3)$ **b)** $(-4q^4)(-6q)^2$ **c)** $(2x^4)^2(2x)^5$

6.5   **18.** Simplify.

a) $12a^3 \div a$ **b)** $(-8b^2) \div 4$ **c)** $21h^7 \div (-3h^2)$

d) $(-18x^4) \div 3x$ **e)** $(-54y^6) \div 9y^5$ **f)** $(-32z^8) \div (-8z^5)$

19. Simplify.

a) $\dfrac{-45y^8}{-5y^4}$ **b)** $\dfrac{36n^6}{4n^2}$ **c)** $\dfrac{25x^7}{-5x^3}$

d) $\dfrac{-24a^5}{6a^3}$ **e)** $\dfrac{-54m^9}{-9m^8}$ **f)** $\dfrac{72b^6}{8b^3}$

20. Simplify.

a) $\dfrac{(12k^2)^3}{(-4k)^2}$ **b)** $\dfrac{(16s^2)^4}{(4s^2)^3}$ **c)** $\dfrac{(-15d)^4}{(-5d)^2}$

6.6   **21.** What product does each diagram represent?

a)    **b)**    **c)**

22. Expand.

a) $4(y - 2)$ **b)** $8(a - 3)$ **c)** $(-4)(x + 2)$

d) $3x(5 - x)$ **e)** $2y(y - 6)$ **f)** $(-5x)(3 - x)$

23. Expand.

a) $(-4d)(3d + 2)$ **b)** $5h(7 - 2h)$ **c)** $3t(6t^2 + 2t + 1)$

d) $(-p)(p^2 - 5p + 3)$ **e)** $2w(2 - w + 6w^2)$ **f)** $6x^2(2x^2 - 3x - 4)$

1. **Knowledge/Understanding** Simplify. Then evaluate for $x = -1$.

   a) $(4x - 2) + (3x + 1)$

   b) $(5x^2 + 3x + 2) - (x^2 - 4x - 5)$

   c) $(x^2 + 5x - 1) - (x^2 + 2x - 4)$

   d) $(2x^4 - 6x^2 - 2) + (3x^4 + x^2 - 3)$

2. Simplify.

   a) $6(-5j)$

   b) $(-a)(8a)$

   c) $(-7y)(4y)$

   d) $(-8g)(-2g)$

   e) $(-4f^2)(-6f^3)$

   f) $(5e^4)(e^3)^3$

   g) $(6k^5)(-3k^4)$

   h) $(-5p^6)(4p^2)^2$

3. Simplify.

   a) $(5r^6)^2$

   b) $(-3d^3)^3$

   c) $(-2s^4)^4$

   d) $(4a^2)^3$

4. Simplify.

   a) $16t^3 \div (-t)$

   b) $(-6w^8) \div (-3w^5)$

   c) $(-28b^7) \div 4b^6$

   d) $\dfrac{54m^9}{9}$

   e) $\dfrac{48k^4}{-8k^2}$

   f) $\dfrac{-42n^7}{-6n^5}$

5. a) Simplify.

   i) $\dfrac{8m^5}{2m}$

   ii) $\dfrac{-15x^4}{5x^2}$

   iii) $\dfrac{-20s^8}{-4s^7}$

   iv) $\dfrac{27h^6}{-h^3}$

   b) **Communication** For each expression in part a, write a related multiplication equation using the quotient. Explain the relationship between the multiplication equation and your results from part a.

6. **Thinking/Inquiry/Problem Solving**

   a) Find the mean of $6x$, $-2x$, and $5x$.

   b) Check whether your answer is the mean for the monomials $6x$, $-2x$, and $5x$ when $x = 2$, $x = -4$, and $x = 0$. Check for any two other values of x.

   c) Repeat parts a and b to find and check the mean of x, $-8x$, $-x$, and $-4x$.

   d) Draw a conclusion about whether your method of finding the mean of monomials always works. Justify your conclusion.

7. a) **Application** The area of a rectangle is $36x^2$ and the length is $4x$. What is the width? Show the dimensions on a diagram.

   b) State the dimensions of 2 other rectangles with an area of $36x^2$. Label the dimensions on a diagram of each rectangle.

8. Expand.

   a) $(-5r)(2r - 2)$

   b) $x(x + 1)$

   c) $3g(6 - 4g^2)$

   d) $(-4y)(1 - 3y + 2y^2)$

   e) $(-2h)(-5h^2 + 3h)$

   f) $4q^2(q^2 + 2q - 3)$

1. Volume of a rectangular solid $= lwh$

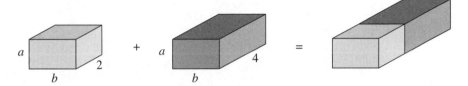

Write an algebraic statement that represents the sum of the two volumes as indicated in the diagram.

2. The algebra tile that represents x^2 is shown.

Create a diagram of algebra tiles to represent $\dfrac{6x^2}{3}$.

Numeracy
Skills Appendix

In this appendix, you will:

- Plan and apply mental mathematics strategies.

- Plan and apply estimation strategies.

- Add, subtract, multiply, and divide with integers.

- Calculate with percent, ratio and rate, and rational numbers.

- Use a scientific calculator.

- Consider whether answers to problems are reasonable.

- Use mental mathematics to decide whether answers obtained from using a calculator and from using pencil and paper are reasonable.

Factors

The *factors* of a number divide into the number with no remainder.

Example

Find all factors of 12.

Solution

To find all the factors, use rectangles.
All the possible rectangles for 12 show all the factors.

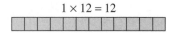

The factors of 12 are 1, 2, 3, 4, 6, and 12.

The factors of 9 are 1, 3, and 9.

The *common factors* of 12 and 9 are 1 and 3.

The *greatest common factor* of 12 and 9 is 3.

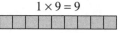

Exercises

1. List all the factors of each number. Draw rectangles if necessary.

   a) 10   **b)** 16   **c)** 6   **d)** 7   **e)** 2   **f)** 15

2. List all the factors of each number.

   a) 24   **b)** 100   **c)** 25   **d)** 8

3. List all the factors of each number. Underline the common factors.
   Circle the greatest common factor.

   a) 4, 12   **b)** 16, 20   **c)** 8, 12   **d)** 3, 9

4. Find the greatest common factor.

   a) 6, 8   **b)** 12, 24   **c)** 20, 100   **d)** 18, 24

Multiples

Example

List the multiples of 2 and 3.

Solution

The *multiples* of 2 are 2, 4, 6, 8, 10, 12, 14, 16, 18, 20, 24, … .
That is, the results of multiplying 2 by 1, 2 by 2, 2 by 3, and so on.

The multiples of 3 are 3, 6, 9, 12, 15, 18, 21, 24, … .
That is, the results of multiplying 3 by 1, 3 by 2, 3 by 3, and so on.

The *common multiples* of 2 and 3 are 6, 12, 18, 24, … .
The *least common multiple* of 2 and 3 is 6.

Exercises

1. List the first five multiples of 6.

2. Write the next 5 multiples for each pattern.

    a) 5, 10, 15, …   **b)** 4, 8, 12, …   **c)** 7, 14, 21, …

    d) 10, 20, 30, …   **e)** 100, 200, 300, …   **f)** 25, 50, 75, …

    g) 12, 24, 36, …   **h)** 9, 18, 27, …

3. List the first 5 multiples for each number in the pair. Underline the least common multiple.

    a) 6, 2   **b)** 3, 4   **c)** 2, 10   **d)** 4, 6

4. Find the least common multiple.

    a) 2, 4   **b)** 4, 5   **c)** 4, 8   **d)** 2, 12

    e) 3, 8   **f)** 10, 100   **g)** 6, 9   **h)** 8, 2

5. Muffins are sold in packages of a half dozen. How many muffins are in each of these?

    a) 1 package   **b)** 2 packages

    c) 3 packages   **d)** 4 packages

6. Veggie burgers are sold in packages of 12. Buns are sold in packages of 8. What is the least number of packages you can buy to have the same number of veggie burgers and buns?

Place Value and Rounding

The area of Canada is approximately 9 975 360 km². The value of each *digit* in this number depends on its position in a place-value chart.

Hundred Billions	Ten Billions	Billions	Hundred Millions	Ten Millions	Millions	Hundred Thousands	Ten Thousands	Thousands	Hundreds	Tens	Ones	Tenths	Hundredths	Thousandths	Ten Thousandths
					9	9	7	5	3	6	0 •				

Example

a) Round 9 975 360 to the nearest thousand.   **b)** Round 0.198 to the nearest hundredth.

Solution

a) Round 9 975 360 to the nearest thousand.
    ↑ The digit to the right of the thousands place is 3.
    Since 3 is less than 5, round down to 9 975 000.

b) Round 0.198 to the nearest hundredth, or 2 decimal places.
    ↑ The digit to the right of the hundredths place is 8.
    Since 8 is 5 or greater, round up to 0.020.

Record 0 thousandths since the number is rounded to the nearest hundredth.

Exercises

1. In 2001, the population of Canada was approximately 31 081 900. Write the digit in each place value for this population of Canada.

 a) thousands **b)** ten millions **c)** hundreds **d)** millions

2. The length of the largest flea is 1.25 cm. Write the digit in each place value for the length of this flea.

 a) tenths   **b)** ones   **c)** hundredths

3. Round to the nearest whole number.

 a) 19.3 **b)** 127.8 **c)** 14 299.19 **d)** 9.52 **e)** 153.099 8

4. The distance from the sun to Pluto is 5 906 376 200 km. Write the digit in each place value for the distance.

 a) ten thousand **b)** million **c)** billion **d)** hundred million

5. The click beetle has a mass of about 0.009 69 g. Write the digit in each place value for the mass of the click beetle.

 a) thousandth **b)** hundredth **c)** ten thousandth

Estimating Sums and Differences

We can use rounding to estimate when we add or subtract.

Example

Estimate each sum and difference.

a)   44 538
    + 26 124

b)   0.932
    − 0.450

Solution

a) Round to the nearest 10 000.

     44 538   Rounds to   40 000
    + 26 124   + 30 000
                             70 000

The estimated sum is 70 000.

b) Round to the nearest tenth.

    0.932   Rounds to   0.9
  − 0.450   − 0.5
                         0.4

The estimated difference is 0.4.

In the *Example* part a, we could have rounded to the nearest 1000 or the nearest 100 to estimate the sum.

When you use a calculator, you can use rounding to check.

Exercises

1. Estimate by rounding.

a)   76 384   b)   2719   c)   4047   d)   54.01   e)   51.6
    − 55 193   + 5832   − 1504   − 13.42   + 52.59

2. Estimate by rounding.

a) $27 802   b)   49.81   c)   0.62   d) $7.70   e)   9051
    + $60 342   − 5.45   + 0.572   − $5.05   + 884

3. Estimate the amount of each grocery bill. An amount less than $1 is not written with a leading zero.

a)

1% MILK 1L	2.06
STONE GR BRD	2.09
STONE GR BRD	2.09
0.480 kg @ 3.73 /kg	
HH TOMATOES	1.79
JP HAMB BUNS	1.79
PINK SALMON	1.39
MUFFINS CARRI	2.97
ENG CUCUMBER	1.49

b)

0.725 kg @ 2.84 /kg	
WT POTATOES RED	2.06
0.360 kg @ 4.39 /kg	
WT SQUASH ZUCCH	1.58
0.600 kg @ 1.52 /kg	
WT BANANAS	.91
.010 kg @ 3.28 /kg	
WT NAVEL ORANGE	3.31
DELI CHEESE	3.64

Example

a) Add mentally. $5 + 7 + 3 + 100 + 4 + 900 + 1$

b) Add mentally. $296 + 7$

c) Subtract mentally. $104 - 6$

Solution

a) $5 + 7 + 3 + 100 + 4 + 900 + 1$

The sum is 1020.

Think: $5 + 4 + 1 = 10$
$7 + 3 = 10$
$100 + 900 = 1000$
Then: $1000 + 10 + 10 = 1020$

b) $296 + 7$

The sum is 303.

Think: $296 + 4 = 300$
Then: $296 + 7 = 296 + 4 + 3$
$= 300 + 3$
$= 303$

c) $104 - 6$

The difference is 98.

Think: $104 - 4 = 100$
Then: $104 - 6 = 104 - 4 - 2$
$= 100 - 2$
$= 98$

When we find sums of 10, 100, or 1000, as in part a, adding mentally is easy.

To add or subtract a number close to a 100, break the number into parts so that the addition or subtraction is easier.

Exercises

1. Add mentally by first finding sums of 10, 100, or 1000.

   a) $8 + 2 + 4 + 6$ **b)** $5 + 1 + 9 + 5$ **c)** $3 + 2 + 5$

   d) $800 + 200 + 4 + 6$ **e)** $50 + 10 + 90 + 50$ **f)** $300 + 200 + 500$

2. Add or subtract mentally.

   a) $96 + 4$ **b)** $96 + 8$ **c)** $205 - 5$

   d) $205 - 7$ **e)** $103 - 6$ **f)** $689 + 14$

3. Add or subtract mentally.

   a) $610 + 101$ **b)** $405 - 402$ **c)** $7912 - 2301$

   d) $1873 - 412$ **e)** $50\ 002 + 10\ 451$ **f)** $35\ 192 - 12\ 002$

Estimating Products and Quotients

Example

Estimate by rounding.

a) 4.07×5.5 **b)** $58\,041 \div 82$

Solution

┌──────── Round to the nearest whole number. ────────┐
a) 4.07×5.5 $\qquad\qquad\qquad\qquad 4 \times 6 = 24$
└──── Round to the nearest whole number. ────┘

The estimated product is 24.

b) $\dfrac{58\,041}{82}$ Round to the nearest 1000. $\longrightarrow$ $\dfrac{58\,000}{80}$ Round to a multiple of 80. $\dfrac{56\,000}{80}$
$\qquad$ Round to the nearest 10. $\longrightarrow$

Think: $\dfrac{56}{8} = 7$, so $\dfrac{56\,000}{80} = 700$

The estimated quotient is 700.

Exercises

1. Estimate by rounding.

  a) 75×51 **b)** 58.24×80 **c)** 61.2×4.2 **d)** 705×38

2. Estimate by rounding.

  a) $612 \div 32$ **b)** $437.2 \div 56$ **c)** $81\,735 \div 75$ **d)** $125.81 \div 63$

3. To compensate for rounding one factor up, you can round the other factor down. Estimate by compensating.

  a) 85×65 **b)** 756×57

  c) 1.93×95 **d)** 4.3×7.4

Round up. $\left(\dfrac{85 \times 65}{90 \times 60} \right)$ Round down.

4. In one second, Earth travels approximately 29.8 km as it orbits the sun. About how far does Earth travel in 1 min?

Mental Math for Products and Quotients

Example

Evaluate mentally.

a) 80×900

b) $72\ 000 \div 80$

Solution

a) Think:

$$80 \times 900 = 8 \times 10 \times 9 \times 100$$
$$= 72 \times 1000$$
$$= 72\ 000$$

b) Think:

$$\frac{72\ 000}{80} = \frac{72 \times 1000}{8 \times 10}$$
$$= \frac{72}{8} \times \frac{1000}{10}$$
$$= 9 \times 100$$
$$= 900$$

Exercises

1. Use mental math and patterns to find each product.

a) 10×1
100×10
1000×100
$10\ 000 \times 1000$

b) 6×7
60×70
600×700
6000×7000

c) 9×30
9×3
9×0.3
9×0.03

2. Use mental math and patterns to find each quotient.

a) $100 \div 10$
$1000 \div 10$
$10\ 000 \div 10$
$100\ 000 \div 10$

b) $56 \div 8$
$560 \div 8$
$5600 \div 8$
$56\ 000 \div 8$

3. Use mental math to evaluate.

a) $64 \times 30 \times 0$ **b)** $1 \times 1 \times 1 \times 1$ **c)** $0 \div 512$ **d)** $0 \div 41 \div 25$ **e)** $823 \times 0 \times 0.734$

4. Use $36 \times 792 = 28\ 512$ to evaluate mentally.

a) 792×36 **b)** $28\ 512 \div 36$ **c)** 360×792 **d)** $285\ 120 \div 36$ **e)** $285\ 120 \div 792$

5. Use $25\ 434 \div 54 = 471$ to evaluate mentally.

a) $2543.4 \div 54$ **b)** $254.34 \div 54$ **c)** $25.434 \div 54$ **d)** $2.5434 \div 471$ **e)** $254.34 \div 471$

6. Think of the number of quarters in $1 to calculate mentally.

a) 4×25 **b)** 4×0.25 **c)** 8×25 **d)** $100 \div 25$ **e)** $1.50 \div 25$

7. Bamboo can grow 40 cm in a day. Giant bamboo can grow 90 cm in a day. How tall can each type of bamboo grow in a week?

$1\ m = 100\ cm$

Integers

Integers are the numbers ... −5, −4, −3, −2, −1, 0, +1, +2, +3, +4, +5, ...

$$\xleftarrow{\hspace{1cm}} \begin{array}{ccccccccccc} -5 & -4 & -3 & -2 & -1 & 0 & +1 & +2 & +3 & +4 & +5 \end{array} \xrightarrow{\hspace{1cm}}$$

Negative integers are less than 0.   *Positive* integers are greater than 0.

−3 and +3 are *opposite* integers.

Example

The highest recorded temperature in Sudbury was 37 degrees above 0°C.
The lowest recorded temperature in Sudbury was 43 degrees below 0°C.
Express each temperature as an integer.

Solution

37 degrees above 0°C is 37 units to the right of 0 on the number line.
So, the highest recorded temperature in Sudbury was 37°C.
43 degrees below 0°C is 43 units to the left of 0 on the number line.
So, the lowest recorded temperature in Sudbury was −43°C.

Exercises

1. Write an integer for each temperature.

   a) 8 degrees above 0°C   **b)** 6 degrees below 0°C   **c)** 35 degrees above 0°C

2. Express each as an integer.

   a) a decrease of 16°C   **b)** an increase of 1°C

   c) a rise of 7°C   **d)** a drop of 9°C

   e) Isura earned $25.   **f)** Max spent $109.

3. Write the opposite of each integer.

   a) +8   **b)** −2   **c)** −1

   d) +24   **e)** +9   **f)** −15

4. Suppose red counters are positive, and blue counters are negative.
   Write each integer.

   a)    **b)**   **c)**

5. What integer is not positive or negative? Draw a number line to show this.

Adding Integers

Example

Add.

a) $(-5) + (-3)$ **b)** $(-5) + (+3)$

Solution

a) $(-5) + (-3)$

Start at -5. Draw an arrow to represent -3. The arrow ends at -8.

$(-5) + (-3) = -8$

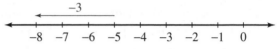

Both integers are negative, so the sum is negative.

b) $(-5) + (+3)$

Start at -5. Draw an arrow to represent $+3$. The arrow ends at -2.

$(-5) + (+3) = -2$

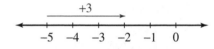

The integer -5 is farther from 0 than $+3$, so the sum is negative.

You can check with a calculator.

For $(-5) + (+3)$, press: (-) 5 + 3 ENTER =

Exercises

1. Add. Draw a number line if necessary.

a) $(+6) + (+2)$ **b)** $(-6) + (-2)$ **c)** $(-6) + (+2)$ **d)** $(+6) + (-2)$

e) $(+3) + (-3)$ **f)** $(-7) + (+7)$ **g)** $(+2) + (-2)$ **h)** $(-1) + (+1)$

2. Add.

a) $(+2) + (+5)$ **b)** $(-4) + (+9)$ **c)** $(+8) + (-1)$ **d)** $0 + (-2)$

e) $(-3) + (-6)$ **f)** $(-7) + (+7)$ **g)** $(-9) + (-5)$ **h)** $(+4) + (-8)$

3. Is each sum positive or negative?

a) a positive integer + 0

b) a negative integer + 0

c) a positive integer + a positive integer

d) a negative integer + a negative integer

e) a positive integer + a negative integer, when the negative integer is farther from 0

f) a positive integer + a negative integer, when the positive integer is farther from 0

Subtracting Integers

Example

Subtract.

a) $(+7) - (-2)$ **b)** $(-7) - (-2)$

Solution

a) $(+7) - (-2)$

Draw an arrow from −2 to +7.
The arrow represents the
difference between +7 and −2.
$(+7) - (-2) = +9$

The arrow shows $(+7) - (-2) = (+7) + (+2)$, or +9.
To subtract integers, add the opposite. The opposite of −2 is +2.

b) $(-7) - (-2)$

Draw an arrow from −2 to −7.
The arrow represents −5.
$(-7) - (-2) = -5$

The arrow shows $(-7) - (-2) = (-7) + (+2)$, or −5.
Check by adding. $(-5) + (-2) = -7$ and $(-2) + (-5) = -7$

You can check with a calculator.
For $(-7) - (-2)$, press: (−) 7 (−) (−) 2 ENTER =

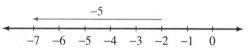

$-7 - -2$

-5

Exercises

1. Subtract. Draw a number line if necessary.

   a) $(+3) - (+4)$ **b)** $(+3) - (-4)$ **c)** $(-3) - (-4)$ **d)** $(-3) - (+4)$

2. Subtract by adding the opposite.

   a) $(-1) - (-7)$ **b)** $(-1) - (+7)$ **c)** $(+1) - (-7)$ **d)** $(+1) - (+7)$

3. Subtract.

   a) $(-1) - (+8)$ **b)** $(-4) - (-6)$ **c)** $(+1) - (+3)$ **d)** $(+8) - (-2)$

4. Subtract.

   a) $0 - (-8)$ **b)** $0 - (+4)$ **c)** $(-1) - 0$ **d)** $0 - 0$

5. Temperatures recorded in Australia range from 51°C on January 2, 1960 to −23°C on June 29, 1994. What is the difference between the highest and lowest temperatures?

Adding and Subtracting Integers

Example

Simplify.

a) $2 + 6$ **b)** $2 - 6$ **c)** $-2 - 6$ **d)** $-2 + 6$

Solution

Use a number line.
To add, move right.
To subtract, move left.

a) $6 + 2$
Start at 6. Move 2 right to 8.
$6 + 2 = 8$

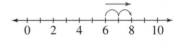

b) $2 - 6$
Start at 2. Move 6 left to -4.
$2 - 6 = -4$

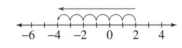

c) $-2 - 6$
Start at -2. Move 6 left to -8.
$-2 - 6 = -8$

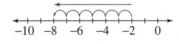

d) $-2 + 6$
Start at -2. Move 6 right to 4.
$-2 + 6 = 4$

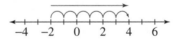

Exercises

1. Simplify.

  a) $1 + 2$ **b)** $1 - 2$ **c)** $-1 - 2$ **d)** $-1 + 2$

  e) $3 + 1$ **f)** $-3 - 1$ **g)** $-3 + 1$ **h)** $3 - 1$

2. Simplify.

  a) $4 - 5$ **b)** $4 + 5$ **c)** $-4 + 5$ **d)** $-4 - 5$

  e) $5 - 4$ **f)** $-5 + 4$ **g)** $-5 - 4$ **h)** $5 + 4$

3. Simplify.

  a) $5 - 3$ **b)** $-6 + 9$ **c)** $3 - 10$

  d) $-7 - 3$ **e)** $4 + 2$ **f)** $10 - 5$

Multiplying Integers

Recall the rules for multiplying integers.

- When two integers have the same sign, their product is positive.
- When two integers have different signs, their product is negative.

$$(+3) \times (+3) = +9$$
$$(-3) \times (-3) = +9$$
$$(+3) \times (-3) = -9$$
$$(-3) \times (+3) = -9$$

Example

Multiply.

a) $(3) \times (-6)$ **b)** $(-3) \times (-6)$

Solution

a) $(3) \times (-6)$
The integers have opposite signs, so their product is negative.
$(3) \times (-6) = -18$

b) $(-3) \times (-6)$
The integers have the same sign, so their product is positive.
$(-3) \times (-6) = 18$

You can check with a calculator.

For $(-3) \times (-6)$, press: ⟨(-)⟩ 3 ⟨×⟩ ⟨(-)⟩ 6 ⟨ENTER =⟩

```
-3*-6
              18
```

A product of integers may be written without a × sign. For example, $(3) \times (-6)$ is written $(3)(-6)$; the brackets indicate multiplication.

Exercises

1. Is each product positive or negative?

  a) $(3)(-3)$ **b)** $(-4)(-4)$ **c)** $(-2)(5)$ **d)** $(1)(7)$

2. Multiply.

  a) $(1) \times (2)$ **b)** $(-2) \times (1)$ **c)** $(-1) \times (-2)$ **d)** $(-1) \times (2)$

  e) $(-10)(3)$ **f)** $(3)(2)$ **g)** $(-1)(-1)$ **h)** $(0)(9)$

3. Write each product. Write the next 3 rows of each pattern.

  a) $(-7)(-2)$ **b)** $(4)(1)$ **c)** $(-9)(3)$ **d)** $(4)(-4)$
      $(-7)(-1)$ $(3)(1)$ $(-9)(2)$ $(3)(-3)$
      $(-7)(0)$ $(2)(1)$ $(-9)(1)$ $(2)(-2)$

4. Use a calculator. Record only the negative answers.

  a) $(16)(-32)$ **b)** $(-48)(-25)$ **c)** $(-57)(62)$ **d)** $(-94)(0)$

5. Multiply.

  a) $(5)(-7)(-2)$ **b)** $(-8)(0)(-24)$ **c)** $(-3)(-3)(-3)$ **d)** $(-6)(-1)(-9)(1)$

Dividing Integers

The rules for division are similar to those for multiplication.

- When two integers have the same sign, their quotient is positive.
- When two integers have different signs, their quotient is negative.

$$\frac{+8}{+4} = +2 \quad \frac{-8}{-4} = +2$$
$$\frac{+8}{-4} = -2 \quad \frac{-8}{+4} = -2$$

Example

Divide.

a) $\dfrac{-42}{7}$

b) $\dfrac{-42}{-7}$

Solution

a) $\dfrac{-42}{7}$

The signs are different,
so the quotient is negative.

$\dfrac{-42}{7} = -6$

b) $\dfrac{-42}{-7}$

The signs are the same,
so the quotient is positive.

$\dfrac{-42}{-7} = 6$

You can check with a calculator.

For $\dfrac{-42}{7}$, press: (−) 42 ÷ 7 ENTER =

```
-42/7

          -6
```

Exercises

1. Is each quotient positive or negative?

a) $\dfrac{10}{2}$ b) $\dfrac{-1}{-1}$ c) $\dfrac{4}{-2}$ d) $\dfrac{-6}{3}$

2. Divide.

a) $\dfrac{24}{6}$ b) $\dfrac{-24}{6}$ c) $\dfrac{24}{-6}$ d) $\dfrac{-24}{-6}$

3. Divide.

a) $\dfrac{-14}{7}$ b) $\dfrac{10}{5}$ c) $\dfrac{-12}{-3}$ d) $\dfrac{36}{-6}$

4. Divide.

a) $\dfrac{15}{3}$ b) $\dfrac{-56}{-8}$ c) $\dfrac{-16}{4}$ d) $\dfrac{20}{-5}$

5. Divide. Record only positive answers.

a) $(-81) \div (9)$ b) $(48) \div (6)$

c) $(-72) \div (-8)$ d) $(63) \div (-7)$

Proper Fractions

In a *proper fraction*, the numerator is less than the denominator.
To write a fraction in *simplest form*, reduce the fraction to *lowest terms*.

Example

Write $\dfrac{8}{12}$ in simplest form, or lowest terms.

Solution

Divide the numerator and denominator by the greatest common factor.

$$\frac{8}{12} = \frac{8 \div 4}{12 \div 4}$$
$$= \frac{2}{3}$$

The greatest common factor of 8 and 12 is 4.
So, divide 8 by 4, and divide 12 by 4.

$\dfrac{8}{12}$ and $\dfrac{2}{3}$ are *equivalent fractions*.

You can check with a calculator.

For $\dfrac{8}{12}$, press: 8 (A%) 12 (ENTER =)

$\dfrac{8}{12}$ of the squares

$\dfrac{2}{3}$ of the rows

```
8 ⌐12
              2/3
```

Exercises

1. Write in simplest form.

   a) $\dfrac{4}{8}$ **b)** $\dfrac{6}{10}$ **c)** $\dfrac{3}{9}$ **d)** $\dfrac{10}{100}$ **e)** $\dfrac{4}{6}$ **f)** $\dfrac{4}{12}$

2. Write in simplest form.

   a) $\dfrac{2}{6}$ **b)** $\dfrac{10}{20}$ **c)** $\dfrac{8}{10}$ **d)** $\dfrac{4}{16}$ **e)** $\dfrac{4}{12}$ **f)** $\dfrac{90}{100}$

3. Simplify. Write only the fractions that are not equivalent to $\dfrac{3}{4}$.

   a) $\dfrac{6}{8}$ **b)** $\dfrac{9}{12}$ **c)** $\dfrac{16}{24}$ **d)** $\dfrac{12}{16}$ **e)** $\dfrac{6}{9}$ **f)** $\dfrac{15}{20}$

4. Simplify.

   a) $\dfrac{6}{24}$ **b)** $\dfrac{25}{100}$ **c)** $\dfrac{10}{12}$ **d)** $\dfrac{10}{15}$ **e)** $\dfrac{8}{16}$ **f)** $\dfrac{5}{20}$

Improper Fractions

In an *improper fraction*, the numerator is greater than the denominator.
An improper fraction can also be expressed as a *mixed number*.

Example

a) Write $\frac{6}{4}$ in simplest form.

b) Express $\frac{6}{4}$ as a mixed number in simplest form.

Solution

a) Divide the numerator and denominator by the greatest common factor.

$$\frac{6}{4} = \frac{6 \div 2}{4 \div 2}$$
$$= \frac{3}{2}$$

The greatest common factor of 6 and 4 is 2.
So, divide 6 and 4 by 2.

b) Divide the numerator by the denominator.

$$\frac{6}{4} = 1\frac{2}{4}$$
$$= 1\frac{1}{2}$$

To write $\frac{2}{4}$ in simplest form, divide the numerator and denominator by the greatest common factor of 2 and 4. $\quad \frac{2}{4} = \frac{1}{2}$

Discuss

In part b, could you have reduced to simplest form, and then changed to a mixed number?

Exercises

1. Write as a mixed number or a whole number.

   a) $\frac{5}{5}$
   b) $\frac{3}{2}$
   c) $\frac{10}{8}$
   d) $\frac{4}{3}$
   e) $\frac{7}{4}$
   f) $\frac{14}{6}$

2. Write in simplest form.

   a) $\frac{15}{10}$
   b) $\frac{10}{8}$
   c) $\frac{2}{2}$
   d) $\frac{8}{4}$
   e) $\frac{14}{10}$
   f) $\frac{24}{20}$

3. Write in simplest form.

   a) $\frac{15}{12}$
   b) $\frac{6}{6}$
   c) $\frac{18}{16}$
   d) $\frac{5}{4}$
   e) $\frac{18}{12}$
   f) $\frac{100}{10}$

Common Denominators

The fractions $\frac{2}{5}$ and $\frac{4}{5}$ have a *common denominator*.

> The *lowest common denominator* is the least common multiple of the denominators.

Example

Write $\frac{5}{6}$ and $\frac{8}{9}$ with a common denominator.

Solution

$\frac{5}{6}$ and $\frac{8}{9}$

A common denominator is a common multiple of 6 and 9.
The lowest common denominator is the least common multiple of 6 and 9.

Multiples of 6 are: 6, 12, 18, 24, 30, …
Multiples of 9 are: 9, 18, 27, 36, 45, …

The least common multiple is 18.
Rewrite $\frac{5}{6}$ and $\frac{8}{9}$ with denominator 18.

$$\frac{5}{6} = \frac{5 \times 3}{6 \times 3} \qquad\qquad \frac{8}{9} = \frac{8 \times 2}{9 \times 2}$$
$$= \frac{15}{18} \qquad\qquad\qquad = \frac{16}{18}$$

Exercises

1. Write each equivalent fraction.

  a) $\frac{1}{4} = \frac{\square}{8}$
  b) $\frac{5}{8} = \frac{\square}{24}$
  c) $\frac{4}{5} = \frac{\square}{10}$
  d) $\frac{3}{4} = \frac{\square}{16}$

2. Write an equivalent fraction with denominator 12.

  a) $\frac{1}{3}$
  b) $\frac{3}{4}$
  c) $\frac{5}{6}$
  d) $\frac{1}{2}$
  e) $\frac{1}{4}$
  f) $\frac{2}{3}$

3. Write the least common multiple for each pair of numbers.

  a) 2, 4
  b) 3, 4
  c) 3, 2
  d) 4, 6
  e) 10, 5
  f) 5, 4

4. Write each pair of fractions with a common denominator.

  a) $\frac{1}{2}, \frac{1}{4}$
  b) $\frac{1}{3}, \frac{7}{4}$
  c) $\frac{2}{3}, \frac{3}{2}$
  d) $\frac{5}{4}, \frac{1}{6}$
  e) $\frac{9}{10}, \frac{2}{5}$
  f) $\frac{3}{5}, \frac{3}{4}$

5. Write each pair of fractions with the lowest common denominator.

  a) $\frac{2}{3}, \frac{4}{9}$
  b) $\frac{7}{10}, \frac{3}{2}$
  c) $\frac{5}{8}, \frac{5}{4}$
  d) $\frac{3}{4}, \frac{5}{12}$
  e) $\frac{7}{6}, \frac{1}{4}$
  f) $\frac{11}{12}, \frac{2}{3}$

Adding Fractions

To add two fractions, their denominators must be equal. Only the numerators are added.

Example

Add.

a) $\dfrac{4}{5} + \dfrac{3}{5}$

b) $\dfrac{2}{9} + \dfrac{1}{3}$

Solution

a) $\dfrac{4}{5} + \dfrac{3}{5}$ The denominators are equal. Add the numerators.

$$\dfrac{4}{5} + \dfrac{3}{5} = \dfrac{4+3}{5}$$

$$= \dfrac{7}{5}$$

b) $\dfrac{2}{9} + \dfrac{1}{3}$ The denominators are different. Find a common denominator.

A common denominator is a number into which 9 and 3 divide.
The lowest common denominator is 9.

Write $\dfrac{1}{3}$ as an equivalent fraction with denominator 9.

$$\dfrac{2}{9} + \dfrac{1}{3} = \dfrac{2}{9} + \dfrac{1}{3} \times \dfrac{3}{3}$$

$$= \dfrac{2}{9} + \dfrac{3}{9}$$

$$= \dfrac{5}{9}$$

You can check with a calculator.

To add $\dfrac{2}{9} + \dfrac{1}{3}$, press: 2 (A%) 9 (+) 1 (A%) 3 (ENTER)

```
2 ⌐9+1⌐3

            5 / 9
```

Exercises

1. Add.

a) $\dfrac{2}{5} + \dfrac{1}{5}$ b) $\dfrac{3}{7} + \dfrac{2}{7}$ c) $\dfrac{7}{9} + \dfrac{2}{9}$ d) $\dfrac{1}{3} + \dfrac{2}{3}$

2. Add.

a) $\dfrac{1}{2} + \dfrac{5}{8}$ b) $\dfrac{11}{12} + \dfrac{5}{3}$ c) $\dfrac{3}{2} + \dfrac{3}{10}$ d) $\dfrac{5}{6} + \dfrac{1}{3}$

3. Add.

a) $\dfrac{3}{4} + \dfrac{1}{3}$ b) $\dfrac{3}{4} + \dfrac{4}{5}$ c) $\dfrac{7}{6} + \dfrac{1}{4}$ d) $\dfrac{3}{8} + \dfrac{2}{3}$

Subtracting Fractions

To subtract two fractions, their denominators must be equal. Only the numerators are subtracted.

Example

Subtract.

a) $\dfrac{5}{3} - \dfrac{2}{3}$

b) $\dfrac{7}{10} - \dfrac{2}{3}$

Solution

a) $\dfrac{5}{3} - \dfrac{2}{3}$ The denominators are equal. Subtract the numerators.

$$\dfrac{5}{3} - \dfrac{2}{3} = \dfrac{5-2}{3}$$
$$= \dfrac{3}{3}$$
$$= 1$$

b) $\dfrac{7}{10} - \dfrac{2}{3}$ The denominators are different. The lowest common denominator is 30.

Write each fraction as an equivalent fraction with denominator 30.

$$\dfrac{7}{10} - \dfrac{2}{3} = \dfrac{7}{10} \times \dfrac{3}{3} - \dfrac{2}{3} \times \dfrac{10}{10}$$
$$= \dfrac{21}{30} - \dfrac{20}{30}$$
$$= \dfrac{1}{30}$$

You can check with a calculator.

To subtract $\dfrac{7}{10} - \dfrac{2}{3}$, press: 7 (A%) 10 (−) 2 (A%) 3 (ENTER =)

```
7⌐10−2⌐3

            1 / 30
```

Exercises

1. Subtract.

a) $\dfrac{5}{2} - \dfrac{3}{2}$ b) $\dfrac{7}{3} - \dfrac{1}{3}$ c) $\dfrac{8}{4} - \dfrac{5}{4}$ d) $\dfrac{6}{5} - \dfrac{1}{5}$

2. Subtract.

a) $\dfrac{3}{2} - \dfrac{1}{4}$ b) $\dfrac{5}{6} - \dfrac{1}{3}$ c) $\dfrac{3}{2} - \dfrac{3}{8}$ d) $\dfrac{4}{3} - \dfrac{5}{9}$

3. Subtract.

a) $\dfrac{1}{3} - \dfrac{1}{4}$ b) $\dfrac{3}{5} - \dfrac{2}{6}$ c) $\dfrac{5}{2} - \dfrac{3}{4}$ d) $5 - \dfrac{3}{8}$

4. How does stating $\dfrac{5}{6} - \dfrac{1}{6}$ as five-sixths subtract one-sixth explain why you subtract the numerators only?

Multiplying Fractions

To multiply fractions, multiply the numerators and multiply the denominators.

Example

Multiply.

$\frac{3}{4} \times \frac{2}{3}$

Solution

$\frac{3}{4} \times \frac{2}{3} = \frac{3 \times 2}{4 \times 3}$

$\qquad = \frac{6}{12} \qquad$ Reduce.

$\qquad = \frac{1}{2}$

Exercises

1. Copy and complete.

a) $\quad \frac{1}{5} \times \frac{10}{8}$

$= \frac{\square}{40}$

$= \frac{\square}{4}$

b) $\quad 4 \times \frac{3}{5}$

$= \frac{4}{1} \times \frac{3}{\square}$

$= \frac{\square}{5}$

c) $\quad \frac{2}{3} \times \frac{9}{2}$

$= \frac{18}{\square}$

$= \square$

d) $\quad \frac{1}{4}$ of 15

$= \frac{1}{4} \times \frac{15}{1}$

$= \frac{\square}{\square}$

2. Multiply.

a) $\frac{1}{2} \times \frac{1}{4}$ b) $\frac{1}{3} \times \frac{3}{2}$ c) $\frac{3}{4} \times \frac{1}{5}$ d) $\frac{1}{2} \times \frac{1}{2}$ e) $\frac{3}{5} \times \frac{5}{2}$ f) $\frac{2}{3} \times \frac{3}{4}$

3. Multiply.

a) $\frac{1}{8} \times 2$ b) $\frac{7}{3} \times \frac{4}{7}$ c) $10 \times \frac{1}{5}$ d) $\frac{5}{9} \times \frac{2}{5}$ e) $\frac{9}{10} \times \frac{5}{9}$ f) $\frac{3}{8} \times \frac{4}{3}$

4. Multiply. What do you notice about the products? Why does this happen?

a) $\frac{3}{4} \times \frac{4}{3}$ b) $\frac{7}{10} \times \frac{10}{7}$ c) $\frac{1}{2} \times 2$ d) $\frac{5}{8} \times \frac{8}{5}$

5. Calculate.

a) $\frac{1}{2}$ of 10 b) $\frac{3}{4}$ of 28 c) $\frac{2}{3}$ of 15 d) $\frac{1}{8}$ of 20

Dividing Fractions

To divide fractions, multiply by the *reciprocal*. To write the reciprocal, invert the fraction.

Example

Divide.

$$\frac{2}{3} \div \frac{1}{6}$$

Solution

$$\frac{2}{3} \div \frac{1}{6} = \frac{2}{3} \times \frac{6}{1} \qquad \text{Invert the second fraction and multiply.}$$

$$= \frac{12}{3}$$

$$= 4$$

Exercises

1. Copy and complete.

a) $\frac{3}{8} \div 5$

$$= \frac{3}{\square} \times \frac{1}{\square}$$

$$= \frac{\square}{40}$$

b) $\frac{3}{4} \div \frac{9}{2}$

$$= \frac{\square}{\square} \times \frac{2}{\square}$$

$$= \frac{\square}{36}$$

$$= \frac{\square}{6}$$

c) $\frac{7}{10} \div \frac{1}{5}$

$$= \frac{7}{\square} \times \frac{\square}{1}$$

$$= \frac{\square}{10}$$

$$= \frac{7}{\square}$$

d) $6 \div \frac{2}{3}$

$$= \frac{\square}{1} \times \frac{\square}{\square}$$

$$= \frac{\square}{2}$$

$$= \square$$

2. Divide.

a) $\frac{1}{2} \div \frac{1}{4}$ **b)** $\frac{2}{5} \div 4$ **c)** $\frac{2}{3} \div \frac{2}{3}$ **d)** $\frac{2}{9} \div \frac{1}{3}$ **e)** $\frac{1}{3} \div \frac{3}{2}$ **f)** $\frac{5}{6} \div \frac{1}{2}$

3. Divide.

a) $5 \div \frac{1}{4}$ **b)** $\frac{3}{2} \div 2$ **c)** $\frac{3}{5} \div \frac{5}{2}$ **d)** $6 \div \frac{3}{4}$ **e)** $\frac{3}{10} \div \frac{3}{5}$ **f)** $\frac{3}{5} \div \frac{3}{4}$

4. Divide. What do you notice about the quotients? Why does this happen?

a) $\frac{1}{6} \div \frac{1}{6}$ **b)** $\frac{2}{5} \div \frac{2}{5}$ **c)** $\frac{3}{4} \div \frac{3}{4}$ **d)** $\frac{1}{2} \div \frac{1}{2}$ **e)** $\frac{7}{3} \div \frac{7}{3}$ **f)** $\frac{9}{10} \div \frac{9}{10}$

Fractions to Decimals

To write a fraction as a decimal, divide the numerator by the denominator.
Use a calculator if necessary.

Example

Write each fraction as a decimal.

a) $\dfrac{100}{6}$

b) $2\dfrac{1}{8}$

Solution

a) $\dfrac{100}{6}$

Press: 100 ÷ 6 ENTER

Draw a bar over the digit that repeats.

$\dfrac{100}{6} = 16.\overline{6}$

> 100/6
> 16.66666667

b) $2\dfrac{1}{8}$

Consider only the fraction part.
Press: 1 ÷ 8 ENTER

Write the whole number, 2, then the decimal.

$2\dfrac{1}{8} = 2.125$

> 1/8
> 0.125

The decimal in part a, $16.\overline{6}$, is a *repeating* decimal.
The decimal in part b, 2.125, is a *terminating* decimal.

Exercises

1. Write each fraction as a decimal.

   a) $\dfrac{1}{2}$
   b) $\dfrac{3}{5}$
   c) $\dfrac{3}{4}$
   d) $\dfrac{1}{50}$
   e) $\dfrac{9}{50}$
   f) $\dfrac{2}{25}$

2. Write each fraction as a decimal. Use a bar for repeating decimals.

   a) $\dfrac{5}{11}$
   b) $1\dfrac{9}{20}$
   c) $\dfrac{1}{4}$
   d) $1\dfrac{2}{3}$

   > A bar can be over more than one repeating digit.
   > $\dfrac{1}{11} = 0.090909...$,
   > so write $0.\overline{09}$.

3. Write each fraction as a decimal. Round to 2 decimal places where necessary.

   a) $\dfrac{10}{9}$
   b) $\dfrac{17}{10}$
   c) $\dfrac{1}{8}$
   d) $\dfrac{7}{29}$
   e) $1\dfrac{9}{23}$

To convert a decimal to a fraction, use the place value of the right-most digit in the decimal.

Example

Write each decimal as a fraction in simplest form.

a) 4.5

b) 0.32

Solution

a) 4.5 means 45 tenths.

$$4.5 = \frac{45}{10}$$

$$= \frac{9}{2} \qquad \text{Reduce.}$$

b) 0.32 means 32 hundredths.

$$0.32 = \frac{32}{100}$$

$$= \frac{8}{25} \qquad \text{Reduce.}$$

Exercises

1. Write as a fraction in simplest form.

  a) 0.75   **b)** 1.75   **c)** 0.01   **d)** 1.01   **e)** 0.2   **f)** 1.2

2. Write as a fraction in simplest form.

  a) 0.25   **b)** 1.05   **c)** 2.2   **d)** 0.97   **e)** 0.33   **f)** 1.9

3. Write as a fraction in simplest form.

  a) 1.35   **b)** 0.09   **c)** 3.75   **d)** 1.8   **e)** 4.5   **f)** 0.6

4. Choose the fraction or mixed number, from the box, for each decimal.

  a) $0.\overline{4}$ **b)** $0.\overline{3}$ **c)** $0.\overline{36}$ **d)** $0.\overline{27}$

  e) $0.2\overline{7}$ **f)** $0.4\overline{4}$ **g)** $0.\overline{3}$ **h)** $0.3\overline{6}$

$\frac{1}{3}$	$\frac{4}{11}$	$\frac{3}{11}$
$\frac{4}{9}$	$\frac{1}{3}$	
$\frac{4}{11}$	$\frac{3}{11}$	$\frac{4}{9}$

A *ratio* is a comparison of two or more quantities with the same units.

Example

In a band, 3 of the 9 members play the guitar. Write each ratio in simplest terms.

a) guitarists to all band members

b) all band members to guitarists

c) guitarists to other band members

Solution

a) The ratio of guitarists to all members is 3 to 9. This is written as 3 : 9.
To simplify a ratio, divide each term by the greatest common factor. 3 : 9 = 1 : 3

b) Ratio of all band members to guitarists: 9 to 3   In simplest form: 3 to 1
                                        9 : 3   3 : 1

c) Ratio of guitarists to other band members: 3 to 6 or 1 to 2
                                        3 : 6   1 : 2

Exercises

1. Why is the simplest form for all band members to guitarists 3 : 1, and not 3?

2. Write each ratio.

   a) rectangles to circles   **b)** circles to rectangles

   c) rectangles to geometric figures   **d)** circles to geometric figures

3. Write each ratio in simplest form.

   a) 5 : 10   **b)** 6 : 2   **c)** 8 : 12   **d)** 6 : 12   **e)** 8 : 4   **f)** 4 : 6

4. Write each ratio in lowest terms.

   a) 2 goals to 3 goals   **b)** 4 games to 10 games   **c)** $100 to $50

5. In the 2002 Olympic Winter Games, the Canadian women's hockey team scored 3 goals while the American team scored 2 goals. What is the ratio of all goals scored to those scored by Canada?

Rate

A *rate* is a comparison of two quantities with different units.

The speed 55 km/h is a rate. The distance in kilometres is compared to the time in hours.

Example

Carole earns $58.50 in 9 h.

a) What is Carole's pay rate?

b) How much does Carole earn in 5 h?

Solution

a) Carole's hourly rate is $\dfrac{\text{earnings}}{\text{time}} = \dfrac{58.50}{9}$
$$= 6.5$$

Carole's pay rate is $6.50/h.

b) In 5 h, Carole earns $5 \times \$6.50 = \$32.50$.

Exercises

1. What is each hourly rate?

   a) $35 earned in 5 h   **b)** $170 earned in 20 h   **c)** $236.25 earned in 35 h

2. How much is earned?

   a) 7 h at $6.25/h   **b)** 10 h at $7.35/h

   c) 18 h at $8.15/h   **d)** 25 h at $6.65/h

3. Whose pay rate is the highest?

   Antonine earns $66 in 8 h.

   Leticia earns $72 in 9 h.

   Keon earns $51 in 5 h.

4. Find each speed.

   a) 300 km in 3 h   **b)** 150 km in 2 h

   c) 920 m in 10 h   **d)** 360 cm in 8 h

5. Which is faster?

   a) 320 km in 4 h or 320 km in 5 h   **b)** 12 km in 3 h or 2 km in 30 min

Percent

Percent means *per hundred* or out of 100.   % means percent

Since 60 hundredths of the square are blue, 60% is blue.

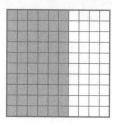

Example

Write 60% as:

a) a fraction in simplest form

b) a decimal

Solution

a) 60% means 60 out of 100, or $\frac{60}{100}$.

$\frac{60}{100} = \frac{3}{5}$

So, 60% = $\frac{3}{5}$

b) 60% means 60 hundredths or 0.60.
So, 60% = 0.6

Exercises

1. Write the fraction, decimal, and percent that is blue.

a) 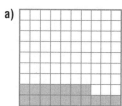   **b)** 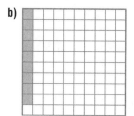   **c)**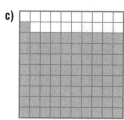

2. Write each percent as a decimal and as a fraction in simplest form.

a) 71%   **b)** 9%   **c)** 20%   **d)** 25%   **e)** 50%   **f)** 5%

3. Write each percent as a fraction in simplest form and as a decimal.

a) Inhaled air is 21% oxygen, 75% nitrogen, and 4% carbon dioxide.

b) Exhaled air is 16% oxygen, 75% nitrogen, and 9% carbon dioxide.

4. Write each decimal as a percent.

a) 0.1   **b)** 0.2   **c)** 0.45   **d)** 0.7   **e)** 0.75   **f)** 0.95

5. Write each percent as a decimal or whole number.

a) 110%   **b)** 200%   **c)** 115%   **d)** 100%   **e)** 101%   **f)** 309%

Mental Math and Estimation with Fractions and Percent

To estimate fractions, or percents, you can predict whether the result will be close to a known value and whether it will be greater or less than a known value.

Example

a) Express $\frac{9}{20}$ as a percent.

b) Use the result from part a to estimate $\frac{9}{19}$ as a percent. Check the result.

Solution

a) $\frac{9}{20} = \frac{9}{20} \times 100\%$

$= 45\%$

b)

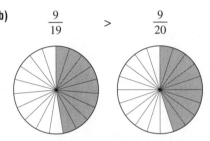

$$\frac{9}{19} > \frac{9}{20}$$

Since $\frac{9}{20}$ is 45%, then $\frac{9}{19}$ is slightly greater, perhaps 48%.

You can check with a calculator.

Press: 9 ÷ 19 × 100 ENTER

    9/19*100
        47.36842105

The estimate of $\frac{9}{19} \doteq 48\%$ is close to its true value.

In a fraction:

- When denominators are equal, the greater the *numerator*, the greater the fraction.
- When numerators are equal, the greater the *denominator*, the lesser the fraction.

Exercises

1. Order these fractions from least to greatest. Check by using a calculator.

a) $\frac{1}{102}, \frac{1}{100}, \frac{1}{98}, \frac{1}{99}, \frac{1}{101}$ **b)** $\frac{22}{23}, \frac{20}{23}, \frac{23}{23}, \frac{19}{23}, \frac{21}{23}$ **c)** $\frac{7}{11}, \frac{7}{13}, \frac{7}{10}, \frac{7}{12}, \frac{7}{9}$

2. Use a calculator to express $\frac{43}{67}$ as a percent. Use the result to estimate each as a percent.

a) $\frac{46}{67}$ **b)** $\frac{40}{67}$ **c)** $\frac{43}{70}$ **d)** $\frac{43}{64}$ **e)** $\frac{21}{67}$

3. In the 2002 Winter Olympics, Canada won 6 gold, 3 silver, and 8 bronze medals. What fraction of Canada's medals were gold?

One Number as a Percent of Another Number

To express one number as a percent of another number, use fractions.

Example

a) Write 3 as a percent of 9.

b) Write 3 as a percent of 2.

Solution

a) Write 3 as a fraction of 9. $\dfrac{3}{9}$

Then write $\dfrac{3}{9}$ as a percent. $\dfrac{3}{9} \times 100\% \doteq 33.3\%$

3 is approximately 33.3% of 9.

b) Write 3 as a fraction of 2. $\dfrac{3}{2}$

Then write $\dfrac{3}{2}$ as a percent. $\dfrac{3}{2} \times 100\% = 150\%$

3 is 150% of 2.

Exercises

1. Write each fraction as a percent. Round to the nearest percent, if necessary.

a) $\dfrac{9}{10}$
    b) $\dfrac{1}{3}$
    c) $\dfrac{1}{2}$

d) $\dfrac{8}{8}$
    e) $\dfrac{7}{20}$
    f) $\dfrac{3}{4}$

2. Write the first number as a percent of the second.

a) 37, 100
    b) 9, 10
    c) 2, 5

d) 11, 11
    e) 0, 15
    f) 1, 4

3. Write each fraction as a percent. Round to the nearest percent, if necessary.

a) $\dfrac{4}{5}$
    b) $\dfrac{7}{7}$
    c) $\dfrac{1}{6}$
    d) $\dfrac{9}{15}$

4. a) Alberta, Saskatchewan, Manitoba, and Ontario are the only provinces that do not have any coastline. What percent of the 10 Canadian provinces do not have any coastline?

b) What percent of the provinces have a coastline?

c) Yukon Territory is the only one of the 3 territories that border the United States. What percent of the territories border the United States?

Percent of an Amount

Example

a) Calculate 24% of $356.   **b)** Calculate 115% of $356.

Solution

a) Write 24% as a decimal.   0.24

24% of $356 = 0.24 × $356   Use a calculator.
$$= \$85.44$$

24% of $356 is $85.44.

b) Write 115% as a decimal.   1.15

115% of $356 = 1.15 × $356   Use a calculator.
$$= \$409.40$$

115% of $356 is $409.40.

Exercises

1. Calculate. What happens when the amount is 100?

   a) 70% of 100   **b)** 135% of 100   **c)** 0.2% of 100 $0.2\% = 0.002$

2. Calculate. What pattern do you notice?

   a) 100% of 400   **b)** 10% of 400   **c)** 1% of 400   **d)** 0.1% of 400

3. Calculate. Round to the nearest tenth if necessary.

   a) 20% of 160   **b)** 18% of 20   **c)** 0.5% of 720   **d)** 115% of 333

4. A pair of roller blades costs $159.98.

   a) Calculate the Ontario Provincial Sales Tax (PST) on the roller blades.

   b) Calculate the Goods and Services Tax (GST) on the roller blades.

   c) Calculate the total cost.

   d) Multiply the price of the roller blades by 1.15.
      What does the result represent?

> Ontario PST is 8%.
> GST is 7%.

5. Calculate the total cost, including GST and PST, for each amount.

   a) $3.50   **b)** $99.99

   c) $249.99   **d)** $0.10

6. The list price of a DVD player is $479.99. What is the cost with taxes for each sale?

a) 10% OFF

b) 75% OFF REGULAR PRICE

c) 50% OFF EVERYTHING

d) 30% OFF TODAY ONLY

Mental Math and Estimation with Percent of an Amount

Example

Estimate the cost of this CD player with taxes.

Solution

Approximate price: $50
GST = 7%, PST = 8%
GST + PST: 15%

To calculate 15%, use 10%, and 5%.
10% of $50 = $5
Since $5\% = \frac{1}{2}$ of 10%, or $\frac{1}{2}$ of $5

Then, 5% of $50 = \frac{1}{2} \times \$5$
$= \$2.50$

Price with taxes: $50 + $5 + $2.50 \doteq $57.
The cost of this CD player is about $57.

Exercises

1. Is each amount greater than 75, less than 75, or neither?

   a) 102% of 75   **b)** 95% of 75   **c)** 100% of 75   **d)** 9.9% of 75

2. Calculate each percent. If possible, write the answer only.

   a) 1% of 60   **b)** 50% of 60   **c)** 100% of 60   **d)** 200% of 60

3. Refer to exercise 2. Estimate each percent.

   a) 2% of 60   **b)** 49% of 60   **c)** 53% of 60   **d)** 145% of 60

4. Calculate. If possible, write the answer only.

   a) 100% of 35.5   **b)** 50% of 40   **c)** 1% of 800   **d)** 200% of 30

5. What is the approximate cost of each item, including taxes?

   a) running shoes that cost $134.99   **b)** a CD that costs $17.99

6. The regular cost of a camera is $249.99. It is on sale for 15% off.
   Estimate the cost with taxes.

Rational Numbers

A *rational number* is a number that can be written as a fraction. This means that a rational number can also be written as a terminating decimal or a repeating decimal.

A rational number may be positive or negative.

These numbers are rational numbers: $3, -5, \frac{1}{4}, \frac{-3}{2}, 0.34, 0.\overline{2}$

Example

State the rational number for each letter on the number line.

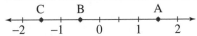

Solution

A is halfway between 1 and 2. So, A is $1\frac{1}{2}$ or 1.5.

B is halfway between 0 and −1. So, B is $-\frac{1}{2}$ or −0.5.

C is halfway between −1 and −2. So, C is $-1\frac{1}{2}$ or −1.5.

Exercises

1. Write the rational number for each letter.

a) 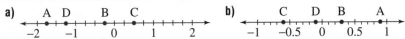   b)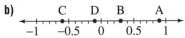

2. Round each rational number, represented by the dot, to the nearest integer.

a)

$$\xleftarrow{\hspace{2em}} \underset{-1}{|} \quad | \quad | \quad | \quad \underset{-0.5}{|} \quad | \quad \bullet \quad | \quad | \quad | \quad \underset{0}{|} \xrightarrow{\hspace{2em}}$$

b)

$$\xleftarrow{\hspace{2em}} \underset{-2}{|} \quad \bullet \quad | \quad | \quad | \quad \underset{-1.5}{|} \quad | \quad | \quad | \quad | \quad \underset{-1}{|} \xrightarrow{\hspace{2em}}$$

3. Round each rational number to the nearest integer.

a) 4.3   b) −1.2   c) 6.7   d) 0.1   e) −3.9   f) −0.2

4. Write in simplest form.

a) $\frac{80}{100}$ b) $-\frac{5}{10}$ c) $-\frac{8}{12}$ d) $\frac{16}{20}$ e) $-\frac{4}{6}$ f) $-\frac{10}{15}$

5. Construct a number line. Mark a dot on the line to represent each rational number.

a) 0.5   b) $2\frac{1}{4}$ c) −3.75   d) $-4\frac{1}{2}$ e) 2.5   f) $-\frac{3}{2}$